Vision Voiced

American University Studies

Series III
Comparative Literature
Vol. 34

PETER LANG
New York • Bern • Frankfurt am Main • Paris

Rev. Edward R. Heidt, C.S.B.

Vision Voiced

Narrative Viewpoint in Autobiographical Writing

PETER LANG
New York • Bern • Frankfurt am Main • Paris

Library of Congress Cataloging-in-Publication Data

Heidt, Edward R.
  Vision Voiced : Narrative Viewpoint in
Autobiographical Writing / Edward R. Heidt.
    p. cm. — (American university studies. Series III,
Comparative literature ; 34)
    Includes bibliographical references (p.) and index.
    1. English prose literature—History and criticism.
2. Autobiographical fiction, English—History and
criticism.   3. Autobiographical fiction, American—
History and criticism.   4. American prose literature—
History and criticism.   5. Point-of-view (Literature)
6. Narration (Rhetoric) 7. Autobiography.   I. Title.
II. Series: American university studies. Series III,
Comparative literature ; vol. 34.
PR756.A9H45   1991   820.9'492—dc20   90-6094
ISBN 0-8204-1245-7   CIP
ISSN 0724-1445

© Peter Lang Publishing, Inc., New York 1991

All rights reserved.
Reprint or reproduction, even partially, in all forms such as microfilm,
xerography, microfiche, microcard, offset strictly prohibited.

Printed in the United States of America.

Contents

An Autobiographical Preface vii

Introduction: Autobiographical Writing as a Genre 1

Chapter One: An Autobiography Unites The Mimetic/
                Diegetic Voices In a Synecdochic Narrative 17
PART ONE: FICTIONAL AUTOBIOGRAPHIES 21
Tristram Shandy 21
Hermione Gart 30
A Man Lying on His Back in the Dark 37
A Ninety-Five Year Old Man About to Commit Suicide 41
PART TWO: NON-FICTIONAL AUTOBIOGRAPHIES 50
Helen Keller 50
Christopher Nolan 56
John Stuart Mill 61
Maya Angelou 71

Chapter Two: A Memoir Compares and Contrasts the Mimetic/Diegetic Voices in a Metaphoric Narrative 79
PART ONE: FICTIONAL MEMOIRS 86
Gogo, Didi, Pozzo, Lucky 86
Tom Wingfield 93
PART TWO: NON-FICTIONAL MEMOIRS 99
William Wordsworth 99
Maxine Hong Kingston 108
Arthur Miller 113
Edmund Gosse 121
Mary McCarthy 126

Contents

Chapter Three: A Confession Reveals Mimetic/Diegetic
        Voices in a Metonymic Narrative 135
PART ONE: FICTIONAL CONFESSIONS 141
George, Martha, Nick and Honey 141
PART TWO: NON-FICTIONAL CONFESSIONS 156
Thomas DeQuincey 156
Norman Mailer 163
Andrew Greeley 170
Perry Edward Smith 176

Chapter Four: John Henry Newman: Confessor,
        Autobiographer, Memoirist 189
His Synecdochic Self: Student and Scholar 191
His Metaphoric Selves: The Quest for Certainty 195
His Metonymic Self: The Right to Private Judgment 206

Conclusion: A Philosophy of Autobiographical Writing:
        A Metaphysics of Presence 219

Bibliography 239

Index 251

An Autobiographical Preface

As a Guidance Counsellor at Andrean High School in Merrillville, Indiana during the 1981-82 school year, I had an experience which I have not forgotten and which has influenced my teaching, counselling and, during these past five years, my graduate studies in English literature and has became the focus of my dissertation and is now the focus of this book. This experience, in keeping with the theory which I explore in this book, is then a synecdochic one for me. It stands out etched in my memory as uniquely representative *for* me and *of* me. It is secondarily a metonymic or metaphoric one to the extent that it is a linking-connecting experience or a replaceable one. It is, however, unique to me.

A parent telephoned me, distressed that his son was doing poorly in his schoolwork. During the course of our conversation, the parent, exasperated with his son and confused about what to do, finally insisted that I, as a guidance counsellor, should know how to motivate this boy. He said, and I quote as accurately as I can recall, that "it was my profession;" I was to be a professional motivator. This evaluation of the role of a Guidance Counsellor, and by association "priest," has stayed with me since that conversation as has the provocative question of how to motivate people.

To be sure, school Guidance Counsellors set up academic programs and courses, recommend colleges and careers, and suggest various avenues of possible interest to their counsellees. But how does the counsellor motivate the student to want to take the courses, attend the college or participate in extracurricular activities? How does a priest or psychologist motivate a person to change a behavior, an attitude, a feeling, a disposition? Why does an individual become a guidance counsellor, a priest, a psychologist?

These questions invited me to explore the wider questions with regard to anybody's interior life (motivations, intentions, attitudes, feelings), which led me to become interested in reading and analyzing autobiographical writing. I came to realize that autobiographical literature can offer valuable insights into motivations, attitude formation and interior life generally.

When I applied to various graduate schools in the Spring of 1984, many of them wanted an "autobiographical statement." I remember clearly (and wrote in the first sentence of the statement) that I had no idea how to write an autobiography and should probably consult some of the "masters" before I attempted doing so. In retrospect, as I prepare this book on a theory of autobiographical literature, I realize that my somewhat whimsical, offhand comment about "consulting the masters" has resulted in just that and the experience of attempting to write my own autobiographical statement becomes, in retrospect, a "synecdochic" one when viewed in terms of this book. At the time, it was written as part of graduate school applications. It is a metonymic statement in terms of the transition to graduate school. But it's first sentence becomes synecdochic in relation to this book. The statement itself becomes metaphoric in the sense that it can replace other statements and letters about myself which I have accumulated.

Without any "reading of the masters," I quite naturally wrote a rather traditional autobiographical statement for the graduate schools. Like most autobiographers, I located one, particular, synecdochic thread (and so naturally excluded others) that went through my life and illustrated that synecdochic, thematic thread with various examples which could metaphorically replace each other in representing the thread.

I constructed a short story, a summary, that illustrated a part of who I was, albeit a favorable, possibly somewhat idealized, part. The metaphorical experiences used to illustrate the thread are idealized. I would need to change the summary into a longer narrative which contains some metonymic, confessional elements; that is, stories about myself that are inconsistent with the ideal presented; stories that are conflictual. On the other hand, I could add stories which repeat the synecdochic idealizations or the metonymic connectors and these serve as metaphors which serve the idealized, synecdochic portrait originally written by adding replaceable, similar stories.

My interest, then, in autobiographical literature flowered when I realized that there was a wealth of material on the subject, and, as my dissertation director, Jay Martin, said, at the defense of my dissertation, biography and autobiography seem to have captured the imaginations of people.

When I first read James Boswell's *Life of Johnson* and his *London Journal* in a graduate seminar in the Fall of 1985, the professor focused on the *person* of Boswell as a biographer and a "journalist" or diarist and his place and the point of view in the narrative. The narrative was not just Boswell's attempt to portray a "pure" Johnson but it was also an attempt to express a little bit of Boswell. The *Journal* was not just a record of what happened, it was the result of an intentional "posturing" by Boswell so that he would have material to write about. It never occurred to me that narratives could represent *persons*: their attitudes, motivations, intentions and points of view. I had always read and taught novels, short stories, poems in terms of a theme, moral or plot structure to which the fictional characters contributed or were a secondary part. In the graduate seminar on James Boswell and Samuel Johnson, instead of reading a sequence of plotted events or series of conflicts leading to a resolution which taught a lesson, I saw that the more central reality in the narrative was the person of Johnson vis-a-vis the person of Boswell and vice versa. And these persons had really existed once in time and space, in history. Although their books may contain fictions, they were not fictions. The subject indeed captured *my* imagination.

In this book, I look carefully at specific people in specific pieces of autobiographical writing where the persons seem to me to emerge so clearly and so uniquely, as only they could emerge, as separate and distinct from the plot. These writers form self-concepts and images and they narrate stories which embody the image or concept. Sometimes the image is idealized, synecdochically significant, while at other times the images interlace, and metaphorically replace each other. At other times, the image or concept contained in a particular narrative is a metonymic connector with one of the metaphors or synecdoches of the self.

I intend this book to be a contribution to the on-going conversation about autobiographical writing as a genre in its own right in which I assert that one of the distinguishing features of autobiographical writing is this strength of personality and character expressed in and through tone of voice, point of view, and the vision of the writer. Secondly, I hope to encourage people not only to study the autobiographical writings of others but to attempt their own autobiographical writing based upon my theory; that is, I invite readers to allow their imagination and creativity full range so that they may sit down and construct and re-construct their own lives in writing. I invite my readers to narrate stories which synecdochically represent them, metonymically connect their various selves or metaphorically replace and reinforce their self-concept and image.

Finally, this book is a significant, synecdochic contribution to my life. It is synecdochic for me because it is my first expression of my particular voice and point of view in a particular discourse community of theoreticians of autobiography, literature and education. I was motivated to study autobiography but I was also motivated to do so as part of my own autobiography, intending to find another voice of my own in the process. My Ph.D. dissertation and this book synecdochically represent metonymic experiences in my life which consist of varieties of stories and experiences which can metaphorically replace each other in representing the metonymic experience of graduate study and the synecdochic experience of dissertation writing.

Individuals need to feel the right to tell their own stories in their own ways, without fear of recrimination, from their own points of view in their own voices. Autobiographical writing contains narratives that have the potential to carry a powerful personal presence because they embody this strong point of view in this strong, highly synecdochic, voice.

Preface

And so, as part of this "autobiographical preface," I wish to end by writing the customary acknowledgements. I wish of course to thank Professor Paul Alkon for the seminar on Boswell and Johnson where my interest was first piqued. I would then like to thank my dissertation director, Professor Jay Martin, for the care and sensitivity with which he read my work and helped me to discern, separate and clarify my ideas, my theory. I wish to thank Professor Ross Winterowd who taught me to understand language, rhetoric and linguistics in a completely new way. His seminar on the Literature of Fact helped to focus even more clearly. Professor Moshe Lazar, in his course on Samuel Beckett, Eugene Ionesco and Harold Pinter, led me to see how their fictional writings could effectively serve to elaborate and exemplify my theory.

The inherent danger, of course, about acknowledgements and thank you's is that the author may omit important people and so hurt their feelings. This danger is magnified in autobiographical writing where the narratives go beyond mere thank-you's and acknowledgements into actual stories about other people which can turn out to be not only hurtful but libelous and slanderous.

There are certain individuals and groups in my life who come strongly to mind and I want to write their names here: my community, The Basilian Fathers, my family (especially my sister Ruthanne), Kathy Schultheis, Paul O'Connor, Marjorie Perloff, Karen Bierman, Connie Destito, Ed Gala, the Lynd family, Art McCarthy, Charles Reynolds, William Marceau, Joe Abend, Ted Baenziger, John McCarthy, Robert McKinnon, Michael Murray and Susan Clarke, Virginia Bertrand, Olga Kravchenko Sliwa, Andrea White, and my dear John Cieslinski. These people know who they are in relation to me and their importance to me and rather than elaborate details here, I let their names stand as my tribute to them, my respect and love for them.

Ed Heidt
St. Mark's College
Vancouver, British Columbia
November 1989

Selections from Edward Albee, *Who's Afraid of Virginia Woolf?*, copyright © 1962 by Edward Albee. Reprinted with permission of Atheneum Publishers, an imprint of Macmillan Publishing Co. All rights reserved.

Selections from Jacques Derrida, *Of Grammatology,* copyright © 1974 by Johns Hopkins University Press, New York. Reprinted by permission of the publisher. All rights reserved.

Selections from Christopher Nolan, *Under the Eye of the Clock,* copyright © 1987 by Saint Martin's Press, New York. Reprinted by permission of the publisher. All rights reserved.

Selections from Vladimir Nabokov, *Speak, Memory: An Autobiography Revisited,* copyright © 1947, 1948, 1949, 1951, © 1967 by Vladimir Nabokov, published by Vintage Books, a division of Random House, Inc. Reprinted by permission of Random House, Inc. and the Estate of Vladimir Nabokov. All rights reserved.

Selections from Eugene Ionesco, *Four Plays: The Bald Soprano, The Lesson, Jack, or the Submission, and The Chairs,* copyright © 1958; Arthur Miller, *Timebends,* copyright © 1987; Samuel Beckett, *Malone Dies,* copyright © 1956; *Endgame: A Play in One Act Followed by an Act Without Words: A Mime for One Player,* copyright © 1958, and *Waiting for Godot,* copyright © 1954, by Grove Press, New York. Reprinted by permission of the publisher. All rights reserved.

Introduction:

Autobiographical Writing as a Genre

I wish to establish a theoretical framework consisting of specific elements or tools by which an autobiographical piece of writing can be recognized and accorded a special place as part of a separate genre in its own right. In my conclusion, I will establish a philosophical framework for autobiographical writing based on the work of Edmund Husserl and Jacques Derrida.

A piece of writing, whether a fictional creation of a character by a writer in a novel, a drama, a poem or a non-fictional narration by a writer in an essay, letter, diary or journal, will have the following characteristics which I shall develop:

There will be (1) some degree of narrative progression, a plot line, however small, where (2) a series of diegetic-mimetic narrative voices communicate (3) the particular, unique voice of the character in the fiction or the author in the non-fiction. My thesis for separating autobiographical writing as a genre in its own right is based on the fact that when these voices unite in the narrative progression of the plot, then the incident being narrated becomes synecdochic for the fictional character or the non-fictional writer and I call this "autobiography proper." On the other hand, when the mimetic/diegetic voices disagree with each other in the re-telling of a particular story, then there is a comparing and contrasting of voices, such that the incidents being narrated by the fictional character or the non-fictional writer become a series of metaphoric replacements of viewpoint and I call this piece of writing a "memoir proper." Finally, when the mimetic/diegetic voices narrating a particular incident discover that a *new*, hitherto unrecognized voice is being revealed, the new voice and the incident being narrated represent a metonymic link for the fictional character or the non-fictional writer and I call this piece of writing "confession proper."

In this introduction, I wish to define more clearly and specifically what I mean by mimetic/diegetic voice and synecdoche, metaphor and metonymy using James Boswell's dual narration of the first time that he met Samuel Johnson. I will then proceed to devote one chapter to each of the following: fictional characters and non-fictional writers who narrate synecdochic incidents which unite their voices, metaphoric incidents which compare and contrast voices and metonymic incidents which reveal and connect voices. In the conclusion, I will discuss the philosophy of Edmund Husserl and Jacques Derrida as applied to Samuel Beckett as a way of locating the nature of the voices narrating the incidents and as a way of constructing a general philosophy of autobiography.

The Narrative Unit

William Labov and Joshua Waletsky discuss the narrative unit as a series of free and restricted clauses.[1] Restricted clauses are those which must be placed in a certain order so that the mimetic chronology of the event is preserved. The free clauses are diegetic and can be re-arranged by the author and placed anywhere.

The sequence of restricted clauses or units in James Boswell's narrative of his first meeting with Samuel Johnson consists of such facts as having tea at Davies' house at a particular time on a particular day, followed by Johnson's arrival and the subsequent conversation. The sequence of free units are Boswell's commentary on the joke about his homeland, the discussion of the actor Garrick or his physical description of Johnson. These free units could be added and re-combined in any number of ways and placed around the restricted mimetic sequence.

The narrative unit is that series of words, clauses, and sentences which combine to build the mimetic/diegetic sequence of the plot. The sequence of events is mimetic when events are arranged chronologically and relate referentially; the reader is able to sequence the events, list the various characteristics of personalities and setting, and generally reconstruct, paraphrase, the particular scene narrated.

Various diegetic sub-themes or motifs may emerge from within the narrative which motifs can be compared and contrasted, like the different physical descriptions that Boswell gives of Johnson. The narrative unit itself can be a sub-theme or motif which separates itself from the entire series of narrative units that comprise the particular work. This narrative unit of Boswell's first meeting with Samuel Johnson itself becomes significant in terms of the series of narrative units that make up both the *London Journal* and the *Life of Johnson* in both of which the narrative of the first meeting occurs.

The narrative unit of Boswell's first meeting with Johnson fits chronologically, mimetically, into both the *Journal* and the *Life* but emerges differently in the diegetic gestalt of narratives in each work. In the *Journal*, Boswell records the meeting as part of his year in London but in the *Life*, he records the meeting as part of a lifelong friendship with Johnson.

My point with regard to narrative is that each word, clause, sentence and paragraph can be read as a trace, a building block, which make up the structure of the narrative itself and then the narrative unit itself becomes a trace, a building block, which makes up the structure of the series of narratives which comprise the work itself. These words, clauses, sentences and paragraphs can be read mimetically, in the order in which they occurred in time and space, or diegetically, with various out of order additions and deletions.

The mimetic narrative sequence of restricted units in both of Boswell's narratives is as follows: He is having tea at Davies house on Russell Street at about seven o'clock when Johnson arrives. They are introduced; the comment about Scotland is made and they sit down to converse together. Boswell leaves at ten for another engagement with Dr. Pringle and he stays that night at Lord Eglinton's.

The narrative unit itself as a mimetic re-telling of Boswell's first meeting with Johnson is synecdochic in the sense that it is a one time, significant experience for Boswell and it is metaphoric in the sense that it is one among many narratives about Boswell's relationship with Johnson. It is metonymic in that it narrates a very important connective event in the Boswell-Johnson relationship. In the unit itself, there are synecdochic, metaphoric, metonymic pieces. The joke about Scotland is a one-time, significant experience for Boswell and it relates to the metonymic revelation that he knows Johnson does not like Scots and wants to hide this fact from him. There are three different physical descriptions of Johnson which can metaphorically replace each other.

Thomas Pison summarizes James Olney's thesis about autobiographical writing as "metaphors of the self" by saying that the essential, what I am calling synecdochic, unity of the self evolves out of and into this balance, poise, or cooperation of opposites and that this union can be communicated only by metaphor or symbol. One topic leads to another, one voice to another, through their similarity (the metaphoric pole) or through their contiguity (the metonymic pole). The final 'metaphor of self' that shapes a life and governs the design of an autobiography [and in effect becomes a synecdoche] must await its formulation after the metonymical relationships of the life lived in time has unfolded. One can readily agree that John Stuart Mill's *daimon* was the rational mind, that Darwin's was the nature of nature as objective fact, and that Newman's was his religious conscience.[2]

Pison adds Wordsworth to this group by saying that Wordsworth's *daimon* was his "philosophic mind" represented in the subtitle of *The Prelude*, "the growth of a poet's mind." What Olney calls the "daimon,"[3] is what I am calling the synecdochic image or narrative which none other can equal or replace. Images or narratives which can replace each other are metaphoric precisely because they are equal in value. The *daimon*, according to Olney, is the personal genius and guardian spirit, the dominant faculty, function or tendency that forms part of the whole but from which there is no escape because it forms an essential part of the self and is thus synecdochic. A metonymic narrative or image could also be synecdochic to the extent that someone could discover something about themselves that has been a part of them but unrecognized. Synecdoches are recognized and not necessarily connected. Metonymies can be synecdoches but they must be connected or form a connection if they are to remain metonymies. Boswell's desire that Johnson not know he is from Scotland is a synecdochic fact about Boswell; he doesn't want people generally to know he's from Scotland; its an important representative part of his personality. This synecdochic fact about Boswell becomes metonymic in the narrative of the first meeting; it connects with Boswell telling Davies "not to tell him where I'm from" and the joke about Scotland.

Olney's autobiography "simplex"[4] tells one, synecdochic story of a career, conversion or achievement focusing on the essential *daimon* and his autobiography "duplex"[5] focuses on a variety of metaphoric, metonymic expressions and narratives of the essential *daimon*.

James Mellard continues this discussion of metaphor, metonymy and synecdoche in relation to autobiography by saying that when an autobiographer selects a certain story to be told, it can be selected metonymically so as to suggest a unity through connectedness to the life story or it can be selected synecdochically to portray an idealized, unified self or metaphorically to present a version, or part of the self.

Mellard uses Henry Adams' medieval virgin as a synecdoche which best represents the metonymic development of events called the Middle Ages. Cathedrals, Thomistic philosophy, Franciscan spirituality are metaphors which can replace each other in representing the age. Mellard then uses Adams' image of the "dynamo" as the synecdoche which best represents the metonymic development of the events surrounding the rise of Industrialism. Pearson's theory of kinesis or Darwin's theory of evolution are metaphors which can replace each other in representing the age. Henry Adam's own image of himself as "accidentally educated"[6] is a synecdoche which best represents the metonymic development of his life story. The specific educational experiences that he recounts in his autobiography are metaphoric to the extent that they can replace each other as representative of his life.

In other words, history can be represented as a series of synecdochic, metaphoric and metonymic events. When considered as evolutionary, history is just one synecdochic unfolding made up of some events which separate themselves as quite unique and representative of an age but even then they become metaphoric replacements for each other as events "which represent an age." If history is broken up into millions and millions of isolated incidents, it can be grouped according to common patterns. And when an event is discovered to be a connective, it becomes metonymic.

The Diegetic/Mimetic Voices

The diegetic-mimetic voices in an autobiographical narrative like Boswell's consist of the spoken words, the locutions, of the narrator and characters in dialogue as well as the various thoughts and feelings, motivations, beliefs and desires of these characters and narrators, their illocutionary acts. The voice is that which articulates the words of the locutions and which originates in consciousness. Boswell voices his thoughts, feelings and attitudes, the illocutionary activity in his consciousness, about this experience in the creation of the words of the narrative in which he also expresses those thoughts and feelings.

I want to ground my use of mimetic and diegetic voice in Platonic-Aristotelian poetics which Gerard Genette has clearly and succinctly summarized in his article "Boundaries of Narrative." Basically, the mimetic voice parallels the mimetic chronology of the event narrated and the diegetic voice parallels the events that have been added or re-arranged or expanded.

Plato divided imitation properly speaking (mimesis) and simple narrative (diegesis) by saying that a narrator "speaks in his own name without trying to make us believe that it is another who speaks (*The Republic*, III, 393a,e)." Plato denies to narrative (diegesis) the quality of imitation (mimesis) and separates them. Narration is at one remove from imitation which is itself at one remove from the reality. The reality of Boswell's first meeting with Johnson is mimetically represented aside from the authorial intrusions.

Aristotle, on the other hand, said that narration (diegesis) is one of two forms of imitation (mimesis). One is the direct representation of events by actors speaking and performing before the public (*Poetics*, 1448a). The other is the power of the narrator to narrate (diegesis) with as much imitation (mimesis) as direct representation (1460a). The reality of Boswell's first meeting with Johnson is not only mimetically represented as Plato suggests but it is diegetically represented as Aristotle suggests because there is another narrative that consists of Boswell's intrusions and commentary which are just as real and important as the chronology.

Boswell's voice is mimetic when it reports directly the words spoken and his thoughts and feelings at the time. His voice is diegetic when it comments upon or evaluates these later.

In this book, I will be looking at the mimetic/diegetic voices of particular non-fictional writers and fictional characters in particular "scenes" of particular pieces of writing and I will be examining how these voices synecdochically unite, metaphorically compare and contrast or metonymically connect and reveal.

A good, single example which I have been making reference to is Boswell's mimetic/diegetic voice in the reporting of the joke about Scotland. Davies had slipped and accidentally said that Boswell was from Scotland and Boswell knew that Johnson was prejudiced against the Scotch so he quickly jumped into the conversation and the mimetic sequence has Boswell saying that he couldn't help being from Scotland which invited Johnson's sarcastic "that, Sir, I find, is what a very great many of your countryman cannot help."[7] This "strike stunned Boswell a good deal"[8] so he proceeds with the diegetic explanation in the *Life*:

> I am willing to flatter myself that I meant this as a light pleasantry to sooth and conciliate him, and not as an humiliating abasement at the expense of my country. But however this might be, this speech was somewhat unlucky; for with that quickness of wit for which he was so remarkable, he seized the expression "come from Scotland," which I used in the sense of being of that

country and, [Johnson was answering] as if I had said that I had come away from it, or left it...⁹

He comments further that he was "stunned, embarrassed and apprehensive" about this and slightly afraid of "what might come next."[10] His mimetic voice reports as nearly as possible what the consciousness remembers of the event and the diegetic voice comments and evaluates thirty years later with a different voice and perspective. In the *Journal*, he mimetically reports the comment and in the *Life* he diegetically comments on it and explains it.

Seymour Chatman differentiates the purely mimetic from the purely diegetic voice by saying that the mimetic voice merely records the words directly as if from a tape recorder or video and most nearly approximates the locutionary act while a purely diegetic voice comments and evaluates, makes additions and deletions, and approximates the illocutionary activity in consciousness which wants to direct the readers attention to certain points and meanings and which wants to explain why the mimetic voice said what it did.

Susan Snaider Lanser distinguishes the diegetic voice in terms of the "status" and "stance"[11] of the voice. "Status," as she defines it, refers to whom the non-fictional writer or fictional character is in relation to the narration and the act of narrating, the event being narrated. The values, attitudes, interests of the writer or character are distinct from those of the various other narrators, writers and characters. "Status" refers to the clarity with which the characters and situation are drawn. Lanser's conceptualization of "stance" refers to the point of view, the perspective, the angle of vision from which the writer, narrator or character sees and so tells the story. This vision or stance and the special status of the writer or character as "autobiographer, memoirist or confessor" are what give the voices in the text their authority to narrate.

The sequence is as follows: the "first" voice is the mimetic one which speaks as nearly exactly as it did at the time of the experience and is recorded that way; the second voice is also a mimetic one which thinks as nearly exactly as it thought at the time of the experience and is recorded that way; and a third voice is a diegetic one which comments on and evaluates these two mimetic voices. The diegetic voice is also double. It can comment at the time and record the comments and evaluations as they occurred in the mind at the time or it can record in retrospect and in terms of accumulated experience as it affects the re-telling. A mimetic voice can be adding a diegetic commentary. The mimetic voice which re-tells the story some years later is itself diegetic to the extent that it alters the sequence.

A purely diegetic comment is one like Boswell's that wants to explain the joke or the significance of the meeting. It is meta-physical, meta-experiential, meta-vocal, a "voice above the voice." A purely mimetic one is one like Boswell's which records the discussion with Davies about the impression he made on Johnson or the sequence of the joke itself or the discussion about the actor Garrick. The purely mimetic voice is the voice on a tape recorder.

I will now give an example of the mimetic voices as they occurred and Boswell's diegetic commentary after the fact. At the time of the meeting, Boswell said to himself that he wanted to engage Johnson in conversation and then he actually did so. The diegetic voice realizes that he may have ruined his chances with Johnson by saying what he did and a later diegetic voice attempts to explain that he probably did deserve "this check."

> Eager to take any opening to get into conversation with him, I ventured to say, 'O, Sir, I cannot think Mr. Garrick would grudge such a trifle to you.' 'Sir, (said he, with a stern look,) I have known David Garrick longer than you have done: and I know no right you have to talk to me on the subject.' Perhaps I deserved this check; for it was rather presumptuous in me, an entire stranger, to express any doubt of the justice of his animadversion upon his old acquaintance and pupil. I now felt myself much mortified, and began to think that the hope which I had long indulged of obtaining his acquaintance was blasted. And, in truth, had not my ardour been uncommonly strong, and my resolution uncommonly persevering, so rough a reception might have deterred me for ever from making any further attempts. Fortunately, however, I remained upon the field not wholly discomfited.[12]

The series of voices that a person like Boswell experienced in his first meeting with Samuel Johnson are the materials from which

Boswell writes his two narratives of the meeting. He examines the interior discourse of voices in his own consciousness and attempts to decide how best to narrate that discourse of voices in a written narrative.

Shirley Neumann argues that a person like Gertrude Stein, and for me, James Boswell, tries to re-create the narrative present of the author's or character's mind in the multi-dimensional spatial-temporal configuration of voices in the narrative.

The external events of the writer's or the character's experience are secondary to their consciousness of the interior voices present at the experience and their consciousness of the voices presently narrating. That consciousness may have wandered back and forth in time and place during the event and thoughts may go back to the past event by the most thin thread; or the consciousness may project into the future into some anticipated event again connected to the present by the slightest link. Thus the narrative becomes interlaced, intertwined, braided, much like the stream of consciousness narratives of a Virginia Woolf novel, but different from a stream of consciousness novel to the extent that in autobiographical writing there are real, external objects referring to real, external events in the consciousness of the autobiographer. The two Boswell narratives evidence this recursive process.

Each associative digression takes the narrator to a different point of beginning. This principle of observing and recording massive compounds of details results in either a relinquishing of control over the infinite variables in any situation or attempting to scientifically structure them and generalize by citing a single significant variable.

Continuous presence is Stein's metaphor for ontological autobiography, according to Neuman. Neuman is reading Stein as I will be reading Beckett in my conclusion and Shandy and Gart in Chapter One, under the umbrella of Derridean metaphysics.

Stein and Beckett both attempt to capture the essence, the consciousness, of the person by capturing the flux and flow of their mental acts. They create selves as phenomena in the narrative but with the twist that synecdochic generalizations and opposing metaphoric variables or metonymic voices are allowed to co-exist in time and space. They admit the past to their consciousness not as recollections or ways of reliving the past but as ways of metaphorically re-creating, synecdochically renewing and preserving, and metonymically re-discovering.

When trying to create this continuous presence in narrative, in a written text, the result is a prolonged, "thick" present of voices because moments do not pass continuously with a prolonged elaboration of the conscious thoughts and feelings. There are two continuous presents intersecting: the historical past moment of the event being remembered and narrated and the present writing, narrating moment.

Stein's and Beckett's way of knowing themselves in assessing the multiple traces and fragments of their life experiences in an atemporal atmosphere is analogous to but different from the Boswell narratives constructed temporally and spatially. The experience of the moment of meeting Johnson as the product of a linear progression creates a portrait which incorporates and extends (is contiguous with) another earlier portrait; there is no denial or annulment of past moments. There is for Stein and Beckett, Shandy and Gart, no connection between the persons and events in their lives except the connections made in the mind and feelings of the autobiographer as recorded in the text.

Daryl Mansell maintains that an autobiographer like Boswell intends to structure himself in words based upon this impulse in consciousness, this impulse to order and bracket and in so doing give purpose and meaning. The story is not being true to the real experience as it actually happened but it is being true to the author's consciousness of it and the impulse to create, order, design, give purpose and meaning to it. The main strength of autobiography is that it is a form which organizes interior life based upon interior, illocutionary force and activities not in correspondence with exterior facts. The phenomenological "truth" of what really happened is in this amorphous activity in the consciousness of the autobiographer.

There are actually two sets of raw materials to deal with in the Boswell narrative. First, there are Boswell's own interior perceptions and intuitions which he attempts to explain in the narrative as well as the variety of external circumstances that were occurring at the time. Both Davies and Johnson might construct completely different narratives with different foci based upon their own interior perceptions and intuitions and their personal remembrances of the external circumstances. This is what Edmund Husserl calls the "natural standpoint"[13] of each of the parties involved. They tell the story from a unique, highly individualized, subjective perspective and they represent their own consciousness by means of the mimetic-diegetic voices in the narrative.

There is an immediate act of consciousness which registers various intuitions, perceptions and memories at the time of the experience as there are a different set when the experience is narrated in retrospect. Boswell calls Johnson "the great"[14] in the *Journal* but then proceeds in the *Life* with an elaborate comparison of Johnson to the portrait done of him by Sir Joshua Reynolds. He examined his initial perception of "great" and after thirty years friendship with Johnson shaped a narrative elaboration of what he meant by "great."

Boswell first wrote in the *Journal*:

> Mr. Johnson is a man of a most dreadful appearance. He is a very big man, is troubled with sore eyes, the palsy, and the king's evil. He is very slovenly in his dress and speaks with a most uncouth voice. Yet his great knowledge and strength of expression command vast respect and render him very excellent company. He has great humour and is a worthy man. But his dogmatical roughness of manners is disagreeable.[15]

And in the *Life* he writes:

> I found that I had a very perfect idea of Johnson's figure, from the portrait of him painted by Sir Joshua Reynolds soon after he had published his *Dictionary*, in the attitude of sitting in his easy chair in deep meditation, which was the first picture his friend did for him, which Sir Joshua very kindly presented to me, and from which an engraving has been made for this work.[16]

Introduction 13

The factual arrival of Johnson receives three diegetic additions: the first, "great," occurs mimetically at the time. The second, the longer physical description in the *Journal* occurs at a later time when he wrote the entry and the third, the comparison to the Joshua Reynolds portrait occurs later again. The Scottish joke and the discussion of Garrick follow a similar pattern of vocal additions and commentaries.

An autobiographical narrative unit like Boswell's dual narrations of his first meeting with Samuel Johnson gives some insight into the understanding of Boswell because of his many diegetic/mimetic voices represented there.

My theory of autobiographical writing as a genre then, in contradistinction to my philosophy discussed in the conclusion, is that pieces of writing are autobiographical and can be considered as part of a genre in their own right when they meet the guidelines that I have elaborated here.

An autobiographical document exists when there are mimetic-diegetic voices in narratives units which represent the thinking of either the non-fictional writer or a fictional character.

An autobiography exists when the narrative units each in its own way represents something unique and significant about the non-fictional writer or the fictional character. The diegetic/mimetic voices unite in the self-portrait (synecdoche). A memoir exists when the narrative units accumulate in such a way that they can replace each other in representing the writer or character (a metaphor). The mimetic/diegetic voices disagree with each other, and compare and contrast perceptions of the incidents narrated.

A confession exists when the narrative units accumulate in such a way that they make significant, important connections in the life story of the character or writer (a metonym). The diegetic/mimetic voices reveal and explain these connections.

An autobiographical document, any piece of writing really, can contain narratives of all three types or of one more than another. But whether the narratives are predominantly a memoirist comparison and contrast of voices and experiences, or an autobiographical attempt to unify significant experiences and voices or a confessional attempt to explain and reveal motivations and intentions, the document and its narratives still separate themselves generically in terms of the synecdochic, metaphoric, metonymic voices.

In Chapter One, I shall interpret eight documents which I consider to be autobiography proper according to my theory outlined in this introduction. In Chapters Two and Three, I shall consider memoirs and confessions and in Chapter Four I shall consider one autobiographical writer, John Henry Newman, as autobiographer, memoirist and confessor.

Notes

1 William Labov, Paul Cohen, Clarence Robins and John Lewis, *A Study of Non-Standard English of Negro and Puerto Rican Speakers in New York City*; Co-operative Research Project No. 3288. Volume II: *The Use of Language in the Speech Community*, (Printed and distributed by the U.S. Regional Survey, 204 N. 35th Street, Philadelphia, Pennsylvania, 19104, 1968), 284-286.

2 Thomas Pison, "Wordsworth's Autobiography: The Metonymy of the Self," (*Bucknell Review*, 23, ii, 1977), 85, 92.

3 James Olney, *Metaphors of the Self: The Meaning of Autobiography*, (Princeton University Press, 1972), 39.

4 Olney, 39.

5 Olney, 39.

6 Henry Adams, *The Education of Henry Adams: An Autobiography*, (Boston: Houghton-Mifflin Company, 1961), 86.

7 James Boswell, *London Journal: 1762-1763*, (New York: McGraw-Hill Book Company, Inc., 1950), 260 and James Boswell's *Life of Johnson*, (Oxford University Press, 1980), 277.

8 Boswell. *Life*, 277.

9 Boswell, *Life*, 277.

10 Boswell, *Life*, 278.

11 Susan Snaider Lanser, *The Narrative Act: Point of View in Prose Fiction*, (Princeton University Press, 1981), 224.

12 Boswell, *Life*, 278.

13 Edmund Husserl, *Ideas: General Introduction to Pure Phenomenology*, London: Collier MacMillan Publishers, 1962, 226-227.

14 Boswell, *Journal*, 260.

15 Boswell, *Journal*, 260.

16 Boswell, *Life*, 277.

Chapter One

An Autobiography Unites the Mimetic/Diegetic Voices In a Synecdochic Narrative

> What else than a natural and mighty palimpsest is the human brain?...Everlasting layers of ideas, images, feelings, have fallen upon your brain softly as light. Each succession has seemed to bury all them before. And yet, in reality, not one has been extinguished....Yes, reader, countless are the mysterious handwritings of grief and joy which have inscribed themselves successively upon the palimpsest of your brain; ...They are not dead but sleeping.[1]

Introduction

The metaphor of the palimpsest for the mind and consciousness is one which figures forth the diversity of the mind, the chemistry of the brain and the complexity of consciousness as a unity. An autobiography focuses on the unity there represented in a synecdochic event or moment; a memoir focuses on the diversity there represented in the metaphoric replacement of significant events and moments with each other; a confession focuses on the revelation of a new, hitherto unrecognized or unacknowledged metonymic connection.

My aim in Chapter One is to investigate eight pieces of writing, four fictional and four non-fictional, which I call "autobiography proper" as opposed to memoir or confession because the diegetic/mimetic voice of the present narrating consciousness of the writer/narrator unites with the diegetic/mimetic voices in the piece, the narration. The series of acts of consciousness which lead to the production of the state of consciousness in the autobiographer who writes the narrative unites with the series of acts and states of consciousness represented in the narrative.

Besides the theorists used in the Introduction, I will use William Earle, Jean-Jacques Mayoux and Georges Gusdorf to clarify and define what I mean by this unity between acts and states of consciousness which makes the piece of writing different from a comparison, contrast or revelation of acts and states of consciousness which I shall define in subsequent chapters on confession and memoir. I will use Tristram Shandy, Hermione Gart, a man lying on his back in the dark, a 95 year old man about to commit suicide, Helen Keller, Christopher Nolan, John Stuart Mill and Maya Angelou as the illustrative documents to support the theory.

William Earle says that the autobiographical consciousness remembers and examines in the present a past series of acts of consciousness about a particular event or experience which acts were bracketed then into a state of consciousness about the experience or event and are re-bracketed, often re-arranged, thus the fiction, in the present re-telling. The present series of acts of consciousness which remembers and examines are autobiographical acts by which the autobiographer re-brackets the material for narrative re-telling. Northrup Frye asserts that "most autobiographies are inspired by a creative, and therefore fictional, impulse to select only those events and experiences...that go to build up an integrated pattern."[2]

In his article "Variations on the Time-Sense in *Tristram Shandy*," Jean-Jacques Mayoux explores Tristram Shandy's autobiographical consciousness which is caught in what he calls a "thick present."[3] Tristram's present series of acts of consciousness, and their attendant voices, are a series of acts of remembering and examining a past series in a complex, internal palimpsest of intuitions and perceptions.

Georges Gusdorf explores the importance of affixing a name to these acts and states of consciousness so as to bracket, organize and unify them. And in support of Gusdorf but from another point of view, Michael Cooke talks about namelessness as a form of annihilation and naming oneself in a text empowers the autobiographer with the creation of a unified, "named" self. The autobiographer preserves the self, saves the life of the self, by naming and organizing the self into a verbal narrative.

Laurence Sterne's fictional piece of writing, *The Life and Opinions of Tristram Shandy*, portrays Tristram in the mimetic act of narrating his past "life and opinions" as a present state of consciousness with which he is united. This piece of writing represents the "thick present" of mimetic associations and opinions in Tristram's consciousness which are voiced and then united with Tristram's diegetic assertion that this narrative is a synecdochic "history of what passes through a man's mind."[4] Like Sterne's Tristram, Hilda Doolittle's *Hermione* also represents a unity of voices amidst a random and confused association of diverse perceptions and intuitions which are mimetically voiced in the narrative and diegetically named and commented on through a series of images to represent synecdochically the unity in diversity.

Samuel Beckett in *Company* portrays a man lying on his back alone in the dark; this is the single, synecdochic image; and he portrays this man in a mimetic series of vocal narrations and commentaries about himself in which the man diegetically divides himself into three separate voices to each of which he attaches a name: a voice, a hearer, and a creator of the two.

Eugene Ionesco in *The Chairs* dramatizes the synecdochic event of a conversation between an old man and his wife on the night of their suicides. The old man mimetically recalls the past events of his life which his present voice attempts to unify and, in a present diegetic voice, to endow with meaning and value. The accumulation of mimetic experiences throughout a lifetime can be mimetically re-presented, narrated, and diegetically edited, explained and evaluated.

Helen Keller in *The Story of My Life* portrays herself synecdochically as the young girl who learned to communicate, read and eventually speak. The series of mimetic activities which led to these achievements and resulted in the diegetic realization that these were the "most important days of her life" are united with

Helen's mimetic, narrating voice which diegetically comments upon them in retrospect.

Christopher Nolan's *Under the Eye of the Clock* unites his consciousness of himself as the quadriplegic narrator/author with the consciousness of his fictional protagonist Joseph Meehan. The mimetic series of activities of the quadriplegic-protagonist Joseph Meehan are united with the series of activities and voices of the quadriplegic-author-narrator Christopher Nolan who diegetically comments on Joseph. The quadriplegia is the synecdoche.

John Stuart Mill explores his mental breakdown as a synecdoche in narrative form in Chapter Five of his *Autobiography* "A Crisis in My Mental History." He mimetically portrays himself as proceeding through various stages, or "rays of light,"[5] on his way back to mental health and he diegetically selects, organizes and gives voice to these particular stages or rays of light in the chapter. He sifts the "thick present" mimetically experienced in and during the crisis and diegetically "names" the highlights in the present act of narration.

In Chapter 12 of *I Know Why The Caged Bird Sings*, Maya Angelou portrays herself in the synecdochic experience of a child sexually abused by her stepfather. Angelou gives mimetic voice to the abused child and unites that voice with the adult, diegetic commentary.

William Earle focuses on the importance of the fact that the autobiographer is examining a past event from the narrative point of view of the present. Georges Gusdorf says that it is very important for an autobiographer to examine the past and gain control over it by naming it. Michael Cooke points out that an autobiographer names and owns personal experiences and states of consciousness so as not to let them slip into the "chaos of namelessness,"[6] Jean-Jacques Mayoux calls Cooke's "chaos of namelessness," a "thick present" of interconnections which the autobiographer separates. Avrom Fleischmann, with Northrup Frye and Susanna Egan, bases his theoretical perspective on his belief that the autobiographical act is an attempt to unify and integrate the life experience and consciousness into a pattern.

Based upon these critics and documents, my theory is that if a piece of writing, a particular narrative unit, unites and gives voice to a series of acts and states of consciousness of the present narrator with a series of acts and states of consciousness of the protagonist, who is the narrator in the past, then the narrative unit is generically a piece of autobiographical writing and should properly be called an "autobiography" as opposed to a "memoir" or "confession." If a series of narrative units in an entire document follow the same pattern, then the document is called an "autobiography."

Each of the documents or narrative units that I have chosen are noteworthy because they each evidence an emergence from a "thick present" of confusion, where the narrator was thrown into silence, overwhelmed by the multiple voices within, into a unified, integrated portrait where the parts of the chaos are separated and named. The chaotic subjectivity inherent in these documents and narratives achieves patterned objectivity when the acts and states of consciousness are cast as phenomenological objects and given voice in narrative.

PART ONE: FICTIONAL AUTOBIOGRAPHIES

Tristram Shandy

The Life and Opinions of Tristram Shandy is a good example of a narrating, authorial act of one who determines the narrative point of view and voice throughout the document. Tristram is the eyewitness to his own thinking, his own perceptions and intuitions. Tristram casts his glance quite naturally at whatever interests him and he organizes his discussion of what he sees in whatever way he wants. He mimetically represents the content of his own mind in sequence, which appears, of course, to be completely, totally disorganized, and diegetically comments upon and evaluates it throughout the entire series of books which become then an autobiographical document.

He diegetically comments on what he is mimetically doing as narrator and protagonist and what he expects and presumes that the reader will do. He says that he is narrating his own opinions and feelings about his own life story. He says the narrative is called his "life and opinions" so that the reader is aware from the start that there will be less "life" in the sense of a mimetic sequencing of the external events as the field of objects under investigation and more the "opinions," in the sense of a mimetic sequencing of feelings and thoughts, perceptions and intuitions, about the events and experiences. His consciousness is objectified as an Husserlean phenomenon in this document as the various acts and states of consciousness are voiced.

The content of the external field of objects from which Tristram receives his perceptions and intuitions are bracketed into isolated units which are insightful and meaningful to him because of the simple fact that they are his.

The fact that he created the story about the problem with the clock on the night of his conception (2) or the problems at his birth (29) and baptism (44) or any of the narrative bits and pieces, the traces, about his relatives are devices through which he can mimetically represent his random thoughts and feelings about these events and experiences and make diegetic points about both the experience and his thoughts. Tristram's narrative subverts the autobiographical assumption that this document will be an accurate, unified sequence of external events or that it will be a clear explanation of these events. His narrative focuses on a sequence of random, incoherent, diegetic and mimetic comments and evaluative remarks as present acts and states of consciousness.

The sequences of persons and events in Tristram's life come into this narrative at random; they are not chronologically sequenced. They are sequenced only to the extent that they trigger reactions in Tristram's present, narrating consciousness. The associations in Tristram's mind control the sequence; his opinions, perceptions, insights, attitudes about his memories of events control the presentation of events: Earle's two states of consciousness examining each other. Past events are narrated, amplified, clarified and sequenced according to the present evaluative comments and associations in Tristram's narrative voice.

The present voice which sets out to narrate this story is one which is a random association of voices which have been grouped and formed into associational "states" or constructs. Tristram's apparently haphazard digressions and multiple voices actually interrelate and connect into an intercalated narrative which represents a unified voice and activity in consciousness. Tristram, in fact, admires his own consciousness, his own digressive ability to inter-relate the past, present and future through associational digression, progression and retrogression (52, 333, 380). He manages to communicate that sense of simultaneity (268-269) of past, present and future, that timelessness, which is part of consciousness, through his mental meanderings. The mental associations in one section of one story lead to a variety of mental associations in another section of another story and the stories, the fragments, overlap because of these minor associations and not because they have any actual, objective connection in time and space or some major synecdochic significance or metaphoric/metonymic similarity.

The events themselves took place or are taking place or will take place in a particular time and location. Each event has a field of objects which occupy or will occupy some kind of position in Tristram's unconscious, preconscious and conscious mind and memory. The details of a particular situation in one story remembered about one event may come to be associated with one or two details from another event in another time and place, joined metonymically, synecdochically or metaphorically in the narrating present of the palimpsest of Tristram's consciousness. These associations in Tristram's conscious mind and memory braid together to form this narrative of his consciousness, his "life and opinions" in this document which serves as a phenomenal object of study which offers access to Tristram's mind.

Tristram constructs and expresses a synecdochic attitude, a stance, based upon his own personal experience and feeling, that people should be allowed to tell their own stories about their own lives in their own way (446). It is not the external events themselves, the sequential activities and experiences, the field of objects viewed, but the person's conscious judgement and feeling about the experiences that matter; the perceptions, intuitions, attitudes formed and bracketed from the experience.

As a fiction, the narration of Tristram Shandy represents an abstraction, an idealization, a model, of the autobiographical enterprise as the act of an individual consciousness examining the perceptions and intuitions of lived experience and the individual consciousness gives voice to those perceptions and intuitions *ad libitum*. The discourse of perceptions and intuitions, ideas, feelings, attitudes, intentions and motivations in Tristram's individual consciousness are language acts recorded in the narratives of the autobiographical document which are metonymic parts of the larger discourse in his consciousness but are removed from consciousness and vocalized for others to hear.

Tristram's "thick present" of voices narrates past events in his life but as he narrates, a detail about the event will remind him of a detail in another event which may have occurred before or after the event being narrated. This activity in Tristram's mind and memory is the activity of a consciousness experiencing itself in the continuous, internal present of interrelated details. The details come from the external past, present and future comprised of events, fields of objects, from which intuitions and perceptions were formed, and they can be narrated as stories with beginnings and endings that can be verified or disproved by other individuals who participated in the event.

Tristram allows the details of the discontinuous, unstoppable, external ever-present field of objects (the mimetic) to pass before him while he participates in the details of a discontinuous, internal present, a field of intuitions and perceptions (mimetic), which he is free to stop and comment on or shape and change or re-structure (diegetic). As Tristram begins to narrate a story with a beginning, middle and end about an external event from his past, a field of objects from which he drew perceptions and intuitions, this narrative of the field of objects of the external event switches to a narrative of the internal field of perceptions and intuitions in consciousness.

He remembers a lecture that his father and Uncle Toby gave on "Duration" which led him to write his own Preface to Locke, the father of "Associationism" (Chapter 18 of Book Three, 137 ff.). Locke's theory of Associationism and Duration undergird Tristram's whole approach to his own life and opinions and become Tristram's own diegetic comment on his own consciousness of his own method of analyzing consciousness. Perceptual-intuitive associations in Tristram's consciousness keep succeeding and bumping into each other and connecting with each other and this record of their succession and connection in Tristram's "life and opinions" allows others access to them. He uses Locke to defend his narrative method.

The continuous present in an individual's consciousness along with an apparent continuous present in the flow of events in time and space create this "thick present" that Mayoux writes about because the external field of multiple objects continues to flow and change as does the internal field of perceptions and intuitions drawn from the external field of objects. Consciousness itself is burdened with this complex pattern, this palimpsest, of intuitions, associations and perceptions of past events held in Freudian-Derridean memory traces which make the present moment of individual consciousness "heavy or thick" with anticipation, pregnant with expectation about the future or weighed down by past accumulations. The memory traces, the expectations and the recollections, run side by side with the disconnected, continuous, random succession of the present associations always already going on and being recorded by memory. Consciousness attempts to break, bracket and integrate in a diegetic construct the disconnected, continuous, random succession of mimetic experiences passing before it into connected, discrete, ordered events, actions and activities, perceptions, intuitions, attitudes giving them beginnings and endings and placing them in memory as little packages, narrative units, states of consciousness. These traces are infinitesimal, microscopic, microcosmic interrelations and intersections that "bump into each other"[7] in random succession (which is suggestive of Derrida's point that such construction is a violent act which point I will develop more fully in the conclusion to this book) but connect in the bracketing done by the act of consciousness. Tristram does very little bracketing, connecting and integrating into narrative units and so is concerned about the welfare of the reader in this random journey through his consciousness. He invites the reader's participation but he cautions the reader to be patient with his digressions. The nature of his narrative is such that it is natural for him to stop and reflect on a particular perception or intuition that comes to mind. This may be frustrating, boring and trivial to the reader who wants to get on with the action, the sequence of events, the essentials of plot, the adventure. He focuses on particular perceptions and intuitions and makes little co-operative effort to connect and organize them for the reader. But, in terms of the autobiographical act as an acquisition and expression of a unified consciousness, the "action," the sequence of events, the plot, the adventure that the reader is looking for is taking place in the mind, the consciousness of Tristram's associations.

Tristram attempts Denis Donoghue's "communion"[8] with the reader by suggesting that there is a "confidentiality," a personal relationship between them because he is relating such personal feelings. His digressions may be burdensome to the reader because they are illogical and difficult to follow and the reader loses his own authority and control as reader except to the extent that he may adventurously try to connect the random thoughts. There is always the danger that the reader will miss Tristram while looking for the plot.

The diegetic point that Tristram is making and a point that is essential, it seems to me, to the autobiographical act is that everything a person is interested in and feels strongly about is a doorway to an understanding of that person's consciousness. Tristram does not want to close off any of these doorways to his consciousness in the name of getting on with a "plot." He warns the reader to be careful because the digressions in the mimetic narrative come fast and furiously and the reader may be lost. Tristram admits diegetically that he really wants to "have thee [gentle reader] in my power (340)" by continually postponing the tale of Uncle Toby's amours and holding that story as "bait" for the reader to keep reading. Tristram mimetically represents the stream of intuitions and perceptions in his consciousness but with very little diegetic selection or editing along the way except to say that he wants the reader in his power and he wants to tell the story in his own way and he likes digressing at random. He does indeed diegetically select from his consciousness but with no apparent rational order so it appears mimetic.

Tristram concludes from his own experience of what passes through his own mind that the subtlety and fine-grainedness of consciousness depend on this immense network of associations, this palimpsest, in the brain from which he selects with no apparent pattern. The experience of his consciousness as a Husserlean phenomenon with the variety of perceptions and intuitions there, becomes the object of study for Tristram and he attempts to represent that object mimetically in his narration.

Tristram says that he can tell the story of any number of events in his life and list the facts, the sequence, the field of objects, as he remembers them, but it is the detail and flourish of the perceptions and intuitions, the attitudes and feelings in his consciousness that give the facts, the sequences of events, their interest. He wants to get past the factual details of the stories, which information anybody could supply, and he wants to get on with his perceptions and intuitions about selected details which may be disordered (61, 104, 300, 443).

He can make points about how he feels, what he thinks, and how his attitudes were formed, and it is this detail and flourish with which he embellishes his interior states that give them their autobiographical, synecdochic significance. The bald statement of a diegetic point either about consciousness and its field of perceptions and intuitions or the external world and its field of objects needs the rhetorical flourish, the mimetic detail, to support the diegetic point.

In Chapters 14-19 of Book 6 (307), Tristram makes a diegetic point, an attitude that he has, and one that I think is important to his autobiographical act, that there is some humor behind this whole endeavor (7, 237). He takes himself so seriously and he wants his reader to take him equally seriously by following carefully every thread of every digression in every detail to its apparent, however whimsical, end point. He admits that there is a certain humor to this kind of delicate handling and mimetic tracing, leading and following. He is sensitive to the meaninglessness and disorganization of the minutiae of this mimesis but he is also sensitive to the fact that this minutiae is the very "stuff" of which his mind is made. He does not want to edit or bracket the progress of these thoughts and feelings through his mind except to say that it's quite humorous.

The serious side of Tristram's activity is his admission that time and chance check us in these interior progress and movements. We think there is order and coherence in our minds and in our lives, he says, but he then mimetically exemplifies his diegetic point that there is neither order nor coherence in consciousness nor in life. Order and coherence are diegetic creations of the consciousness. The bracketing and reducing acts of consciousness hinge on the multiple, mimetic, sequential associations of perceptions and intuitions which accompany events and experiences. The diegetic bracketing and associating of the interior perceptions, intuitions, ideas and attitudes into braided narrative units create coherence in consciousness.

But as serious as this realization may be, Tristram still reminds his reader that there is this "fancifulness (156, 161, 218, 260, 307, 413, 421, 433) or humor to such an endeavor. A focus on mimetic triviality and detail calls to mind that one is free to focus on the details in any way and for any length of time and one is also free to organize and bracket them or not. The humor about it, and Tristram's diegetic, synecdochic point is, that a person not be obsessively tied to the mimetic, cause-effect detail or the fact that time and chance check us in our progress or the fact that we are compelled by necessity, predestination, or fate. But he makes the very important Derridean point that we are indeed each free to "play" creatively with the detail and imaginatively organize and unify (the Husserlean bracket) the interior, eyewitness traces, fully aware of inaccuracies and aberrations but also fully aware that the facts are not the controlling feature, the person is.

Tristram invites the reader to join the random journey through his own consciousness by doing such things as inserting a blank page on which the reader can sketch a picture of the Widow Wadman (330). Tristram invites the reader to sit back and enjoy, through laughter, the absurdity of this "cock and bull (457)" story, which opens the lungs and heart (257), he says, and forces the blood to circulate and the whirl of life to run.

Tristram intends that his readers feel just as free to speak and narrate as readers as he is as the writer. He suggests that just as the readers are able to be good-tempered, patient and humorous about this frustrating, endless succession of his associations so they should be able to be as good-tempered, patient and humorous with the flow of associations in their own minds (77, 104, 164, 333, 380, 435) which *his* associations provoked.

The multiplicity of perceptions and associations in consciousness can create a very real, frightening sense of "panic" though, as one tries to arrive at constructions, visions or states with which one can be comfortable. Personal memories of past experiences, voices and events which appeared at the time to be insignificant traces may be recycled, re-voiced, in any number of ways in an attempt to unify, make significant.

Unlike Tristram, Hermione Gart unsuccessfully attempts to bracket and give some kind of order, coherence, and structure to the chaos and multiplicity of her own consciousness. She has become a stranger to the range of perceptions and intuitions in her own interior life and her narration of her consciousness becomes an act of consciousness which randomly explores the confusion. She is much more serious about the digressions in her than Tristram is about his.

Hermione Gart

Hermione articulates a wide range of perceptions, attitudes and intuitions, some of which are bracketed into states and named, most are not. Like Tristram, she is lost in this "thick present" of interior associations and voices. But unlike Tristram, her voice is "frequently overwrought"[9] and imitates the experience of interior confusion and fear brought about by what she diegetically explains as an uncontrollable and disorganized interior chaos.

Hermione finds it extremely difficult to modify, combine or reconstruct a single perspective or point of view. Her mimetic voice in the text articulates a consciousness in suspension, in transition, and in the very process of re-examining the suspension, from her own unique, natural standpoint, she diegetically perceives the dissolution or disintegration of past perceptions, intuitions, formulations, constructs and states as the essence of the transition.

There is an essential, phenomenal consciousness represented here; a consciousness who is aware that she is in a series of acts called transition, changing, becoming. The diegetic voice examines the utterances of the mimetic voice's perceptions, intuitions with a view to coming to some renewed sense of self.

"It feels like dementia (6)," she says. She knows that she would be considered "certifiably insane (6)" because of these "worlds forming worlds (6)" within her. There were some acts of combining, modifying and re-structuring in consciousness but not in the sense of arriving at anything conclusive. Her mind was a "patchwork of indefinable associations (24)," she says, "breaking up like molecules in test tubes....Some plants give birth by breaking apart, by separating themselves from each other (31,118, 178)." Hermione needs to creep back into her shell, like the hermit crab, so that she too can moult and emerge full-fledged (221), the renewed being arisen from the phoenix ashes.

She envisions her consciousness as an object which is "octopus-like (61, 71-72)." The extended octopus arms reach out to re-modify and re-combine, structure and re-structure, in an attempt to collect the chaos of perceptions, intuitions and feelings within and make sense of them but these attempts at structuring only make her feel more remote and distanced from herself. The octopus image suggests that her consciousness is immersed in the depths of some metaphoric sea and the raw materials of her perceptions and intuitions and the various bracketings and reductions already done are the tentacles of the octopus which reach out helplessly in an attempt to re-organize, re-connect.

This synecdochic image of Hermione's consciousness as an octopus flailing its arms coupled with the image of this same octopus flailing its arms in a sea that is "frozen (161)" and motionless is for Hermione an effective visualization of her mimetic consciousness. If the sea is considered as the field of external objects from which consciousness draws new perceptions and insights, intuitions and attitudes, then the image of the sea as frozen suggests that the field of objects in Hermione's vision, the natural standpoint that she is taking on reality, is also frozen, motionless. She can receive no more raw materials until consciousness has "thawed," processed, and bracketed what is there. "Divided we [the multiple and as yet unbracketed perceptions and intuitions within] probably would stand," she asserts (78).

Hermione needs to cling to some state or construction of consciousness of herself, some thing or idea to hold onto as a nucleus, a core, a unified, organic sense of self. One way for her to do this is in the assertion of her name, Hermione Gart (4, 32, 28, 64, 70, 73), which she does throughout the narrative.

The voice which names the self or parts of the self is a diegetic voice which reduces or brackets the multiple components of the self into the name, as a unit, and a statement of fact. The act of naming is that act of bracketing or reducing whereby one creatively utters the words which represent the self. The names uttered are acts of consciousness similar to Husserl's bracketing. The names are a frame in which to place the object. Naming confers an essence, an identity, a singularity, on consciousness, on individuality, on personhood. Hermione is reduced to an essential kind of self-consciousness in the simple utterance of her name. Her awareness of her radical, interior division of previous reductions and namings and the chaotic multiplicity of perceptions and intuitions and past formations are highlighted by the fact that she breathes forth a variety of forms of her name for herself throughout the book. She is aware of a multiplicity by using different names but she is also aware that the name is a common denominator. "I am the word AUM. God is in a Word. God is in Her. I am the word AUM" (64, 119, 175-6, 193, 197, 198, 210).

Hermione's constitutive "I" expressed in her name is in self-conscious interaction with other "I's" and names in the document. The self-conscious "I" in dialogue with various past "I's" become the subjects, the heroines, the organizing principles in the document.

This kind of autobiographical document represents a consciousness examining itself in public in writing. But the 'public Hermione' examining herself in the written document is the same as the private Hermione who is in the process of interior turmoil, painful introspection. The public Hermione in the document who is experiencing all of this difficulty and disorientation is a heroine; her attempt to unify and re-structure her consciousness is given heroic status in the book.[10] Consequently, the experience of the real Hermione, the private person, who wrote or narrated the story, receives an equally heroic status. Her personal acts of consciousness, of re-structuring and re-organizing, become externalized in the public figure in the document so that her personal consciousness becomes an object with its own field of perceptions and intuitions and acts of bracketing and reduction for others to read and interpret in the document.

Hermione says that "a person only has to address a thing by its name and it would do anything (200)." She needed to have this image, this construction of herself, no matter how fluid, negative or inchoate, that her name represented. Sometimes she says that she felt so very strong, so right. Nothing hurt. And other times she felt choked with tears of humiliation (175). What at once feels like a great strength turns into a nothingness, an emptiness and then a fear. She thinks that if she just stops and stares hard enough in an act of consciousness that concentrates, trying to bracket and reduce, trying to arrive at systems and constructs of herself, then she

An Autobiography Unites the Mimetic/Diegetic Voices   33

will have evolved out of the nothingness and fear. She meets the Derridean absence, the void within while attempting the Husserlean bracket of the self. "The rest" to evolve is a "heart," an ability to feel again, she says (183, 186); a spiritual-emotional heart that would beat in rhythm with her own physical heart. In the document, her confusion is named a "hollow space (186)" where she wants heart and feeling and sense of self to be. Her first sense of a multiplicity (in which there is also a void, or a number of voids) occurs when she becomes conscious that she is stagnating, suffocating, embedded, forever "moss-grown (116)" yet at the same time starving for an inner vision, trying to break away, expand, grow. She "hugs HER to Hermione. The feeling was odd, queer and distorted, like being jerked out of the mellow width of space, out of the length and breadth of people, out of black trouser legs (135)." The predominant sense was that she was being "galvanized to extinction (13)," turned inward, thrust backwards. Like Beckett's man in *Company*, three personalities dialogue with each other when "*She* feels that something in *Her* should have warned *Hermione*."

Her perception of what was really happening to her was not in keeping with her vision of a future definition, a growth. She felt half of herself would be forever missing (16, 56, 200) and she feels that she desperately needs that missing half if she is to modify, re-combine and re-construct the whole. She says that it feels like one presence was torn from her and another alien presence was left alone within her. She could not know who she *was* nor *is* because she is really only half there; she has let the other half go. She did not feel at home in herself nor did she feel at home outside of herself. She feels as if she were the mercury about to burst out of the top of the thermometer (59); rising higher and higher, pulsing and beating, reaching for degrees which are beyond its capability. She feels as if she is shut up in a submarine (87) or in a bomb that is suddenly ready to explode. She obsesses about finding herself and she is aware that she is obsessed with the obsession itself (33); but she realizes that giving up the obsessive search was itself too frightening. It is easier to cling to memories overgrown. She would grope about (with the octopus-like tentacles of her consciousness) in the search forward but there was no sign in the world to give her direction. The tentacles of the octopus of her mind later become a "mental cobweb (59, 188)" that she herself (or some self within her) has woven.

She does have some sense of hope which occasionally emerges, but she wonders, when "this" shaping, this apparent bracketing and reducing, will be over (136); when will this play they call "Pygmalion" be finished (138). She determines that "incandescence" is that quality of soul which gives it its shape and centrality. Words constructed and breathed forth as names for acts of consciousness make that state of consciousness incandescent. There is always, in the heart of a new consciousness forming, just that center, that pin point of "incandescence" that holds it together (206, 215). And Hermione does very often feel as if she is the Eliza Doolittle character being formed in *Pygmalion* or a character in a bad novel where there is no reality (168-9, 173, 190).

She needs to move about and re-arrange her life "like doll house furniture (55, 151)" but she can't do it. She feels like she's the doll who has been set down by someone else in a window. This state brings about a negativity, a self-consciousness that is painful because it can't define and name itself. She is not doing the shaping and molding.

When asked what she would "take up next (51)," she responds that she does not know what this "take up" means. She is lost in the present interior journey through multiple perceptions and intuitions, past constructs and visions, and does not care to "take up" anything except to perform the acts of consciousness which will give her the authority to sort out the multiplicity within; nor does she even know how to go about "taking up" anything new. Others still suggest that she ought to do something because she looks too odd, distracted, worried, and "not right here (96, 196)." They want to know where she is going. She agrees that everybody seems to be "taking something up" and "caring for something (82)" but she wonders when this will happen for her. She rather feels continually beaten down when she tries to "take up." She focuses on the incidental and the trivial, the molecules and triangles of her mind fetched in by the octopus arms.

The confused state causes her to generalize and conceptualize in such a way that it feels like a construction to her, but it also feels like something she has created rather than been forced upon her. "All your life (52)" may be spent in vain looking for glory or fame, wisdom or happiness but she feels as if she can't love anyone and her brain is a lead block, a frozen sea, when she tries to remember having loved or cared for something or someone. She wonders what she ever "took up" and what she *was* when she took it up? And what is she now?

As a matter of fact, *now*, she says, is raging down upon her like a "great lumbering bullock (54, 237)," half formed, dangerous. The confusion tossed her about in the undulation of the *now* and she could not re-comprehend, re-organize, re-order. *Now* is the very thing that made this experience of confusion so difficult. She would sit with the moment, the now, the fraction of waiting, and lose it. Nothing could bring back that lost moment. No words could make the thing solid, visible and something with which she could successfully cope. Hermione seeks the solid and the visible in the invisible, amorphous neurochemistry of her brain. She wants to touch, feel and experience the intangibles, the absolutes, the Platonic universals. She is tremendously conscious of significant, solid, visible moments transcending themselves and passing into "all moments" and thus losing their specificity, uniqueness and tangibility (214-216).

The day, like her consciousness, is divided into these moments from dawn til dark. One moment divides early morning from exact morning, as another moment has divided it from dawn. Zeno-like, Hermione divides herself and everything else infinitely in two. Like Beckett's "millet grains of sand,"[11] in *Endgame*, the pile of sand represents the essential wholeness of being and unity of consciousness at the same time that it is comprised of this infinite number of these grains of sand. Hermione sees herself, her consciousness, as divided into moments which are each standing upon the other, like grains of sand, each moment connected to the other, saving the other. This petty pace of infinite divisibility, she says, echoing Shakespeare's Macbeth, will creep on into tomorrow as it did today, making all her yesterdays and tomorrows into an infinite, frustrating divisibility of moments (216). She stood now as part of next year and part of last year but not totally either (225); she could feel the moment about to pass on to the next moment and then into all moments. But each of those moments, taken together, gave her consciousness its incandescence, its wholeness, its centrality.

"People *do* get lost, don't they," she asks (232). We've all come to the end of something and when we look back at it, it appears to be a "heap of things," piled up, millet grains, infinitely divisible. Like Vladimir in Beckett's *Godot*, Hermione wonders where she is, where her own voice is, her own reality, in "all of this." She knows that there is within her that one grain, that one atomic, minute, center, that core of pure, incandescent truth that will unite her division.

Later in the book she wonders why she ever did "go on with it (191)" and she determines that the something that she got on with was a someone, herself. She wonders why she ever did get on with herself because herself turned out to be a series of others within her who tampered with each other. The very multiplicity and complexity of the range of intuitions and perceptions in consciousness are like a "delicate mechanical instrument (191)" and should not be tampered with unthinkingly because such tampering is disrespectful to the complicated, sensitive mechanism.

She concludes that she should not have really bothered with all of this analysis of the "thing behind the thing that mattered" which is her essential self-consciousness, her incandescence (193, 198). If she had just gone on saying and doing the same things or perhaps just let go and drifted along, perhaps then, she and the others within her would have come to realize that the thing (the phenomenal consciousness, the vision, as an object of study, the person, the unified self) behind the thing (the exterior field, the surface, the physical, the multiple perceptions and intuitions, the voice) was what mattered.

An Autobiography Unites the Mimetic/Diegetic Voices

In Hermione's vocalizations of her acts of consciousness, she creatively and mimetically constructs them from the perceptions and intuitions that make up her consciousness. She conveys the state of multiple self-consciousness that is keenly aware of itself. She talks about judging the entire tree by one leaf (56) like one may judge an entire person from one conversation. She sees the forest (the whole pile of sand) of her consciousness or the trees (the millet grains) or both or neither. She pictures herself in the forest primeval (98) and talks about herself as a little bird which has no wings, beak or feathers or the sort of thing a caterpillar would be before it is born (144).

A Man Lying on His Back in the Dark

In the document *Company*, Samuel Beckett mimetically represents a man "who is on his back in the dark"[12] by creating three separate voices or personae for the man. The man diegetically comments that he acknowledges these entities for the sake of the company they bring. Besides hearing the voice, the man is also aware of visual changes in the degree of blackness which make up the darkness in the room when he opens and closes his eyes and he is also aware of spatial changes in that he can vary his physical position.

He hears this voice "telling his past (8)" but the information given by the voice "cannot be verified (7-8)." The voice alludes to the present fact that the man is lying on his back in the darkness and rarely alludes to the future but the voice appears to be a "devising for the sake of company (8)."

The man lying on his back in the dark says that the voice is addressing him as "you" and telling stories about his past. The man decides that he will refer to the voice as "he" or "that cantankerous other (9)." He wonders if this voice might be talking about someone else present in the dark room or if the voice is speaking to him or someone else in the room or "to another of that other or of him. Or of another still. To another of that other or of him or of another still (14)." He concludes that the voice is in fact speaking to him about himself because he recognizes the stories as accurately describing him, his past and his situation. He wonders why the voice is speaking if there is no one else to hear and benefit from the stories (61). The only one to benefit is the hearer himself. He hears the stories about himself and then is left with silence punctuated by his own breathing. The hearer leaves, stops listening, because the voice stops speaking. The man remains on his back in the dark and he reminds himself in the silence that both the hearer and the voice are creatures, figments of his imagination (63). He himself on his back in the dark is the one who created them, who devised them for company to counter and temper the experience of the void within, the silence, the nothingness (64). The "devised deviser devises (64)" the voice and the hearer for the sake of company. Whether the deviser is the man himself or the voice or the hearer, they "devise" each other as entities who are created for the sake of creating, devising, as an activity, something to do.

Because the voice is speaking to him as a second person, he assumes that the subject matter of the narrative, the anecdotes, must be about him or the voice would use the third person. But all of this is a "lower order of mental activity (15)" to him but it is good to the extent and degree that it offers some degree of company, a feeling of communion with someone else, himself, his own multiple consciousness.

The voice comes to him from various quarters of the room, "from all sides and levels with equal remoteness" but "at no time from below (43)," reminding him that he is indeed lying on his back on the floor in the dark with his ears in the center of the room so that the voice can fill the 180 degrees around his head, on both sides of his ears (44). The voice is sometimes a faint murmur in his ear, which ebbs farther and farther away (19). It may change direction or flatten its tone (26). The voice may retreat into a long silence at which time the man is left with his breathing. The voice may repeat a story with a minor variant. It may remind him of the time he had his own voice, when he could speak in the first person singular rather than create a voice who speaks about him as a

An Autobiography Unites the Mimetic/Diegetic Voices   39

second person, a "you." The voice affirms, negates, interrogates, explains and exclaims (26).

He thinks sometimes that he will be on his back in this darkness and silence forever at which time the voice returns to penetrate the silence and darkness. This lying on his back in the dark may be a metaphor for death and this text could actually be continuation of *Malone Dies* but titled *Malone Dead*.

He decides later in the document to name himself as the one who hears the voice; he is also the one who breathes when the voice is silent. He calls the breather H. Aspirate and informs the voice that this is his name. But he abandons the naming plan because essentially it really doesn't matter; there is an unnameable voice and an unnameable hearer and an unnameable breather who are each part of the one man's consciousness. But he changes his mind again (59) and decides to call the hearer "M" and himself, the breather, "W" and the voice remains the voice. He devises all this not only for the sake of company but also for the sake of referential clarity, organizational structure.

He wonders if he should try to utter something himself, as the breather, the creator, W. His voice would at least be an addition to the others and hence add more company. A name, as I pointed out with regard to Hermione, is a hook, an organizer, a way to focus. He concludes that the voice telling the stories about him must be his own because the stories are so accurate. The voice must be a device of his own for the sake of company in the silence and darkness. He concludes "for the time being" that he is actually "speaking of himself...which of all the imaginable positions has the most to offer in the way of company (34, 35)."

He wants himself as hearer of his own voice to become more "companionable and human,...more alive (35-36, 45-46)" by an attempt at "reflexion, recall and even speech (36-37)." He is looking for some trace of emotional response, some sign of character. Later, he wonders if the voice, as well as the hearer, could be improved and made more companionable, less flat, repetitious, faint (45). He would like the voice to find an "optimum position from which to discharge itself with ideal amplitude for the greatest effect (46)."

When the voice tells him stories about himself from his past, the stories weary and confuse him. He imagines himself as the hearer who is apathetic (71) and mentally inert (70) unless the voice is telling a story. He wonders if all his crawling around in the darkness or straining his eyes to see in the darkness are perceptual experiences that could set these creative, storytelling voices into motion. Taste, touch, and smell appear to have "long-since dulled (72)" but sight, movement and hearing are still working.

He switches from himself as hearer and voice to himself as the deviser, the creator, W, and wonders if he is as mentally active and companionable as he wishes *them* to be (72). He sees himself crawling around in the dark trying to see. The creator in him is mentally alert to any clues that the hearer or the storyteller might offer to indicate to him the nature of the place where his imagination has consigned him (74-5).

The craving for companionship revives when he has been lying in silence for awhile. He needs to hear the voice again tell him a story about himself (77). Whether the voice is telling the truth or not, whether the voice is selecting and distorting the facts, the creator in him finds the innumerable ways and anecdotes of the voice most endearing (78). He learns to permute the three voices in a companionable way (79) just as he learns to take various physical positions as he lies in the darkness (80). The varieties of voices and positions "wax and wane" with each other (83) and this "waxing and waning," beginning, fading and ending seem to be the only constant. The dialogue of the voices in consciousness and the change in physical position and degrees of darkness are what make the void, darkness and silence less fearsome and more companionable.

He imagines every so often in the dialogue of voices in consciousness that he is not alone in the darkness of a meaningless void (86) of consciousness. The others within him "wax" about their respective interior positions and points of view until they "wane" into silence and come together in a unified consciousness, only to split again and start later. They slowly cease their laboring for words and images and fabling for stories and dialoguing about truths and "he in his consciousness is as he always was...alone (89)."

The diegetic voice tells him that his mind is less active than it has been but the present "activity of mind however slight is a necessary complement of company (11)." The important fact about this document is the dialogue of the three voices in consciousness which offer different angles and viewpoints, intuitions and insights. The three voices are complementary as well as supplementary in their construction of narratives and self-concepts.

The value of this document as autobiographical is in the quality of mind and spirit, the consciousness of the man and the degree to which the reader is admitted to these acts of consciousness.

Hermione, Tristram and Beckett's man are examples of the metaphysical, phenomenological, and what I call the autobiographical, compulsion to find and be true to one's own self, perceptions, and consciousness. They are each motivated to discover and uncover an innermost structure to their consciousness that will unify them. The documents do not represent "states" of consciousness so much as they do a dialogue among states of consciousness, which dialogues are acts of consciousness themselves. The relationship between this interior life, this dialogue between states of consciousness, is the story. Hermione, Tristram and the man in the dark are attempting to come to a "selbstbesinnung,"[13] an inner, self-understanding of their own consciousness. The autobiographical writer is metaphysically urged to search for the interior essence, the root, the inner self on which a life (and a synecdochic narrative or document of some kind) can be based and built.

A Ninety-Five Year Old Man About to Commit Suicide

Eugene Ionesco's 95 year old man in the play, *The Chairs*, is also attempting, on the night of his suicide, to come to some degree of self-understanding as Hermione and Beckett's man are by remembering and examining in a series of acts of consciousness, the mimetic details and events, the intentions and motivations, the raw materials of various past acts and states of consciousness in his life with a view to bracketing them and reducing them and making a diegetic, coherent, synecdochic statement about the meaning of his life.

He has hired a professional orator, a biographer, so to speak, who, on the night of this suicide, will deliver a speech about the meaning of the man's life. But the orator turns out to be mute which suggests to me that no one, including the individual, can really capture a philosophy of life, much less a life itself, in a diegetic, bracketed evaluation of that life in a speech or document, in a single, synecdochic narrative or series of narratives.

The old man has hired the orator to do this because he says that he has "difficulty expressing himself...it isn't easy for him...but he must tell all."[14] His wife insists that its easy for most people to express themselves once they've made up their minds to do so. Diegetic formulations, constructions and deductions about the meaning and significance of particular events and experiences come naturally, according to William Labov and Joshua Waletsky's research, from the person's examination and review of the raw material of lived experience.

The central irony in this play is that the words which the man utters about himself are constituted in the raw material of perceptions and intuitions in the man's consciousness and they do indeed, contrary to his protests, come easily for this old man, as in a spontaneous overflow. He doesn't really need the orator and he can express himself quite well. The audience listens to the mimetic flow of the man's consciousness but the man's ability to bracket diegetically the empirical data of the perceptions and intuitions of a lifetime into a single message or meaning is what is difficult for him.

The narrative unit in the play that begins "Then at last we arrived...(115 ff.)" is the beginning of a story that has always made this couple laugh. For the 75 years of their marriage, she has loved hearing him tell this story every evening but he has tired of it. She calls this story, "the story of his life, which fascinates her (115)" because "its her story too" and she says that she intentionally makes herself forget everything as though her mind were a "clean slate (115)."

The raw materials of the sequence of external events in this story have become lost and distorted. Facts and numbers do not fit together and the sequence is confused and disordered. The mimetic sequence is not a reliable representation of what happened. But something about the story unifies the consciousness of this couple.

The story goes like this: They first arrive at a fence. They are cold and wet and have been so for a very long time. "Someone" would not open the gate and let them into the garden where there was a path that led through a village to a church. He thinks in diegetic retrospect that they were in some city which "no longer exists" or maybe they were in Paris because he remembers the song "Paris will always be Paris" but he has no idea how they got there or what road they used or why he remembers this particular song. The sequence of memory traces in separate acts of consciousness from separate time periods and experiences interlace in the man's present act of consciousness.

As they both lose themselves in the process of remembering this story, he suddenly remembers why he started this whole story after all---then at last we arrived---it was this moment of "arrival" that both of them will never forget because they "laughed til they cried, the story is so idiotic." At this point the facts disintegrate into meaningless units of what Husserl calls phenomenological data, residuum, sedimentation, like "pot-bellied idiot, trunk full of rice, rice and idiot fall on the ground, his bare pot-belly shows." The phenomenological residuum is the fact that they always remember laughing hysterically at this event and its subsequent re-tellings and they remember the first line, "then at last we arrived."

In terms of phenomenal consciousness as an object of investigation, this man and woman are trying to recall something that happened to them 80 years ago but this "something" has been lost due to the fact that it has been told so many times that the sequential perceptions and intuitions of the initial experience which have been made into this narrative sequence have been lost and all that remains is selected, isolated facts and this "synecdochic" good feeling that makes them laugh. The story has that mythic element that often happens to a story when it is re-told repeatedly. Some event seems to have occurred but the important facts of the event have been lost and others re-arranged and transitions lost such that the mimetic sequencing makes little diegetic sense, unless that sense and meaning are bestowed on it by the author.

The construction of the story is a series of acts of consciousness that each time have reduced it to its essential nature as a time for them that was and has remained very important because it has made them laugh and obviously held their marriage together in some way.

This story sets them off on their hour and a half journey in the play to unify their perceptions of their lives. The old man's wife seems to think that he had some kind of "ideal [or goal] for his life (119)" but "things were not easy for him (120, 150)" so he couldn't reach his ideals and goals and he had to settle for the job of "general factotum (125, 127, 149)," a janitor. He tries to explain and defend why he had no ambition or will power and why he didn't get along with various people but again, these stories also become isolated fragments, phenomenological data. Multiple events and their multiple associations and perceptions occurred in his life and he has bracketed particular mixtures of these intuitions and perceptions. What has been bracketed and reduced in his consciousness does not reflect what actually happened in the external, sensory experience, the mimetic reporting, but does reflect his diegetic sense of himself.

He recalls a fight with his brother because he said (and Ionseco has the old man quote his brother directly): "My friends, I've got a flea. I'm going to pay you a visit in the hope of leaving my flea with you (119)." Clearly, something is missing from this story that would cause him to get so angry with his brother that he would quarrel with him. All that he recalls is this direct quote. The quote triggers the feeling. The feeling has become detached from the actual event and motivates him permanently to dislike his brother.

Or the story of his anger with a friend, Carel, whom he again quotes directly: "I know just the word that fits you. I'm not going to

An Autobiography Unites the Mimetic/Diegetic Voices   45

say it, I'll just think it (119)." This infuriated the old man but his wife saw no harm in either of the comments of the brother or Carel.

With the arrival of each invisible guest during the course of this evening, more information is given about the old man. The bits and pieces of mimetic evidence, direct quotes and traces, accumulate into multiple phenomena, unbracketed, from the man's conscious reflections about himself. He hopes that the orator will do the bracketing, the reducing, the diegetic creating of meaning and significance.

The old man has become somewhat "misanthropic" and reclusive. He seems only to enjoy fishing, reading a good book and recalling these "memories of a lifetime (126)." He lives "a modest life but a full one (126)" and he "spends two hours every day working on his message (126)."

The arrival of a fictional Colonel (a fiction within the fiction) allows the old man to tell a "war story" and again there are only fragments of a story with which to suggest a sequence or meaning. He can't remember who won the last war but he recalls "killing 209 of them (129)." He diegetically needs to prove to himself and the colonel that he was a good soldier and is still capable of bearing arms.

An old girl friend, Belle, arrives with her husband, a photoengraver, and the old man "can scarcely believe his eyes (129)" that she is there. His romantic reminiscence of "when we were young (132)" is his fictional re-creation (if we suspend our disbelief and assume that the action of the play is non-fictional) of the mimetic events of the past with Belle in an "if only we had dared (132)" story. The diegetic voice unites him with the memory of those days, which he has fictionalized, romanticized, and cannot re-capture. The diegetic voice remembers and re-tells the feeling as if it were yesterday. But the mimetic voice is inaccurate. His feeling for this woman is as fresh and new as ever in his consciousness and it is this "feeling" that causes the facts to be distorted and motivates the fictionalization and romanticization. Time has left his marks on their skin (132) and destroyed their memory of the mimetic details and "surgeons can't perform miracles.... When we were young, we were like gods...perhaps we still can be...if we see into the beauty of the heart that the skin has lost (132)." The man chooses to select and remember a particularly strong, good feeling about this romance with Belle that he enlarges to represent the whole experience.

He then begins his diegetic, philosophical exposition of his "philosophy of life" (the "message" he has been working on) to Belle. He tells her what "alone has saved him...the inner life...peace of mind, ...austerity...scientific investigation, ...my message...(133)." The diegetic voice is one that tries to assign value here.

The room is beginning to fill with more invisible guests and newspaper reporters and the old man and woman are finding the "entertaining" tiresome because there are too many people. He is trying to establish some kind of order in the room as he is with his life by getting everyone seated in a "chair." The couple now spend time selling programs and snacks, clearing the aisles, introducing people, seating people, giving the impression of a giant auditorium filled with hundreds and hundreds of people all of whom the old man and woman are trying to organize and direct.

Guests keep yelling random questions at him to which he responds and his responses become an accumulation of more of these isolated, fragmented revelations of his message, his self and his consciousness. He has formed a number of beliefs in his life: "uninterrupted progress;...that lots of money will prevent the exploitation of man;...that pure logic does not exist, all we've got is imitation;...that dignity is only skin deep---one always needs to save face (144-145)." He tells one guest that he has invited them there in order to explain that "the individual and the person are one and the same (145)." He says he is "not himself but another" and then he is "one in the other (145)." In "absolute silence," he experiences life as a "perfect circle...complete...nothing lacking...but there are holes through which one can escape (145)." These beliefs and assumptions are given randomly and are the raw data, the interior perceptual material for the conscious construction of a mental state, a system of belief, a philosophy of life, an autobiography.

During the course of these interchanges, when one of the guests tries to re-state or interpret something the old man has said, he quickly corrects any errors he hears with "that's not my opinion at all (145)." He says that he's had rich, multiple experiences at all levels of thought and all walks of life. He's not an egoist but he wants humanity to profit from what he's learned. He's perfected a real system for which he has suffered greatly (146). His system and his instructions will save the world. He possesses the one truth for all; he's arrived at a sense of absolute certainty. He is conscious that his mind wants to take the diverse experiences and combine and mix them in such a way that they form a system of belief which synthesizes and centers him and will immortalize him and mediate his "message" to others.

The surprise arrival of the emperor brings further acts of consciousness, revelations. The emperor is clearly a "god-figure" of whom the old man asks mercy and forgiveness before he dies but in the course of his talking to the emperor other versions of what has been said and still more raw perceptual and intuitive data about the old man are supplied.

The general theme of his speech to the emperor is a diegetic commentary about the fact that he's been "humiliated (150)" in his life. Nothing has ever really worked out for him. He is proud to serve the emperor and he is very glad that the emperor has finally arrived because they had almost lost hope and the emperor, as God, is his "last recourse (150)." All the rest of his life has been suffering and humiliation. People have hated him for the right reasons and loved him for the wrong ones (150). His enemies have been rewarded and his friends have betrayed him. He's been persecuted and never able to revenge himself (150-151). No one ever pitied him; he was too good (151). He's been robbed, supplanted, assassinated---a collector of injustices (151). He wanted to be a sportsman and attain to great heights in a career but everything was refused him. He was never given considerations nor was he sent invitations.

Part of the message that the orator will give, he says, is the inclusion of these evils that the old man has suffered in the last quarter of a century. The presence and approval of the emperor (the god figure) will make his life, his message and his suicide meaningful, ratified, approved.

The arrival of the orator functions as that moment of realization for the man and the woman that now is really the time of their death. Both of them have lived a life together that they have tried to communicate mimetically to their guests and they want their lives to be meaningful, to have a message for others, which is what the orator will do. No one could "hope for more (155)," says the old man, than to talk about his life and have its meaning explicated and then die happily, peacefully.

The man introduces the orator and proceeds to go through copious "thank you's" until he comes to yet "another" speech which is the actual speech that the orator, or a biographer of this old man, might give. The old man has supplied the autobiographical raw material, the phenomenological data throughout the play from which the oration could be written and this final speech takes its force.

In his final address, he acknowledges the fact that their life on earth, mimetically represented in a number of stories, is over. They have had long and peaceful years and the years been filled to overflowing and his mission is accomplished. He does not feel that any of this was in vain because now other people know about it and will carry on what good he did.

In the play, what is mimetically represented is that moment of recognition, acceptance, honor, fame when all who have underestimated this man will see him and his greatness in truth. He diegetically imagines in this final speech that his life has somehow been extraordinary and that his philosophy will illumine the universe. He would have liked the mimetic sequence of past experiences to have been different (he would liked to have remembered it more clearly) but he can now redeem any disappointments and mistakes with his diegetic commentary and evaluation about meanings and messages.

An Autobiography Unites the Mimetic/Diegetic Voices 49

In fact, his life was probably just as ordinary as anyone else's and just as meaningful as the greatest of lives. He feels that this death is the "supreme sacrifice (157)" not so much because he is some great person who is leaving but because, like any ordinary person, he does not want it to end; he does not want to die and make the "supreme sacrifice" of having to leave. Whatever his life was, whatever the sequence of facts and experiences, he doesn't want it to stop and to say diegetically what it meant to him; that it was more than it appeared to be or to say what he was trying to do in it are just ways of saying that he does not want to leave what has been; he wants there to be more.

He feels that this time to die is another moment of the mimetic sequence and his diegetic comment is that he will become a legend and have a street named after him (158). The reality of his life as he revealed it in bits and pieces throughout the play are idealized in the illusion that he will have a street named after him. He even idealizes his marriage at the end. He proclaims that he and his wife will lie together in unity, in eternity, just as they had lain together in time and space, in adversity (158). They will now die together.

He has examined the fragments of his life, various series of acts and states of consciousness, recalled many incidents and made diegetic statements about them. The mimetic reality of his life as he lived it was different from the mimetic sequencing that he recalled. The diegetic statements about what it all meant are idealizations which, if anything, allow the present consciousness of the old man to surface in the series of acts of consciousness that remembers, narrates, idealizes, unifies and structures. He is doing the same thing that Beckett's Malone is doing in *Malone Dies*.

The ordinariness, simplicity and the apparently commonplace uselessness of the multiple events and continuous experiences in the old man's life, like Tristram Shandy's and Malone's and even Hermione's, are secondary to his conscious formulation of the synecdochic, often unachieved, goals, visions and ideals that he perceived and bracketed for himself, however fictional and modified they are.

PART TWO: NON-FICTIONAL AUTOBIOGRAPHIES

Helen Keller

According to *The Story of My Life,* Helen Keller apparently experienced a rich interior life of hidden associations, perceptions, intuitions and attitudes hidden because an illness as an infant left her deaf, mute and blind but experienced in this autobiographical document. Though mute, she, like Beckett's man in the dark, had voices within her speaking to inner ears and giving her motivation and vision. Even though she couldn't see, she crawled around searching and investigating. Her experience of isolation may not be as radical as Hermione's nor may her thoughts be as complex and convoluted as Beckett's man on the floor in the dark but her autobiographical document re-tells a number of synecdochic events about her in her own diegetic/mimetic voice.

> ....Many incidents in those early years are fixed in my memory, isolated, but clear and distinct, making the sense of that silent, aimless, dayless life all the more intense.[15]

When recalling the experience of a canoe ride, she remembers "fancying" that she could "feel the shimmer of the moon on her garments (101)." She is conscious of the spaciousness of the air and "luminous warmth (101)" that surrounds her. Her impressions and emotions about nature are those which are most deeply embedded in her consciousness as the raw materials about which she feels most strongly. The "subconscious memories (102)" (registered there from before her illness) of the "green earth and the murmuring waters (102)" are common to everyone and her "darkness did not blot them out (26)" for her. She believes that this interior activity of sensitivity to nature is an "inherited capacity, a sort of sixth sense, a soul-sense which sees, hears and feels, all in one (102)." Communion with nature, like the subsequent communion with others which she would experience when she learned to speak and read, are synecdochic experiences by which Helen represents herself in her emergence from her handicap. There were significant experiences occurring in her before she could communicate them and her autobiographical document tells about them.

Maintaining harmony with nature, learning to communicate, speak, read and write became central goals in Helen's life. Helen's raw instinct to expand her knowledge through reading motivated her to "stretch out her hands (86, 92, 106)" to the Braille letters or the fingers of her teachers as others "stretch out their eyes" to print in reading and to behavior in observation. Helen narrates her own story in her own voice about her instincts, her desires, her learning experiences with which she is fondly united at the time of the narration.

She likens her way of allowing the hand of another person to brush the letters gently over her hand to the way sighted people allow their eyes to pass over the letters of words or, if deaf, to read the quick movements of lips. She says her "thoughts beat against her fingertips like little birds striving to gain their freedom (59, 334-335)," until the prison door was opened through speech and they were allowed to escape and the thoughts "eagerly and gladly spread their wings and flew away (60, 335)." Before she learned to speak and read, she remembers feeling the impulse, the instinct, to do so. She remembers feeling like she was "creeping" and she wanted to "soar (335)," thus the frustration and tantrums. She was immersed in the multiplicity of thoughts, feelings, perceptions and attitudes which served as the raw material for the construction of a later perseverance and determination and she narrates both the multiplicity and the determination.

She was afflicted with the illness just when the "unmeaning babblings of the child were beginning to be formed into meaningful words (330)" and her earliest, initial motivations were those where she fought, she persevered, in her efforts to come out of the silence that ensued into the world of communication.

This journey to full communication and language acquisition is the synecdochic subject of her autobiography and the experiences of the journey are experiences with which she is united at the time of the writing because they were experiences which defined her so radically as a person. The value of autobiographical documents like Helen's, which Sterne, Doolittle, Beckett and Ionesco portray fictionally, is that they are records of interior journeys; the raw material of the autobiographer's thoughts and feelings along the way. Being deaf, dumb and blind and emerging from these handicaps into the world of language and communication is an experience of bracketing, systematizing and giving voice to the multiple, varied sensations, perceptions and intuitions in a narrative complete with the diegetic, synecdochic commentary, additions and deletions that unite the autobiographer/narrator with the protagonist/heroine.

As the 19 year old autobiographer, Helen's narrating voice is in communion with the inner voice of the six year old protagonist about whom she is narrating and she can diegetically pick the best, synecdochic examples to communicate that consciousness locked in silent detachment and she can comment on and evaluate and highlight these.

She has a funny thought and she runs about the room feeling the lips and faces of her parents to see if they are having the funny thought too (228). She is keenly aware that she is unable to communicate her thoughts which results in increasing tantrums and crying due to the frustration of being unable to get these things out. She compares the feeling that accompanied this interior state of chaos to a ship at sea in a dense fog, groping its way toward shore which image serves as a single synecdoche within a particular synecdochic narrative.

Her trip to Boston in May, 1888, differed from her trip to Baltimore two years earlier because on the first trip she was the "restless, excitable, irritable child requiring the attention of everybody on the train to keep her amused (49)" whereas on the second, she sat quietly beside Miss Sullivan, taking in with eager interest all that was told her about what was passing. On the one trip, Helen is overwhelmed by the constant stream of thoughts, perceptions and awarenesses that were passing through her and her inability to organize, combine and correlate this material resulted in the panic and frustration that had become her daily bread. But once she learned how to direct and modify the information and communicate through language use, she was less restless and excitable. She could take the information in her consciousness, the raw materials of multiple perceptions and intuitions, and bracket and organize them as she pleased.

The arrival of Annie Sullivan on March 3, 1887, becomes then, in retrospect, along with the day that she learned that the finger play meant something else, what Helen diegetically unites under the synecdochic title the "most important day in all my life (34)." Her memory of the experience of these days is important because they were the days when she was released from the prison of silence. She mimetically re-constructs the story, making use of imagination and memory, to establish the diegetic fact that this indeed was the most important day of her life because this was the day that she learned that things have names. There is a unity of voice and perspective in the narrative here. The actual sequence of the events of those days are remembered in an undistorted way by Helen because they are so important to her. She can re-tell the story as accurately and clearly and truly as can be expected because there is very little distance from it. The experiences at the time, on the day, were so keenly etched in her mind that her consciousness brings them up just as keenly in the present.

When she experienced states of frustration and discouragement while learning to read, write, speak and communicate, she would perform another series of acts of consciousness in which she would steel her patience and perseverance, for example, with the dream, the incentive, that one day she would be able to speak to people, especially her mother. There are three voices here: the one which is struggling and frustrated, the one which perseveres and the other which speaks to the first two by reminding them of the goal. They are all three mimetic, occurring in an order and a context, chronologically, but the one which remembers the goal is a diegetic one which comments upon and adds to the first two. The "rugged paths, the obstacles, the backward slips are overcome when the beautiful goal is kept in mind (335)." Helen's perseverance and singlemindedness of intention in the pursuance of a goal are conscious constructs, wilful shapings, that Helen executed based upon her random memories of her experience of life's manifold sensory contents.

Helen makes it clear in her autobiography that her motivations "were strong, active, and indifferent to consequences and she knew her own mind well enough and always had her own way (28)." Actions, facial expressions and gestures invariably indicated interior states and when she learned to communicate these interior states, she became even more goal-oriented and persevering, doing more reading and more speaking.

Her philosophy professor at Radcliffe College, Ralph Barton, points out that

> Helen Keller may have lost her sight and hearing but she did not lose her mind, her consciousness and her ability to form states of consciousness based upon activity there. She can think, compare, remember, anticipate, associate, imagine, speculate, and feel (16).

Barton notes that when "you communicate with her you know that you have reached her 'inner ear' and the eye of her mind (17)."

Helen learned that there was a deaf and blind girl named Ragnhild Kaata in Norway who had actually been taught to speak and this information fueled her own motivation to learn to speak. She started lessons in March, 1890, and in the first hour she learned six elements: M,P,A,S,T,I. She would feel her teacher's tongue and lip positions for each sound and when she uttered her first connected sentence ("it is warm"), her consciousness was then aware of another new strength, a new organizing ability, an act of consciousness, besides the reading, that would free her to express the multiplicity within in yet another new way (60).

The natural exchange of ideas through conversation, reading or writing is denied a handicapped person like Helen Keller. She was only left with the stream of random, multiple perceptions and sensations which she was unable to bracket and organize. The blind person is denied access to the expression on the speaker's face and eyes which are said to be the "windows of the soul (42)." The deaf child is denied access to nuance in tone of voice and modulation.

An Autobiography Unites the Mimetic/Diegetic Voices   55

The expression on the face, the tone of voice, are consequences of the interior acts of consciousness. A reader is like a blind person in the sense that they too are also denied access to facial expression and tone of voice except to the extent that the writer can communicate these through the words. Therefore, the written words on the page when carefully selected and structured can fill that gap created by the physical absence of facial expressions and tones of voice.[16]

Helen says that

> The great difficulty with writing is to make the language of the educated mind express our confused ideas, half feelings, half thoughts, when we are little more than bundles of instinctive tendencies. Trying to write is very much like trying to put a Chinese puzzle together. We have a pattern in mind which we wish to work out in words; but the words will not fit the spaces, or if they do, they will not match the design (68).

One of the disadvantages that Helen talks about while at Radcliffe was that she had no time to think, to reflect, "my mind and I."

> We would sit together of an evening and listen to the inner melodies of the spirit, which one hears only in leisure moments when the words of some loved poet touch a deep, sweet chord in the soul that until then had been silent. In college there is no time to commune with one's thoughts (85).

The same experience occurs with her teachers. She says that "the lectures were spelled out in her hand as rapidly as possible, and much of the individuality of the lecturer is lost to me in an effort to keep in the race (86)." Helen was learning a great deal of information from the lecturers but there were other aspects of the lecturer which are outside the realm of academic information; aspects that communicate personality and attitude. If she could have had the information spelled more slowly into her hand, she might have been able to appreciate the personality, the character of the teacher and allowed the material to sift more gradually through her own consciousness. The particular words that the lecturer uses and the way the lecturer arranges the words not only communicate diegetic, bracketed, academic information but may also communicate the flow of the present, mimetic consciousness, the personality.

Besides persons, she learns to communicate with and understand "abstractions" like love, justice, peace---those "things" which have no object in nature but can be "touched" in a different way. This insight into abstractions came one day when she was stringing beads. She became frustrated because she kept doing it wrong. Miss Sullivan requested by spelling into her hand that she "think." Helen remembers that it was then that she knew that she could solve problems and have varieties of different avenues open to her through use of her own thought processes, through varied acts of consciousness forming states which offer solutions. Helen's knowledge grew beyond just naming objects and as more and more words were learned and more and more connections made in the palimpsest of her consciousness, more and more questions were being asked and her field of inquiry broadened as did her motivations, attitudes and interests (40).

Helen's multiple words and actions express specific, synecdochic unities of her consciousness and the multiple words and actions are empowered by a comparable multiplicity of sensations, of raw materials, in her consciousness. Helen has a diegetic point to make to her readers about her motivations and goals, her heroism, her values and ideals, which she attempts to construct in the autobiography and which is based on a multiple interlace of perceptions, attitudes and intuitions.

Christopher Nolan

Christopher Nolan is handicapped by quadriplegia from birth and he decides to tell the story of that experience because of the notoriety he had been receiving for a book of poetry he published. He wants to bracket the person, foreground and construct the consciousness of himself as a quadriplegic, the person behind the book of poems. Like Helen Keller, he was unable to speak and communicate until he found a way to type: his mother holds his head while he taps out the letters on the typewriter with the help of a "unicorn" stick strapped to his forehead. He organizes the perceptual/intuitive elements of his consciousness in the autobiographical document from the "natural," however different, viewpoint of a quadriplegic. Like the old man in *The Chairs*, both Nolan and Keller felt paralyzed at their apparent inability to communicate their interior lives, their thoughts, feelings, and beliefs; their expectations and hopes. They need to tell the story about what's going on (or went on) inside them.

Unlike Helen Keller but like the old man's orator in *The Chairs*, Christopher Nolan, tells his life story through a narrator and a persona, Joseph Meehan, as another state of consciousness. Critics have agreed that it was a wise decision to separate himself in this way.[17] The distance seems to have enabled him to write more freely than if he had used his own name and it reflects the detachment of the autobiographer who stands outside of himself in order to paint a unified portrait. This document also bridges the gap between my two-part division in this book. The fictional autobiography of "Joseph Meehan" (or Tristram or Hermione) becomes a non-fictional autobiography when Christopher Nolan says that this story is his own and this Joseph Meehan is himself.

But in so standing outside of himself in this way, he risks the dangers that the old man in *The Chairs* falls into: his voice also "stands outside of itself" as he speaks from the margin, about himself as a third person, but still present to his own solitude and silence where "detachment encounters all of the jangled emotions it must serve."[18] The danger in fictional autobiographies is that they are always at that Platonic one remove from the reality. If the Platonic one remove from "real," is the actual life of the individual and the third remove is the representation in writing of the life story, then a fictionalization of the life story is a further remove again.

John Carey, a Professor of literature at Oxford, prefaces Christopher Nolan's book much like Radcliffe professor Ralph Barton prefaced Helen Keller's by saying that Nolan "plummeted into language like an avalanche, as if it were his escape route from death---which, of course, it was."[19] John Carey says that words were the objects that freed the consciousness from the prison of paralysis and silence and so both Helen and Christopher approached them as another child might approach an overturned truck of candy. Their autobiographical documents are distinguished because they come from that unknown planet of the paralyzed and speechless, the handicapped.

Nolan expresses himself through Meehan as one who indeed "had honestly yearned for a means of communication, ...(3)." He continually pondered how he could "overcome his muteness (4)." Like Helen, "Joseph" developed a "spine of iron (9)" and a "volcanic wish (9)" to become more adept at communicating. Like Helen's teachers and parents, Joseph's teachers and parents could only read the mute Joseph's facial expressions, eye movements and minimal body language.

When he was accepted into the Mount Temple Comprehensive School, he was "as one about to levitate. He felt a surge of happiness rush through his heart, it melted all over his many rejections and schooled his resolves not ever to fail...(16)." Christopher Nolan's autobiographical document captures a consciousness, a discourse of a mind in diegetic, 'stream of consciousness' language, as critics suggest, is reminiscent of Joyce:

> Dark night was always waned by golden visions and the night of 20 February 1979 was no different. Just as always happened, Joseph Meehan saw his life pass before his sensitive mind's eye. Free-falling, he created grand gospels of boyish certainty. Washed by sedentary, snared sacrifice he descended within easy reach of hell, but severe despondency never could stop Joseph's mesmerized woldwaddling in ink-blue heaven's busy mobility of secrets.
>
> Cassettes played back the day's happenings sadly beckoning him towards despair, but fending off fright he beckoned instead towards students frolicking in dreamland and stole yesses from them before they ebbed notional no (24).

Nolan says that he was really seeing his own life recoil before him as if he were a third person, an extratextual diegetic narrator to a story that he was witnessing about someone else. His document exemplifies more clearly than the others William Earle's two states of consciousness. Joseph Meehan represents Nolan's memory of himself growing up as a quadriplegic and Nolan the author/narrator represents the present consciousness connecting with and re-creating the memory of himself as another character, another person. This is another good example of the interlace between diegetic/mimetic voices and synecdochic events and experiences. Christopher Nolan remembers his mimetic experiences and as he writes them out he diegetically selects and edits, adds and subtracts what he wants. As he attempts to represent his own real, mimetic voice from the past in a present narrative, he makes diegetic additions and comments. He remembers himself as another person whom he creates and this other person, this Joseph Meehan himself becomes a synecdoche for Nolan.

He liked the idea of casting himself in this frame of Joseph Meehan and "pranked (28)" himself a storyteller. Nolan prides himself on the fact that he is a good storyteller, a good narrator of his own life story, one who is able to sequence the events and voices logically, clearly and creatively. He intends the reader to look and feel deeply the limitations of the handicapped life, the cruel frustrations of uninvited paralysis and enforced silence but above all not to look so deeply that, like Tristram Shandy suggests, they and he be unable "to laugh the lovely laughter that vanishes the wounds of disability and pride (28)."

Even in school, his problem was always how to get the "whet words (31)" out that were entrapped in his mind. His only language up to this time was "nodding-headed, eye-darting....eyes busy in conversation (36)." He wanted so desperately, like Helen, to communicate some of the more sophisticated discourse of his mind, specific acts of consciousness that would reveal the intricacies of his personality and thought. He calls the interior silence: moments of "fear...mixed with caesuras of despair...mesmerizing himself with the pleasures of life (40)." As the poetic muse descended upon him, he "waxed and waned his creative thoughts in secret (41)." He soon found release in writing and his subsequent awards for the poetry book and the advances in computer science and word processing "gave him voice" and "others who are similarly afflicted with this intelligence lying dormant, stand the chance of being free (84)." Quadriplegics are denied freedom of movement; all they have are "busy, jerky, muffled (85)" movements. But they have the freedom of the discourse of their minds.

Nolan describes the labored process of communication:

> Calling his mother to sit down in front of him, he got to work with his eyes. He conveyed to her that he wished to talk about himself. She nodded and with a broad grin said, "What's new?" He dismissed her barb and became serious in his expression. He nodded towards the telephone. He beckoned her with his eyes to wheel him into the study. He bowed towards his writings and then towards his books on his shelf. All of his clues serve to build up his request to have her telephone the publisher in London for him (90).

The significance of Christopher's and Helen's autobiographies is their "birth as authors (92)" as speakers of the word, as narrators of their own stories. The acts of consciousness which allow them to acquire a language with which to voice their interior lives and so emerge from "the private world that was so private that the demon despair dallied always at the door (93)" also allowed them to express the intuitions, perceptions, attitudes and beliefs which were so integral to their consciousness of themselves.

But now, after publishing his first book of poems, Nolan "cackled to himself" because he "shared the same world as everyone else; he could choose how much to tell and craftily decide how much to hold back. His voice would be his written word (93)." His "bloody frustrations" were alleviated by allowing others "inside his frame" where the words arise from the "depths of his numbness (96)." A "handicap of the body does not mean a handicap of the mind as well (98)."

Christopher Nolan invites his readers into the interior life and consciousness of the quadriplegic but he ends the autobiography with the suggestion that he, like Helen, is a person who is motivated to achieve a great deal and possibly become another James Joyce or W.B. Yeats, as the critics have said.[20]

This autobiographical document celebrates this artist's present consciousness, the creative power to dramatize the self as hero and present his consciousness as object. For nothing is more intense and real to persons than the experience of their own unique, individual selves and the power to give voice to these selves.

John Stuart Mill

In the narrative unit Chapter Five of his *Autobiography*, "A Crisis in My Mental History," John Stuart Mill concisely and clearly narrates the mimetic sequence of the mental breakdown that he had when he was in his early twenties but he does so by diegetically selecting specific, salient events from the five year experience. Mill reflects in retrospect on the multiple perceptions and intuitions he has about this particular experience and diegetically brackets some of them into the narrative unit in his autobiography which he names a "'crisis' in his mental history."

The predominant voice is the diegetic one, selecting, commenting, evaluating and naming the crisis but this diegetic voice is united with the mimetic, narrating one and he presents a unified, synecdochic portrait of a consciousness which experienced this transition.

Mill's father had educated him, trained him and "conditioned (98)" him to be a reformer in Victorian England but when it came time to move into that society and participate in the work of reform, Mill lost all desire or interest in such a pursuit. This loss of desire and feeling for something for which he had been trained frightened him. His father had equipped him with a language system and a set of values with which to express himself argumentatively and rationally, but which no longer meant anything to him. Like Helen Keller or Christopher Nolan, Mill was subjected to silence but unlike Keller or Nolan, he was subjected to a silence after being allowed to communicate freely in the language he learned from his father. He needed to find a new language of his own, new words for new ideas, with which to express new awarenesses, and new states of consciousness and so he needed to be silent for awhile.

His training equipped him with an intellect that was "irretrievably analytic (98)," mechanically conditioned to analyze, synthesize and associate the "permanent sequences of nature (97)." The motivation he lost was his "delight in virtue (98)" and his concern for the common good. His attitude toward himself and his interior life was one which was keenly aware of this loss of a "desire, drive and motivation (98)." He may "intend" to work for reform and he may have the intellectual equipment and language with which to do so successfully, effectively, but he did not desire it. There was a felt loss, a gap, in his consciousness where something new was being created. He divides Chapter Five into a series of significant, diegetic "rays of light (99)" which Mill says carried him through the crisis. This "ray of light" imagery throughout the chapter contrasts with the darkness of the consciousness which experiences itself as having no motivations, no desires. The darkness, the lack of interior motivation and drive, actually became the motivation by which he pulls himself out of the darkness. The "ray of light" imagery is another way to talk about the diegetic voice. He divides the chapter into a series of diegetic voices in particular synecdochic experiences.

Jonathan Loesberg says that Mill's reading of Marmontel's *Memoires* is the central, introductory event that shook him out of the depression and silence and Loesberg connects Mill's identification with Marmontel based on the mutual death of their fathers.[21] Mill saw himself as heroic as the "mere boy" Marmontel who, at his father's death, became filled with a "sudden inspiration" to "be everything" to his family now by "supplying the place they had lost" in the death of the father. Mill was "moved to tears" at the "vivid conception" of this scene created by Marmontel (99 ff.). His interior "hopelessness and oppression died." The "vivid conception" which moved him to tears was the heroism of the boy who would take his father's place. This heroism so inspired Mill that he too could now "exert himself again for the public good." He says that he began to "find enjoyment,...sufficient for cheerfulness." Marmontel's father died and Marmontel was then called to a new life, a new role, to which he responded wholeheartedly; he was called to be a new person in his household with new responsibilities. Comparably, Mill's father's language and education had "died" within Mill and, like Marmontel, Mill was called to discover a new language of his own through which to express new states of consciousness; he was called to express himself, his consciousness of his vocation, in his own unique way (99).

He arrives at a major plateau, a first "ray of light:"

> But I now thought that this end (happiness) was only to be attained by not making it a direct end. Those only are happy (I thought) who have their minds fixed on some object other than their own happiness;...aiming thus at something else, they find happiness by the way (100).

He had previously come to identify his interior happiness with this one object in his life: his education by his father to be a reformer of the world. But as he involved himself in the "cultivation of passive susceptibilities,...intellectual culture,...dull balance among the faculties,...(101)," he came simultaneously to realize that if all the changes and reforms in institutions and opinions that he wanted were completely effected, his "irrepressible self-consciousness (94)" told him that he would still not have "great joy and happiness." All of his happiness and all of his energies, his acts of consciousness, he says, were being directed to the "one" end of reform (93-4). Consequently, and quite naturally, other states of "irrepressible self-consciousness" would insist that other energies and interests be recognized.

He was overwhelmed by the demands made upon him. All of his internal activities and energies were being directed each day to the external activities of reform until which time he was forced to realize that there were more internal activities in other states of consciousness in him which were not finding expression in external words and behaviors.

Poetry and art, especially the reading of Wordsworth's poetry "in the autumn of 1828 (103)" came to be the second "ray of light (99)" in his progress back to mental health because of the simple fact that the poems excited enthusiasm in him. He saw in Wordsworth's poetry a second, key insight that

> the imaginative emotion which an idea, vividly conceived, excites,...is not an illusion but a fact, as real as any of the other qualities of objects;...the intensest feeling of the beauty of a cloud lighted by the setting sun, is not hindrance to my knowing that the cloud is vapour of water, subject to all the laws of vapours in a state of suspension (106-7).

Wordsworth's poetry showed Mill that it was possible to conceive an idea in one act of consciousness that would excite an emotion as another act of consciousness which would find expression in a piece of poetry, as a representation of that state of consciousness which conceived the idea and experienced the emotion.

The action then works in reverse for Mill when he reads the poem. The poem triggers a series of acts of consciousness in Mill which action is the exciting of imaginative ideas and emotions which may or may not be similar to the one excited in Wordsworth, who wrote the poem. Mill's excitement of imaginative emotions and ideas "vividly conceived" are joined by the series of acts of consciousness that motivate him to communicate this activity in consciousness and the activity introduces him to other acts of consciousness in and about himself that he had never met before because he was singlemindedly devoted to the reform for which he was trained. The text of a Wordsworth poem or Monmartel's *Memoirs* and the text of Mill's narrative of his mental crisis are observable, objective "facts, as real as any of the other qualities of objects (107)" and they represent series of acts of consciousness of Marmontel, Wordsworth and Mill forming states of consciousness about a parent, an idea, an emotion, a crisis.

The interior activity of the phenomenal consciousness can be observed scientifically as phenomenon, an object of study, as this chapter from Mill's *Autobiography* attempts to do.

The interior activity in consciousness is complex in that it involves the formation of ideas and emotions in particular acts of consciousness which are new to Mill and it involves the formation of the intention to communicate these ideas and emotions in Chapter Five as another act of consciousness and the refinement and development of that intention in acts of consciousness over a period of 20 years.

He compares this diegetic study of his own synecdochic, mental crisis in Chapter Five to the study of a cloud as a vapor which is subject to the laws of science and is an object which has its own criterial list of identifying marks (107). He is motivated to pursue a scientific, phenomenological investigation of his own consciousness as an object of study and he intends to be as exact, honest and accurate as if he were a scientist studying the vaporous cloud. The imaginative emotion excited in him by a vividly conceived idea is just as viable an object of study as is the cloud beautifully illuminated by the setting sun. He is motivated to be just as exact, honest and accurate in his communication of a criterial list of identifying marks of the emotions, ideas, states and acts of consciousness within him as he would be to communicate a criterial list of identifying marks of a "cloud as vapor." The criterial list expressing Mill's consciousness in Chapter Five is this diegetic series of "rays of light" experiences.

A third "ray of light" occurred when he withdrew from his Debating Society in 1829 (110). This withdrawal from the Debating Society is a significant moment, a synecdoche within the synecdochic chapter, in his journey towards mental health because it initiates the period of silent withdrawal and signifies the beginning of re-examination. He is motivated to communicate the state of consciousness behind the act of withdrawal.

Basically, he says that he was tired of speech-making and preferred "private studies and meditations (110)" where he "wove anew the fabric of his new self and taught opinions which gave way to new ones in many fresh places (110)." New ideas were adjusted and juxtaposed with older ones, particularly his father's theory of government, since it came into conflict with "other schools of political thought." His father's theory made no room for others (110). Mill's crisis, emotionally kindled by Marmontel and Wordsworth, caused him to return to the interior world of rationality and cognition and re-apply the analytic ability which he learned from his father to his father's own teaching and views. As he read more widely in political theory and philosophy, he realized that his father's system had no regard for or interest in continued experimental investigation and research. An apparent silence and withdrawal was actually a very vibrant, vital, interior conversation.

Mill read a critique of his father's "Essay on Government" by Thomas Macaulay who criticized the document because it was a theory deduced from philosophical speculation as opposed to empirical investigation. The elder Mill's premises were too narrow and included only a small number of general principles on which politics might depend (110-111). The elder Mill's major premise was identity of interest between the governing body and the community at large as the only principle on which good government depends.

The elder Mill responded to Macaulay's critique and argued that Macaulay's reasoning was faulty which made the younger Mill suspect even more strongly that the father himself was actually in fundamental error based on the same accusation of faulty reasoning he was levelling against Macaulay (111). The younger Mill exercised his own faculty of logical reasoning in which his own father had trained him and he came to see his father's error which was the error of using deductive reasoning based on limited philosophical premises where he should have used deductive reasoning based on empirical, scientific investigation and philosophical speculation (111), a variety of premises. A true system of principles for a political philosophy is much more complex and many-sided (as Mill discovered his own consciousness and emotions were) than any one system could hold. A system of principles for a philosophy of politics needs to supply practical guidelines along with theoretical principles by which governments can constitute themselves. Part of Mill's progress through his crisis involved this need to disagree with and re-evaluate his father's political theory and establish his own hierarchy of perspectives.

He was led to a fourth "ray of light" with the insight that the human mind, consciousness, like political systems and philosophies, has a certain order or progress, in which some experiences precede others and some follow others. He was led to this insight not only through his reflections on his father's "Essay on Government" and the varied reading he had been doing in political theory but also specifically through the "new mode of political thinking" of the Saint-Simonian school in France which he had been reading in 1828-9 (114).

The writers in this school of political thought presented him with an organic, synecdochic, "connected view" of the natural order of human progress which divides history into organic periods where mankind accepted with firm conviction some positive creed and the society flourished and progressed under this creed until these values and creeds were rejected and rebuilt during a succeeding critical period. Greek and Roman polytheism was an organic period succeeded by the critical/skeptical period of the Greek philosophers. Christianity was an organic period succeeded by the Reformation (115). By extension, Mill himself has the organic period of being educated according to his father's system and this is followed by the critical period of re-examination, crisis and growth narrated in Chapter Five. These succeeding "organic" periods can be understood as "metonyms" in the sense that they are connected periods of "transition." Or they can be seen as "metaphors" in the sense that they represent a critical period in the history of the world or a particular country but they can replace each other depending upon the degree of significance and impact. They would be "synecdochic" if their significance is unparalleled, as Auguste Comte suggests, and Mill's "crisis" could be considered synecdochic since there was not anything else like it for him and it was so significant in his development.

Auguste Comte, a positivist member of the Saint-Simonian school of thought, was a fifth "ray of light" who permitted Mill to see human knowledge as developing according to three synecdochic stages: the theological (feudal, Christian and Protestant Reformation), metaphysical (tenets set by the French Revolution), and positivist (yet to come) (116). Through Comte, Mill was able to recognize that the moral and intellectual characteristics of an age of critical cultural transition were not the normal moral and intellectual characteristics of a particular organic period because the age was perceived as "transitional" and not "organicized." Frank Kermode calls this kind of thinking "Joachism"[22] where transitions, organic wholes and parts, normal and abnormal moral and intellectual characteristics, beginnings, middles, ends, crises, transitions are consequences of acts of consciousness of individual people who bracket external experiences into these sections and give them names and characteristics. According to Kermode's way of thinking, everything is always in transition.

Mill himself was in a metonymic period of transition during his mental crisis and the Saint-Simonians' point of view on historical development helped him to recognize and understand his own development and the transitional nature of his own moment of crisis. His training by his father was an organic, synecdochic, educational experience which was metaphorically replaced by another organic, synecdochic period but both can be considered metonymic, transitional.

In keeping with Georges Gusdorf's and Michael Cooke's analysis of the importance of "naming" which I discussed in the beginning of this chapter, Anne Norton of Princeton University in the Clark Library lecture series of 1987-88[23] developed a thesis that the memory of an event or an experience, the memory of a particular act or state of consciousness, is formed and maintained by the actual occurrence of the experience of the act itself in time and space and then the inscription of it in writing, in a text, in contradiction to Plato who says that the inscribing makes the memory lazy and forget the experience or Derrida who says the inscribing actually makes the reality of the event "absent."

The narrating and naming of the act or event in writing make the reality more fully present according to Ms. Norton. She said at the lecture that the act and the written document can be separate ways of remembering and she uses the examples of the French people who remember the French Revolution by the act of storming the Bastille and the American people who remember the Declaration of Independence from England with a written document. The event is remembered in the naming, "the storming of the Bastille,"

An Autobiography Unites the Mimetic/Diegetic Voices 69

on July 14th the "signing of the Declaration of Independence" on July 4th.

John Stuart Mill remembers the experience of his mental crisis by naming different activities during that period and by narrating them in a written document. The autobiographer generally is attempting to remember acts and states of consciousness through inscription in a document. The memory is of the event and then its inscription or both.

Another interior problem which was causing Mill difficulty at this time was the "incubus" of the doctrine called Philosophical Necessity which presented him with the absurdity that he was "conditioned by antecedent circumstances, a slave to them, wholly in their power and control, having none of his own (118-119)."

Necessity is a name for the doctrine of cause and effect but when applied to human action and consciousness, according to Mill, this definition may be misleading (119). Character is not formed by the happen-stance cause and effect of natural circumstances according to Mill but by the personal desires, motivations and intentions of the characters who can shape the happen-stance cause and effect circumstances and hence shape the self. Free will inspires and enables one to have power over the formation of character. The doctrine of Necessity, the continuous flux of cause and effect, need not be fatalistic, as Tristram Shandy attests to and as Hermione Gart fell slave to. Mill does not allow the cause and effect randomness to shape his character and construct a self. He argues that the person is free to construct a self by picking and choosing from among the many causes and effects which randomly occur. The mimetic narrative of Mill's individual consciousness could have recorded a random cause and effect sequence of the five years; or he could have recorded a completely different set of rays of light. The diegetic narrator selects particular "rays of light" which are then sequenced into the narrative which is Chapter Five of his *Autobiography*. He is not a slave to necessity. He constructs by picking and choosing, editing and re-writing.

The sixth and final "ray of light" in Mill's progress through his mental crisis was his return to publication in 1830-31 when he wrote five "Essays on Some Unsettled Questions of Political Economy" and a series of articles on "The Spirit of the Age (122)" in which he expressed some of his new opinions about the anamolies and evils of an age of transition in society and likened them to some of the difficulties of changing one's personal set of worn-out opinions for another in a personal period of transition. An act of consciousness produced a document for publication after a time of silence and introspection where the acts of consciousness were examining themselves. When Kermode intimates that everything becomes transitional, such an absolute statement invites contradiction. The point is that at certain times, disorganization, chaos, novelty, re-organization seem to be the predominant mode of operation where at other times the disorganization appears to settle into a coherent, unified range of activities. According to Kermode, the one latter period is "less transitional" than the other; it is more even, clear, and centered.

Mill states clearly that "in giving this account of this period (118)" in his life, the few selected points that he includes are only a very insufficient, representative idea of the quantity of thinking which he carried on respecting a host of subjects "in these years of transition (118)."

In summary, Chapter Five of Mill's *Autobiography* accesses Mill's consciousness of his own mental crisis. Mill records and illustrates his progress by making a series of six diegetic points about six mimetic experiences and concludes with the assertion that he started to publish again at the end of the crisis.

Rather than an exact, mimetic replication of every detail in the sequence of the five year crisis, Mill narrates diegetically, like the old man in *The Chairs*, selecting points and constructing diegetic narratives with which he asserts these major points about this life experience of a "mental crisis."

Whether the story is true to the actual life experience in all its triviality and detail is not as important as Mill's remembrance, reconstruction and re-conceptualization of it. The conscious mind which forms intentions, makes inferences and draws conclusions is a consciousness, according to Husserl, whom I shall discuss more extensively in my conclusion, who posits a unity of apprehension about itself, a synthesis of various modalities with which it identifies most strongly.

Maya Angelou

Maya Angelou's narration of being raped by her stepfather when she was nine years old is a narrative unit from the pages of Chapter 12 of her autobiographical document, *I Know Why The Caged Bird Sings*. The narrative involves Maya's adult re-examination of this childhood experience so there are a number of voices here. The adult voice of the autobiographer narrates mimetically in the present time about this experience from the past and so the mimetic narration becomes a dregetic one. She gives mimetic voice to the child in the experience in the narration. The child's thoughts and feelings are verbalized. The adult voice of the autobiographer brackets and reduces the experience to its essential, synecdochic core, a detachable mental state, posited as an organic whole in this narrative unit and she remembers various diegetic comments, evaluations and feelings in the child as part of the mimetic sequence.

This rape sequence follows the story of the child's retreat into a silence, withdrawal and loss of the use of language and the inability to communicate, like many of the other writers I have treated in this chapter. The child loses her ability to speak, seeks refuge in silence but re-emerges, re-acquires language, as part of the healing process. Her consciousness was handicapped by these acts of violence and a symptom of the handicap was the silence and withdrawal. Helen Keller and Christopher Nolan were silenced by physical handicaps which affected their consciousness. John Stuart Mill's voice was silenced by a mental-emotional breakdown.

There are two points that I would like to make about this synecdochic narrative in Maya Angelou's life: first, the child's perception of the rapist, her stepfather, and then the child's perception of herself. These perceptions are given voice in the autobiography and the fictional device of separating herself from the child, like Christopher and Joseph, serves the fuller, non-fictional narration.

The autobiographer, the adult, the diegetic narrator, has the child-protagonist notice that the stepfather's eyes stare blankly, "kind but still and unblinking." The adult writer captures the child's accurate perception of the rapist who is radically unconcerned about the child.

She portrays the rapist as at first being gentle, persuasive and playful but the child's silence and distance reinforce that there is something wrong here. She needs to be forced and she is warned that if she screams she would be killed and if she tells anyone about this her brother Bailey would be killed.

Her relationship with her brother becomes a synecdochic thread within this synecdochic narrative unit because her deep love for her brother contrasts with the lack of love and brutality of the stepfather and further forces her into silence. She doesn't want to lose her relationship with her brother so she must now hide this important, traumatic experience and retreat into the silence of repression. This retreat into silence and hiding suggests that acts of consciousness are occurring which aren't being voiced.

Angelou charts the child's journey back to self-expression. As she recalls this experience, she is able to become one with the time and herself as a child at the time but at the same time she can separate herself and comment as the adult-autobiographer and narrator. The separation of her adult self from her child self is a fictional technique that serves the non-fictional narrative.

The adult autobiographer comments that "the child gives, because the body can't, and the mind of the violator cannot."[24] This sentence is central to the narrative because it portrays the pain of physical rape mixed with the emotional pain that results when a child is forced to care for someone in a way that a child is not yet emotionally prepared to do.

A child should be given *to* and cared *for*; a child is not prepared to be put in a position to care for and feel responsible for the emotional health of his or her parent but this is the position in which this little girl finds herself. She perceives her stepfather as someone who needs to be cared for but she also perceives this need as aberrant because he is asking her for this care, which she thinks she is giving, and then he says that he will kill her brother if she tells anyone about this love and care she is giving him. The confusion and fear throws her into silent re-examination of something she does not understand.

It is this interior life of the little girl and her acts of consciousness that are crucial to the mimetic representation here and the reason why I am using this unit in this chapter.

In the mimetic sequence of events, she faints and remembers waking up with her stepfather washing her. He was shaking and apologizing to her and reminding her not to tell anyone about this. She should just go to the library as she planned and come home when her mother gets home and "act natural (66)." All she remembers wanting to do is sleep (a beginning sign of the retreat into silent depression) and being afraid to tell him what she wants. He is not about to meet any of her needs. She is there to meet his needs. She just doesn't want herself or her brother physically hurt. As she walks to the library, she is conscious of the tremendous physical pain she is experiencing so she just quietly slips back home and goes to bed.

Her confusion (which first caused her to retreat into the silence of sleep) now erupts into the natural desire to run away and if not that, then the desire to die. When her bed was changed and the blood-stained underwear was found, she was taken to the hospital where the fact that she was raped is discovered by the doctors. When the situation becomes public, the retreat to silence is even more pronounced.

The courtroom sequence intimates, while the little girl is on the stand, that she doesn't know what rape is but she does know that her stepfather did something wrong and she feels that she helped him to do it. Angelou represents her apprehension and fear as a "whirlwind of thoughts going round her mind," such that she could only retreat into silence (70). She not only felt that she might be an accomplice with her stepfather but she also felt that she would be considered like "the harlot in the bible (71)" if she said that this had occurred before. Her mother and her brother would be disappointed in her and she again feared losing their love. Her brother would realize that she had been keeping secrets from him at a time when he thought that they agreed to tell each other everything (71). So, in the courtroom, on the stand, she lies and says "no" but a lump quickly thickened in her throat and cut off her air. The pressure erupted in a screaming fit of anger at her stepfather because he was the one responsible for putting her in this silent, deceiving position.

The stepfather was sentenced to a year and a day but his lawyer got him released that very afternoon at which time he was apparently "kicked to death" and dropped in a field (72). This news contributes to the pressure that the little girl was already under and now she feels responsible for his death as well.

She thinks that she is going to feel forever guilty and lose her place in heaven. She feels the evil in her body and thinks that if she keeps her teeth clamped tightly shut then the evil won't get out and contaminate others--thus the silence. She feels that she has sold herself to the devil and can talk to no one because her very breath by which her words are carried would poison others. She found that she could achieve perfect personal silence "by attaching herself leechlike to sound (73)."

Maya Angelou mimetically represents the consciousness of the withdrawn, sullen child who has removed herself from all contact with people and people quite naturally stop talking when they are around her because they feel sorry for her and want her to start talking. They understand that her experience was a painfully violent and traumatic one and it would take awhile for her to process it and begin speaking again.

But the autobiographer catches the child's consciousness and interprets the silence from the point of view of the child. She fantasized that when she went into a room where everyone was talking and laughing, she would simply stand there in the midst of this "riot of sound" until her silence rushed in upon the room "from inside her and ate up all the sounds (73)." And the room would be silent because she made it so not because everyone was looking sympathetically at her, wishing she would speak, play and run like a normal little girl.

This synecdochic narrative shows mimetically the trauma involved in the act of raping of a child. It voices the mimetic/diegetic discourse of the child's mind in the action. And in so doing, the narrative makes a diegetic point about this handicap of being forced into silence, however violent the force. The adult autobiographer-narrator Maya Angelou, in her own mimetic/diegetic voice, represents the mimetic/diegetic discourse of the mind of the child, her consciousness, through the language of the narrative.

Conclusion

The fictional and non-fictional documents that I have used in this chapter are examples of writers who attempt to integrate, unite and give voice to William Earle's idea of past and present experiences and the states of consciousness which accompanied them. These experiences and states are enveloped in Jean-Jacques Mayoux' idea of a "thick present" from which the writer/narrator takes Georges Gusdorf's suggestion to name those states, give voice to them, in the writing of an autobiographical document. Non-fictional documents like Angelou's and Nolan's show how fiction serves non-fiction when Angelou and Nolan create "Marguerite" and "Joseph" to represent them. Helen and Mill may write about a similar, past, fictional self but they don't consciously create and acknowledge that fiction like Angelou and Nolan do.

The synecdochic moment for each of these writers or narrators rests with the fact that they were each handicapped in some way. Each of them was immersed in the silent withdrawal of the "thick present" during which they re-examined their experience of the states of consciousness which revolved around a particular event and they were able to understand them, give them meaning, organize them, integrate them and name them through writing, through narrative.

The fictional pieces focus on the mimetic chaos of the "thick present" in the narrator's consciousness which consciousness attempts to diegetically separate, organize and unify. Tristram Shandy wants to tell his own story in his own way which in effect means that he is going to tell us about the mimetic chaos and disorganization. Similarly, Hermione Gart is not sure how to tell her story or where her life story seems to be proceeding. Beckett's man on the floor in the dark attempts to deal with the mimetic chaos in his mind by distinguish the three voices within and Ionesco's old man also tries to make sense of his life at its ending by remembering it as a series of disconnected, chaotic events.

The non-fictional pieces focus on the mimetic chaos in consciousness caused by a handicap which forces the consciousness to re-examine and re-think in silence and re-emerge in the voice in the autobiographical document. Helen Keller tells about the journey out of the silence of being deaf, mute and blind. Christopher Nolan tells about the same journey for a quadriplegic. John Stuart Mill tells about the same journey for a person who is mentally-emotionally ill and Maya Angelou tells about an experience of violence which forces her into silent re-organization.

I shall now look at what I call the metaphoric memoirist who gives mimetic/diegetic voice to consciousness about events and experiences but places the focus on the diversity of voices and experiences, the interlaces and braids between voices and experiences in the palimpsest of the "thick present" in consciousness rather than uniting the voices and naming the synecdochic unity that is there. The narratives in a memoir name and represent the different strands of diversity and each narrative has the power to replace the other and so is metaphoric rather than synecdochic.

"What else than a natural and mighty palimpsest is the human brain?"[25]

Notes

1 Thomas DeQuincey, *Tales and Prose Phantasies*, Volume XIII, *The Collected Writings of Thomas DeQuincey*, ed. David Masson (Edinburgh: Adam and Charles Black, 1890), 346.

2 Northrup Frye, *Anatomy of Criticism: Four Essays*, (Princeton University Press, 1957), 307.

3 Jean-Jacques Mayoux, "Variations on the Time-Sense in *Tristram Shandy*," in Laurence Sterne *Tristram Shandy: An Authoritative Text, The Author of the Novel, Criticism*, edited by Howard Anderson, (New York: W.W. Norton and Company, 1980), 578.

4 Laurence Sterne, *Tristram Shandy: An Authoritative Text, The Author of the Novel, Criticism*, edited by Howard Anderson, (New York: W.W. Norton and Company, 1980), 61. All further references will be to this edition.

5 John Stuart Mill, *Autobiography of John Stuart Mill* (New York: Columbia University Press, 1924. All further references will be to this edition.

6 Michael Cooke, "Do you Remember Laura?" or, The Limits of Autobiography," (*Iowa Review*, 1978 ii), 61.

7 Mayoux, 583.

8 Denis Donoghue, *Ferocious Alphabets*, (Boston: Little, Brown and Company, 1981), 25.

9 Hilda Doolittle, *Hermione* (New York: New Directions, 1927)), ix. All further references will be to this edition.

10 Monica Blasing, *The Art of Life: Studies in American Autobiographical Literature* (Austin: The University of Texas Press, 1977), xv.

11 Samuel Beckett, *Endgame: A Play in One Act followed by Act Without Words: A Mime for One Player*, (New York: Grove Press, Inc., 1958), 70. Also *Malone Dies*, (New York: Grove Press, Inc.), 50.

12 Samuel Beckett, *Company*, (London: Jack Calder, 1980), 7. All further references will be to this edition.

13 Roy Pascal, *Design and Truth in Autobiography*, (Harvard University Press, 1960), 182.

14 Eugene Ionesco, *Four Plays: The Bald Soprano, The Lesson, Jack, or The Submission, The Chairs*, trans. Donald M. Allen (New York: Grove Press, Inc., 1958), 118-119.

15 Helen Keller, *The Story of My Life*, (New York: Doubleday and Company, Inc., 1954), 26, 30. All further references will be to this edition.

16 Donohue, 12.

17 John Gross, A Review of Christopher Nolan's autobiography *Under the Eye of the Clock* in *The New York Times*, February 26, 1988, Section C, 33.

18 Patricia Hampl, "Defying the Yapping Establishment," (*The New York Times Book Review*, March 13, 1988), 9.

19 Christopher Nolan, *Under the Eye of the Clock: The Life Story of Christopher Nolan* (New York: St. Martin's Press, 1987), xi. All further references will be to this edition.

20 Linda Joffee, "A Voice From a Mute World Sings," (*The Christian Science Monitor*, January 27, 1988), 6.

21 Jonathan Loesberg, *Fictions of Consciousness: Mill, Newman and the Reading of Victorian Prose*, (Rutgers University Press, 1986), 58-59.

22 Frank Kermode, *The Sense of Ending: Studies in the Theory of Fiction*, (Oxford University Press, 1966), 101.

23 Anne Norton, "Writing, Violence and Revolution in Memory," (The 1987-88 William Andrews Clark Library Lecture Series: "Violence and Order, Revolution and Constitution: Bicentennial Reflections," Los Angeles, May 27, 1988).

24 Maya Angelou, *I Know Why The Caged Bird Sings*, (New York: Atheneum Press, 1975), 65. All further references will be to this edition.

25 DeQuincey, 346.

Chapter Two

A Memoir Compares and Contrasts the Mimetic/Diegetic Voices in Metaphoric Narratives

> Everlasting layers of ideas, images, feelings, have fallen upon your brain softly as light.[1]

Introduction

In this chapter, I want to distinguish the narrative voice in a memoir from the voice in an autobiography or confession, by examining how these "layers of ideas, images and feelings" which have "fallen upon the brain" are mimetically/diegetically vocalized by the memoirist in a series of metaphoric narratives.

The crucial distinction to be made about these "layers of ideas, images and feelings" is that they are a compilation of an infinite number of sensations registered on the conscious, unconscious, subconscious mind. The memoirist perceives the multiple otherness within and attempts to represent that variety and alterity in a number of metaphoric narratives which can replace each other as equal in value.

James Goodwin supports the idea that there are multiple "other" acts and states of consciousness in people in his exploration of the myth of Narcissus, who came to love himself as "another," and Goodwin relates this myth to autobiographical writing. Steven Marcus compares Freud's explanation of interior conflicts in consciousness as an attempt to resolve childhood conflicts with Heinz Kohut's explanation that these conflicts actually arise because of the presence of a void, an absence created in childhood which consciousness continually tries to fill and resolve. Following upon this "void" idea, Jacques Derrida discusses how Friedrich Nietzsche's states of consciousness eternally return to each other so as to meet and reconcile the presence of the various void within; Derrida contends that the present consciousness acts in such a way as to formulate a state to fill voids created in the past.

Samuel Beckett dramatizes how the conscious mind compares and contrasts various interior states in his play, *Waiting for Godot*, where the characters' mimetic interactions in Act One of the play are analyzed diegetically by them in Act Two. Act Two is also a mimetic interaction of voices but the mimetic voices are performing a diegetic examination of a previous set of mimetic voices and experiences which are compared and contrasted, replaced and re-positioned, remembered and re-organized. The series of mimetic activities performed in Act One cannot be remembered in a series of mimetic activities in Act Two which are diegetic commentaries on the first set of activities.

Like Beckett, Tennessee Williams also dramatizes Tom Wingfield's attempts to remember the mimetic circumstances under which he left home to join the Merchant Marine in *The Glass Menagerie*. The series of mimetic activities and voices which led to his leaving are admittedly not clear to his present diegetic, narrating voice. He compares and contrasts remembrances in a series of metaphoric scenes in the play.

In *Speak, Memory*, Vladimir Nabokov highlights what the "fictional" Tom Wingfield is doing when Nabokov "stacks" (his own word) his memories in a series of chapters but admits that he feels as if he is falling into a "transparent abyss" of multiple acts and states. Nabokov admits that his present diegetic act of narration can indeed create apparently mimetic narratives in these chapters which represent past voices and experiences but he knows that they are metaphoric versions of many possible voices and experiences.

William Wordsworth, in *The Prelude*, portrays himself mimetically in a state of depression due to the feeling that he has lost his creative impulse as a poet. His solution is to return home where three separate, metaphoric experiences from childhood balance themselves against the present depressed state and he gives mimetic voice to these experiences but arranges them in such a way that he can make an inferred, diegetic point about his depression. The synecdochic experiences of depression and loss of poetic voice are resolved in the metaphoric narratives of three memories from childhood. In Wordsworth, my definitions of memoir and autobiography intersect. He is remembering, comparing and contrasting three experiences from childhood as a way to make a present, diegetic point about a very significant experience in his life--his loss of his poetic voice, his depression and his desire to write the great philosophical epic poem.

As pointed out by Derrida, Friedrich Nietzsche's concept of "the eternal return" is a highly significant one for the memoirist enterprise. In his *Ecce Homo*, Nietzsche argues that every time he tries to remember mimetically, as in "exactly," a past act or state, he in fact is diegetically commenting that his present consciousness is in effect returning to the past, as if "eternally," in order to resolve or end, supplement the void or complement the other, and actually finds some new void or other each time.

In *The Woman Warrior*, Maxine Hong Kingston has one chapter entitled "Shaman" in which she tells a story about her mother from the time when her mother was a teenager. The story, then, is one that has been told by the mother to Maxine and Maxine reports it, as in a biography. But since this is Maxine's "memoir of a girlhood among ghosts," this story emerges as her own story about her own mother. Assuming that Maxine experienced her mother like most children do, there would be multiple, metaphoric stories to report. But Maxine's memory reduces the multiplicity to this one synecdochic story about her mother. It is a synecdochic, autobiographical account of a mimetic experience which the mother had but it is a metaphoric, memoirist account of a series of mimetic experiences that Maxine had of her mother. As she wrote this memoir, she "eternally returned" to stories, mimetic experiences, and memories of her mother and so bracketed and reduced them to this one story where she diegetically represents herself as her mother's biographer.

Arthur Miller, in his life story, remembers his infamous relationship with Marilyn Monroe. He remembers in particular the writing and filming of the movie *The Misfits*. His diegetic voice selects particular mimetic voices and experiences and he compares and contrasts these for validity and believability. The narrative of the filming of *The Misfits* becomes a metaphoric narrative which represents and could replace other experiences and narratives of his relationship with Marilyn.

Like Maxine Hong Kingston, Edmund Gosse remembers his father in his autobiographical document, *Father and Son*. He remembers specifically his mother's illness and her subsequent death from cancer and his baptism. These narratives become metaphoric replacements and examples of his relationship with his father. Like Maxine, he, for all intents and purpose, becomes his parents' biographer, but, also like Maxine, he distills a number of memories in these particular metaphoric narrative units in which his mimetic voice and diegetic commentary represent his relationship with his parents.

Mary McCarthy in her *Memories of a Catholic Girlhood* narrates the mimetic sequence of events and voices of an unjust discipline she received from a mean uncle when she was nine years old in a story called "A Tin Butterfly." But in a series of diegetic "postscripts" to the story, she re-examines the mimetic events and voices and questions their accuracy. Other events and voices may have occurred which she has forgotten. The diegetic postscripts become metaphoric replacements for particular parts of the story. Whether her voice spoke one set of words or another or whether certain events occurred or did not occur or in what order, they can replace each other in the re-telling and re-structuring of a coherent, believable story.

James Goodwin sees the specific aim of an autobiographical document, like a memoir, as a way for the writer to explore the multiple parts of the singular, individual self and the multiple parts of, in some cases, a great variety of experiences, and come to express that self-understanding in a narrative which communicates the perceptions through the person's own voice. In such an exploration, as in a memoir, there is a necessary self-alienation that occurs when memory seems to fail and difficulty distinguishing and differentiating occurs which is essential to the process of re-constituting, re-integrating the self. The writer meets new selves and integrates them in what Goodwin calls a "narcissistic self-objectification"[2] which is necessary for the journey back to integration. Robert Langbaum notes that ours has become an "identity society,"[3] where people are more narcissistically concerned with personal consciousness than success at a career. He notes that the typical patient in psychoanalysis nowadays focuses on this narcissistic pursuit of self-consciousness and self-fulfillment. Every interior relation becomes a power struggle as persons seek to experience and know these other parts of themselves as real objects, each with its own multiple parts with whom they can maintain strong relations, significant, meaningful dialogue. Langbaum, with Goodwin, says that the autobiographical writer who is a memoirist, like the patient in psychoanalysis, recognizes these radically other selves as new selves whom the writer wants to know so as to love the whole self better (88-89).

Steven Marcus gives another perspective to this issue in his article "The Psychoanalytic Self" where he focuses on Heinz Kohut's thesis that deeply embedded in the anatomical, physiological, neurological matrix of the unconscious are these inexplicable blank spaces, inconsistencies, and contradictions which have never been addressed by the person.[4] Goodwin says that the autobiographer as memoirist is a person who meets these, reconciles them and comes to love and appreciate them as metaphorical parts, voices, of the self. Kohut says that there may never be any reconciliation or "love" but only a continual dialogue, a nietzschean "eternal return." Kohut says that when the individual discovers an irreconcilable inconsistency or contradiction, these two (or more) "horns of the dilemma" dialogue with each other in the memoirist text or the psychoanalyst's couch.

Kohut disagrees with Freud who says that these gaps, inconsistencies or contradictions were created in childhood and the adult attempts to reconcile them. Freud says that two or more distinct, unconscious states are formed in the child and evidence themselves in a conscious way in adult neuroses. Kohut, on the other hand, says that the warring states in the adult are an attempt to supply a state that was missed, not created, in childhood through healthy child-parent interaction. The gap or lack of an important "state" which was supposed to be created in early childhood and was registered in the unconscious evidences itself in the adult warring states and dialogues with various selves in order to fill the blank or resolve the conflict between two or more distinct states.

Jacques Derrida in *The Ear of the Other* addresses this question of the blank or absent state which should have been created in childhood with his discussion of Nietzsche's idea that an individual, like a memoirist, will "eternally return" to this state in an attempt to fill it.[5] Derrida accents the idea that the memoirist playfully differentiates the multiple selves, the gaps or voids within, when one "self" giving ear to the other self creates a portrait of the other self. Derrida says that the constructed self dialogues with the multiple others within and another self may be constructed which can again be deconstructed in a new "eternal return" and re-discovery of someone else. These newly constructed, metaphoric selves sometimes are used to fill the place of the absent self when the absence is recognized.

The problem with the void or the gap within is that there is nothing, no one, with whom to dialogue. Derrida compares this to the process of mourning the death of a loved one (57-58). When someone dies with whom a person has been particularly close, the person experiences this as loss and void. There is no one to dialogue with any more. The survivor may retreat to the place of silence and emptiness in the void, the place where the person used to be, as part of the mourning process, the acceptance of this loss, the lack within.

Derrida says that a similar process occurs with parts of the self that have died or never existed. He suggests that this void within be looked at in terms of the loss of the loved one where the "surviving selves" need to retreat to the silence of the emptiness as part of the acceptance of that loss, or lack, or void within. Another self can be constructed to replace the loss or the loss, the void, can be accepted as an new addition, a part of the structure of the self.

In "The New Model Autobiographer," John Sturrock reiterates Derrida's point about this fear of death and extinction, the fear of the recognition of these voids and gaps within, as the motivation for autobiographical, memoirist writing.[6] The autobiographer desires to record some synecdochic, representative form of a self that will ensure a permanent place in time, in historical record. The experience of various voids within, as little deaths, are countered with the concerted effort of the self to fill the gaps and re-assert existence in the face of and fear of oblivion. If individuals experience parts of themselves as empty, void, containing "nothing," the natural desire is to find a someone, a something, or a variety of metaphoric "things" to fill this space.

Based on what I have found useful in Goodwin, Marcus, and Derrida and correlatively in Langbaum and Sturrock, and as I apply them to the narratives chosen, my theory of memoir writing, as distinct from autobiographical or confessional, is that it is a narrative in which the mimetic narrating voice articulates a series of other voices from past events and experiences held in memory and the present voice compares and contrasts the accuracy of these.

The multiplicity of remembered voices and experiences overlap each other and in effect "bury" each other, as DeQuincey intimates in his palimpsest metaphor. The key distinction among memoir, autobiography and confession is that the voices and experiences are buried but not eradicated: in autobiography, they are synecdochically united; in memoir they are metaphorically compared and contrasted; in confession they are re-discovered and metonymically linked.

PART ONE: FICTIONAL MEMOIRS

Gogo, Didi, Lucky and Pozzo

Estragon, Pozzo, Lucky and Vladimir in Samuel Beckett's *Waiting for Godot*, participate in an experience, a series of acts and vocal exchanges, in Act One which become vague, incoherent memories in a series of acts and vocal exchanges in Act Two when they try to remember what happened; the events are completely forgotten by Pozzo and remembered differently each by Gogo and Didi as a series of isolated, unconnected facts and incidents. Lucky and the audience are silent eyewitnesses to these "facts" in Act One. If there were an Act Three and an eternal return of Acts and these characters kept meeting again and again, Beckett suggests that these characters would continue to remember only isolated metaphoric-synecdochic facts, pieces and traces, about the previous meetings and the new meeting would create another set of overlapping metaphors and synecdoches in memory which they would try to make into a metonymic, synecdochic, metaphoric narrative of mimetic/diegetic voices later.

This drama by Samuel Beckett exemplifies my theoretical perspective about the memoir, based on the work of Derrida, Marcus and Goodwin, that these characters in this play are returning to an experience in an attempt to make sense of it but the return only results in a conflict of opposites and missing pieces. When familiarity with the remembered circumstances and details sets in, they may arrive at a narrative like Maxine Hong Kingston's about her mother which will capture the essence of their experience for them.

Vladimir might be conceptualized as the creative, artistic person as well as the historical researcher, the investigator, the diegetic commentator and evaluator. He remembers the significant bits and pieces, the raw materials of various perceptions and intuitions, and he wants to reconstruct a story, a metonymic sequence of events, like an historical annalist, a chronicler, but he is confounded because he gets no eyewitness support from neither Estragon nor

Mimetic/Diegetic Voices in Metaphoric Narratives 87

Pozzo in Act Two and he can't make the metonymic connections between the events, situations and objects remembered so that he can bracket them into a sequence of metaphors and synecdoches representative of experience generally which give it "meaning."

At the beginning of Act Two Estragon and Vladimir embrace each other because they have missed each other after the evening's sleep. There is a general discussion about their almost being beaten up the day before and about the general state of their relative unhappiness and discontent as they wait. Vladimir sees the tree and recalls that they considered hanging themselves from it yesterday and so he decides to reconstruct, narrate the day, based upon the memory prompt of this tree. Estragon recalls none of this. He embodies Derrida's idea of the void. He says Vladimir dreamt it. Vladimir is amazed that Estragon would forget something so serious as wanting to commit suicide. Estragon says that he usually either "forgets immediately,"[7] which he did with this suicide business with the tree, or he "never forgets (39)," in which case he too elaborates his own "dream" or fiction.

Vladimir wonders if Estragon also forgot about the visitation of Pozzo and Lucky yesterday. He remembers Lucky as "a lunatic who kicked him in the shins (40)" and he recalls that Pozzo gave him a bone. These two isolated facts in Estragon's memory neither synecdochically represent nor metonymically capture the sequence of the experience of Pozzo and Lucky in Act One but they indeed serve as metaphors of the experience because they are what give meaning to the experience for Estragon. They become metonymic when he connects them with other facts and builds a story. They become synecdochic after the narrative is created in that they stand out from all the rest.

The mimetic voice of the narrator attempts to give metonymic sequence to selected facts by putting them in an infallible, chronological order while the diegetic voice of the evaluator attempts to give metaphoric-synecdochic sequence to the selected facts by admitting that there are gaps in this order, which make these particular facts significant because they were remembered over the others.

Vladimir and Estragon finally agree that they need to take things "calmly (40);" it's not enough just to "live their lives" and "wait for Godot (41)," they need, somewhat compulsively, to talk about their lives and reconstruct them, as objects. They want to give their lives some kind of metonymic sequence, a logical order of significant events which are metaphorically-synecdochically representative and meaningful.

They try to start a conversation; they try to "have an idea, a thought (42)" until which time Estragon asks Vladimir to try to remember what they were saying when they began this particular day in Act II. He thinks that they began this day by trying to recall what happened yesterday. Vladimir finds this activity of remembering to be particularly challenging, being the type of a creative-artistic man and an historian. He wants to reconstruct the beginning of the day by a kind of brainstorming, a Shandy-esque word association, by which he can make sure it existed and can have some kind of control over it: "embrace...happy...waiting...happy ...tree (42)!" He perceives the tree differently from yesterday which makes Estragon believe that they weren't there yesterday; this is a different tree in a different place.

With the thought of "yesterday," then, Vladimir returns again to ask himself what he "did" yesterday. Estragon says they probably just "blathered (43)" about nothing, like they usually do, waiting for Godot. But Vladimir, the historian, wants something more specific; he wants a metonymic sequence of "facts and circumstances" that he can put his finger on in recall and synecdochically hang meaning and coherence on---he wants to know that "something happened" in his life yesterday; something significant which would indicate that he "means something." For Estragon, such a series of acts of consciousness as remembering and reconstructing is "torment (43)." Like the characters in Sartre's *No Exit*, he would rather just eternally get on with the mimetic sequence of raw perceptions and intuitions gathered from the field of objects continually passing before him than stop to examine, analyze, evaluate and re-construct.

Vladimir begins another word association in which Estragon participates half-heartedly and the word association this time takes them back to Pozzo and Lucky: "...the bone...the kick...Lucky gave the kick (43)." Vladimir, the historian, asks Estragon to show the spot on his leg where he was kicked as proof. Vladimir notices that Estragon has no boots on and discovers the boots are at the place on the stage where they had left them at the end of Act One when they went to sleep. He accepts this as historical proof that the two of them were there in that same spot yesterday with that tree. But Estragon discovers that they are not his boots because they are the wrong color. Vladimir wants them to be his boots because he wants this to be the same spot so that he can construct his story, his sequence and make his life meaningful.

So he leaves his role as chronicler and historian and becomes the novelist, the artist who creates the fiction that someone came and took Estragon's boots and left these. These boots, the bone, the kick, the tree are the metaphors from the mimetic sequence with which Vladimir will form the sequence of his new narrative and the diegetic voice endows them with a synecdochic/metonymic meaning that they don't have by themselves. They can stand for each other or replace each other to the degree that they represent the experience for Vladimir. The tree reminds him of the suicide. The boots remind him that he was there yesterday which reminds him that Estragon was kicked by a lunatic which reminds Estragon that the lunatic's friend gave him a chicken bone. The "being kicked" is significant especially since Estragon confuses it with another beating by another person not witnessed by the audience in Act One.

The next piece of "evidence" is Lucky's hat. Vladimir finds Lucky's hat and he and Estragon participate in a pantomime of hat exchanges after which Vladimir decides that "for something to do" for the sake of "company or diversity," they could "play" at being Pozzo and Lucky. They have the "bone" and the "kicking" and the hat as the facts on which to base their pantomime, their imitation. But then Vladimir suddenly remembers something else: the visual image of Lucky sagging under the weight of his master's, Pozzo's, heavy baggage and so he begins his imitation of Lucky based upon this visual image. Estragon does not know what to do; he does not know how "to be" Pozzo; all he remembers is "the bone" which Pozzo gave him and so Vladimir must coach him, direct him: "curse me,...tell me to think,...tell me to dance (47)." Estragon does not want to play so Vladimir plays both parts until he realizes Estragon has left, is not participating in his game, and so misses him and rushes to embrace him. Vladimir, the artist, re-creates the moment and the experience by imitating it.

But the mimetic "embracing" and the "waiting," not the analytical, diegetic remembering or imitating, are the central issues in this play for the consciousness of Estragon and Vladimir. The essence of their experience is that they care for each other as they wait and the mimetic storytelling and diegetic commenting are quite secondary endeavors which comprise the content of the caring and waiting. Vladimir does not care to go on with the pantomime if Estragon leaves.

They go back to their play-acting but this time they play themselves; they yell at each other and call it "abuse." They argue with each other and happily call it "contradicting." They hug each other and say they "made up (49)." They have experiences, they imitate these experiences, name them, connect them, narrate them, forget them, diegetically comment on them and return to them to fictionalize them.

When Pozzo and Lucky return to meet Vladimir and Estragon again in Act II, Vladimir sees this staggering, helpless Pozzo, who yesterday was the triumphant commandant, and his companion Lucky, and he thinks of them as "reinforcements, help (49)" while they all wait for Godot; someone else to embrace, to remember with, to share stories. "They are not alone (50)" in the wait.

Vladimir thinks that Pozzo may have another bone for Estragon and Estragon has no idea what Vladimir means by "bone" when not moments earlier the bone was Estragon's only memory of Pozzo. Estragon wants proof that this was really the same man who gave him that bone. Vladimir suggests that Estragon get this proof by "asking him (50)." Pozzo meanwhile is groping, writhing, groaning, beating the ground in pain and asking for help. He can't get up. He is quite radically changed from the day before but Vladimir and Estragon do not notice; they only want the bone and see him as a "help" to them.

This persistent memory of the bone makes no sense in terms of what happened the day before nor does it make sense in terms of what is happening now, indicating the possibility that a strong memory may indeed be only an isolated, tangential, superficial part of the real experience but an author may make it central in his retelling of the experience--a synecdoche that has lost its significance or a metaphor that can't replace.

As the two deliberate about the deranged Pozzo, Vladimir says he is worried that "Lucky might get going again (51)." Estragon does not remember a "Lucky." In fact, Estragon connects Lucky with an entirely different experience from the day before when we "almost were beaten up" which the audience did not witness. Estragon here confuses two similar events: one of almost being beaten up and another of being kicked by Lucky. Vladimir points to Lucky standing immobile and tells Estragon that "here is the one who kicked you yesterday (51)." He is ready and willing to "run amuk (51)" again, at a moment's notice. Vladimir and Estragon are not conscious of Lucky and Pozzo as they are in that moment, on that day; they only perceive them as they remember them. They can't see them as they are.

An entirely new scenario of activity and dialogue now takes place between the four characters which will be the raw data, the brute facts, for a remembrance in Act Three, if there was an Act Three. Estragon attempts to kick and hurl abuse at the motionless Lucky; Pozzo worries that Lucky will be hurt. Vladimir, the ever-vigilant historian, again hears this as proof: Pozzo's oral testimony that this man is Lucky because he called him by that name, the same as yesterday. Pozzo remembers nothing of yesterday but he also knows, he says, that he won't remember anything of today when tomorrow comes. Vladimir reminds Pozzo about what Pozzo was doing yesterday, bringing Lucky to the fair to sell him along with the dancing, the thinking, Pozzo was not blind yesterday etc.

Pozzo allows Vladimir his fiction ("as you please (57)"). He just wants to move on into the transparent abyss of the successive quantity of accumulating moments. He remembers none of what Vladimir is saying.

Vladimir has created a story which he believes to be true based upon his eyewitness, first-hand experience but he receives no support from Pozzo nor Estragon. Vladimir wants Lucky to sing and think and recite again like he did yesterday. Pozzo has no idea what Vladimir is talking about because Lucky is now "dumb (57)." Obviously more than one day has passed for Pozzo because he says "one day he went dumb,...one day I went blind,...one day we'll go deaf,...one day we're born, one day we shall die (58)." For Pozzo, there seem to be many years between the experiences of Act One and Two. For Vladimir, the day itself is like many years. He tries to recall every detail, every event, every moment. Vladimir is like Beckett's Malone or Doolittle's Hermione who go through every millet grain of their lives trying to make meaning out of each moment and sense out of each day and experience.

Pozzo and Lucky leave and Vladimir, the historical analyst, wonders if Pozzo is "really blind." He thinks that the blindness he just witnessed may have been an act, a pretense of Pozzo's because he feels that Pozzo really "saw him (59)." Estragon, on the other hand, accepts Pozzo's testimony on faith; "he told us he was blind (58)," therefore he really was. If Vladimir doesn't believe Pozzo and thinks that he really wasn't blind, then that is Vladimir's own "dream," fictional creation, diegetic bracket. Estragon believes Pozzo's testimony and creates his narrative based upon that faith.

Vladimir returns full circle and wonders what he will say about this day and this experience when he wakes up tomorrow. The waiting...Pozzo and Lucky passing by...in all of that "where is the truth?...Where is the meaning?...What have I said;...What will I say (58-9)?" Will each of them return again tomorrow and not know each other or will each of them know metaphoric-metonymic-synecdochic bits and pieces, Derridean traces and Kohutian gaps, which each of them will use to construct his own meaningful, albeit fictional, memoir.

Beckett's play accents the series of acts of consciousness that eternally return to a previous state of consciousness to examine the interplay of acts and states there and gives voice to these in his drama. In a memoir, consciousness attempts to fill voids, reconcile opposites and generally compare and contrast memories.

Tom Wingfield

Tom Wingfield's mimetic voice narrating in the present constructs a story in which he represents himself mimetically, speaking and acting in the past event. His narrating, mimetic voice is also diegetic to the extent that he asserts that his memory may be fictionalizing some of the circumstance of the event. The play is set "now and in the past."[8] His mimetic voice speaking at the time of the event also makes various diegetic comments throughout as well.

Williams' describes Scene One:

> The scene is memory and is therefore nonrealistic. Memory takes a lot of poetic license. It omits some details; others are exaggerated, according to the emotional value of the articles it touches, for memory is seated predominantly in the heart (27).

He describes a "fourth transparent wall" and transparent gauze portieres of the dining room arch (28)." The gauze portieres and the concept of transparency become synecdoches or metaphors for memory itself.

Like Williams, Vladimir Nabokov speaks of memory as a "transparent abyss"[9] in his autobiographical document, *Speak, Memory*. Nabokov also uses these images of gauze curtains and transparency for memory when he says that

> with lips pressed against the thin fabric that veiled the windowpane, the pane through which nostalgia longed to peer, the windowpane on which his tongue could only taste the cold of the glass through the gauze but prevented him from entering fully into that transparent abyss of memory. (73, 89, 107)...The cradle rocks above an abyss, and common sense tells us that our existence is but a brief crack of light between two eternities of darkness (19).

He writes about remembering the Nabokov family coat of arms "with great clarity" as a "great chessboard (50)" and then he corrects the memory because after looking it up he discovers that only about one-sixteenth of one square contains part of a chessboard.

In the following passage, Nabokov attempts to remember his childhood tutors and the passage represents how memory can distort and blur the reality. Tom Wingfield attempts to remember the circumstances around the time that he left home to join the Merchant Marine and he too admits the possibility of the same kind of blurring and distortion but also "an essential completeness and stability...an innate harmony...gather and fold the suspended and wandering tonalities...into consummation and resolution (see quotation here following)."

> In thinking of my successive tutors, I am concerned less with the queer dissonances they introduced me to in my young life than with the essential stability and completeness of that life. I witness with pleasure the supreme achievement of memory, which is the masterly use it makes of innate harmonies when gathering to its fold the suspended and wandering tonalities of the past. I like to imagine, in consummation and resolution of those jangling chords, something as enduring, in retrospect, as the long table on summer birthdays and namedays used to be laid for afternoon chocolate out of doors....I see the tablecloth and the faces....exaggerated, no doubt, by the same faculty of impassioned commemoration, of ceaseless return, that always makes me approach that table from the outside,...through a tremulous prism, I distinguish features,...I see...I note....the pulsation of my thought mingles with that of the lead shadows and turns Ordo into Max and Max into Lenski and Lenski into the schoolmaster, and the whole array of trembling transformations is repeated. And then, suddenly,...a torrent of sounds comes to life: voices speaking all together...the confused and enthusiastic hullabalo,...like a background of wild applause (170-72).

Nabakov's voice is mimetic to the extent that he is telling the reader exactly how he remembers these situations. He looks through the gauze curtain of the window at his mental picture of the past and mimetically sees the experiences but when he narrates, he evaluates diegetically the specificity and clarity of the recollection and, like Mary McCarthy, he questions its truth because as he looks through the gauze curtain at the picture, he feels as if he falls into an uncontrollable, chaotic "transparent abyss."

Tom Wingfield also narrates mimetically in that he tries to remember the mimetic details of a specific situation and the gauze portieres that enclose the Wingfield apartment are like Nabokov's gauze curtains on the windows and Tom, like Nabokov, or later, as I shall point out in Mary McCarthy's "postscripts," narrates diegetically through them when he questions the accuracy of his memories. As he looks through the "gauze portieres" into the dining room of the apartment, this fourth wall is "transparent" so as to allow him to narrate while looking through it:

> I am the narrator of the play and also a character in it....The play is memory. Being a memory play, it is dimly lighted, it is sentimental, it is not realistic. In memory everything seems to happen to music. That explains the fiddle in the wings (29-30).

In this opening speech, Tom explains his theoretical, diegetic stance before he attempts a mimetic narration.

> Yes, I have tricks in my pocket, I have things up my sleeve. But I am the opposite of a stage magician. He gives you illusion that has the appearance of truth. I give you truth in the pleasant guise of illusion (29).

There will be reference later in the play to a real magician, Malvolio, whom Tom sees at a stage show. Malvolio is also the name of Lady Olivia's steward in Shakespeare's *Twelfth Night* who fantasizes that he might marry her. She has no interest in him; he is so serious and somber that he is an easy prey for Sir Toby's elaborate tricks and jokes. "Shakespeare" is a nickname given to Tom because he writes poetry. I would like to connect this interlace of magician, Shakespeare and Malvolio with Tom. They are different diegetic elements in Tom's consciousness that compare and contrast who he is.

As a narrator who creates this story, this mimesis, this illusion, and is able to make it sound real, he is the stage magician. As Shakespeare, the artist, the writer, he is not only able to make the drama sound and look real, he is also able to make a diegetic point with his creation.

As Malvolio, he is duped into thinking that the illusion he has created is the reality, that he is responsible for his sister's well-being, for example. Tom, the writer, magician and dupe, has the diegetic power to return again through narrative, through dramatization, and change the mimetic memory, the reality and create an illusion but at the same time come to terms with it.

Tom tells his sister that the stage magician Malvolio poured water back and forth into pitchers and turned it into wine, which Tom of course volunteered to taste and as he more often than not does, proceeds to get drunk. Malvolio the stage magician also gave Tom a magic scarf with which he can turn a canary cage into a goldfish bowl and the goldfish fly away as canaries. He gives his sister the scarf in hopes that it will be able to make magic in her life, change her and make her happy.

But the most "wonderfullest trick of all was the coffin trick (56)." Malvolio was nailed into a coffin and got out of the coffin without removing one nail. Tom reflects diegetically at home aloud to his sister that its easy to get yourself nailed in to a coffin, like he is nailed into the coffin of his home, the coffin of his own personal illusions about himself, continually putting off, excusing and ignoring the abuse and manipulation of Amanda and in the process, he walls himself up, nails himself in, and loses all sense of himself and his own motivations and needs. He is in many ways "silenced."

Tom comes to his most keen, clear, perceptive, diegetic insight: it's easy to get oneself nailed in, walled up, closed off, lost, but how does one get back out of the coffin, out of the corner, out in the open, back into contact with a healthy sense of self without going through the pain of removing one nail, without asserting oneself such that illusions will be shattered. He knows that by leaving and joining the Merchant Marine, he may hurt and lose his sister, neither of which he wants to do nor is he able to do. She will not be hurt nor will he lose her. He must "remove that nail" to be free.

Malvolio, the stage magician, makes the reality look easy. Tom, the narrative magician, makes the illusion that he is responsible for his sister so difficult to shatter. Malvolio the magician is, of course, not *really* nailed into the coffin; it is a trick, an illusion; he looks like he's nailed in. So getting out is no problem.

Tom makes it "look like" he's nailed into that house with his mother and sister; he narrates mimetically this illusion. And if it is an illusion, it should be easy to shatter. The reality is that he's not forced to stay there; he is free to remove the nails and leave. He narrates this diegetic "reality" that he is free to leave under the guise of the mimetic "illusion" that he is nailed in, forced to stay. Like Malvolio, the magician, Tom can remove the nails quite easily. Like Malvolio, the magician, Tom is not really nailed into that house. He makes it "look like" he's forced to stay there and he is tied to that illusion as if it were a reality. He shatters the illusion, discovers the reality, and leaves to join the Merchant Marine.

When his mother refuses to believe the reality that he "just goes to the movies" every night, he creates a fiction, an illusion, for her. He narrates a long, elaborate, magical story about himself as an underworld spy, El Diablo, and other stories about his gang-related activities. The truth is, the reality is, that he does in fact go to the movies and get drunk but the fiction, the illusion, is more fun, more believable, more magical, more delusional. The truth is that Tom is responsible neither for his sister's nor his mother's health and happiness but the illusion that he is responsible for them makes him appear responsible, caring, even heroic. And when the reality that he is free emerges and the illusion of being responsible, caring and heroic is shattered, Tom's self-esteem and self-image are shattered because he then thinks that he is uncaring and irresponsible.

Tom later tells his friend, Jim, the "gentleman caller" who nicknamed him Shakespeare, that he is tired of sitting in a theater watching the illusions on the movie screen of fictional people having fictional, magical adventures. He is equally tired of the illusion of his own life. He wants to participate in the reality of "moving" himself and having a real adventure, a life, for himself, and so is motivated to join the Merchant Marine. He is tired of creating stories, illusions, about where he goes each night which attempt to imitate the reality that he desires and he's tired of living with this illusion that he is responsible for his mother and sister.

The mimetic sequence of dialogue and words spoken by Tom in the play are accompanied by this diegetic sequence of comments and evaluations, especially to his friend, Jim, on the balcony before the dinner.

The magician image is synecdochic in that it is representative of Tom generally; Malvolio, the stage magician, and the writer are metaphoric forms or versions of the magician image. They overlap, braid and substitute for each other. Malvolio, the magician makes the illusion that he is nailed into the coffin look real; Tom is the magician who narrates the illusion that he forced to remain in that house look real. Malvolio, in *Twelfth Night*, creates the illusion that Lady Olivia loves him and they will marry and Tom creates the illusion that he is responsible for his sister when in fact, she is actually quite aware of her mother's needs and she also has the opportunity to renew her high-school relationship with Jim and when she learns that he is engaged to be married, she does not break but manages to survive quite well. She can get along quite well without Tom.

Shakespeare is the writer who creates mimetic fictions, illusions, through which he makes true, diegetic points about real life. Tom is the writer who creates this fiction of his own life through which he makes a point about it.

The Glass Menagerie is an example of a metaphoric memoir of comparative/contrastive mimetic/diegetic voices because Tom is remembering an event, the circumstances around which he left home to join the Merchant Marine. He is remembering the mimetic series of activities that he experienced at that time and he is narrating them in terms of a present series of realizations which become the diegetic commentary and evaluation. The mimetic circumstances remembered are admitted by him through various metaphoric images to be illusory dialogues and situations created which he feels will imitate the reality but he knows they do not so he adds various diegetic commentary and evaluation. The metaphoric, synecdochic image of the magician/writer is a diegetic device by which Tom represents various narrative voices and viewpoints from his past and present. His narrative is a way for him to reconcile opposites, fill the voids and clarify confusions, however fictional.

PART TWO: NON-FICTIONAL MEMOIRS

William Wordsworth

William Wordsworth returned to the Lake District to renew "those latent essences by which [his] mind [was once] moved with feelings of delight."[10] The Lake District, his "beloved Grasmere," is that place where he was first "fed by lofty speculation and never-failing joy and passion (2, 49-51)." So he returns there to renew those lost essences and his consciousness is once again fed and moved by lofty speculations and never-failing joys and passions which were formed in childhood and are again re-kindled by three childhood remembrances which result in three separate but, I propose, braided, metaphoric narratives in *The Prelude*.

The three narrative remembrances are metaphoric narratives because they can each replace the other in his conscious remembrance of his mimetic experience as a child at Grasmere and they are his diegetic comment about the source of his creativity. His creative spirit was renewed in this return to his birthplace. Wordsworth's crisis in his personal life involved this loss of his poetic creativity which led him to return to the Lake District and there re-discover his roots. The experience of the loss of creativity is itself synecdochic for him and he situates its importance and significance through the mixture of voices in these various, metaphoric narratives from experiences held in memory.

He "read...with clearer knowledge (4, 212-214)" the book of nature there in his homeland and narrated in his autobiographical poem, his diegetic interpretation of what he mimetically saw there. He mimetically re-experienced the area as if he were a child again and he mimetically re-experienced the perceptions and intuitions recorded in consciousness which were re-activated again upon the return and he diegetically connects these with this present feeling of loss and in so doing retrieves his creative impulse. He experiences one of these voids, an absence, a lack of the creative impulse which lack frustrated him because he had also been creative and productive; and he attempts to fill that void by returning home and the memories there serve to re-kindle the creative impulse.

He walks about and recalls those "rapturous times (1,430)" when he was able to be alone with nature who "employed such ministry (1,467-8)" on him that his creative talent was born and nurtured. The elements of this place animate and agitate his creative spirit with their "noises, mists, convergences, kindred spectacles of sound, shape, and place (9, 1)." These "unfading recollections (1,491)" of nature "people his mind with form sublime and fair and making him love them (1,546)." These "first born affinities in the dawn of [his] being constitute [him] in a bond of union (1,555-8)." He remembers now, as he walks, that nature "spoke memorable things to him (1,587-8)" then, in his childhood. His hope now as he walks about is to "fetch those invigorating thoughts from those former years (1,621-2)." He "makes no vows, but vows were made then for him...that [he] should be...a dedicated Spirit." And he walks on in "blessed thankfulness" that this Spirit still "survives" in him (4,334-8)." A diegetic voice creates a self-consciousness based upon past mimetic voices and experiences.

Wordsworth takes his own advice from his *Lyrical Ballads* and recollects himself in tranquillity and allows this tranquillizing spirit to "press" on him and fill the vacancy between his past creativity and present loss (2,27-29). These reminiscences of childhood experiences, former acts and states of consciousness, were stirred in the painful act of returning to interrogate them about the present loss. An expected anger or discontent results rather in a "pleasurable recollection" because he "gives himself over" to these recollections in pleasure and tranquillity such that any pain, compulsion or driven-ness of an interrogative, angry spirit gives way to a freedom that allows him to write freely and creatively again.

Walking around the Lake District, he realizes that he had built his life into a great assembly hall, a system, a state, and in so doing he forgot the first stone, the cornerstone of childhood, where creativity began (2, 199). He distanced himself from these origins and took control of his own intellect and powers and parceled them out by "geometric rules (2,204)." "He had transferred his delight to inorganic natures (2,392)" and he came to commune habitually "with little enmities and low desires (1, 432)."

And so he sits, recollected in tranquillity, and by his glance, from his particular Husserlean natural standpoint, his consciousness ceases to be a formed state, a system, and begins to bend, "act" and re-act again as he allows the beauty and inspiration of the Lake District to re-enter his soul and re-kindle past acts of consciousness.

The conscious act of returning to the Lake District triggers the unexpected memories of past experiences which serve as metaphors like his return there after being away at school during his first year at Cambridge. These two acts of returning, first as a student and now as the adult, depressed poet, parallel and substitute for each other. He is reminded of this first exit to and return from Cambridge and he writes the narrative of that return home after a first year away at school which is an earlier form of this second, more significant return. He remembers being so overwhelmed by a feeling of communion with nature that he made "two circuits around the Lake (4,138)" and was able to "pull the veil from his soul and stand naked in the presence of God (4,151-2)." This "external scene (4,160)," this place where he had been born and raised and was separated from for the first time, tapped his "inward hopes and swelling spirit (4, 162-2)." As the adult writer who has lost his creative impulse, he returns and remembers how once before he had returned and felt renewed. "Lake, islands, promontories, gleaming bays, a universe of Nature's fairest forms instantaneously burst" upon him in their "magnificence (4,7-11)." He "speeds" up "the familiar hill,...with exultation...towards that secret valley where [he] had been reared (4,17-19)." Here was an "emblem (4,61)" (a synecdoche) of his life. He met and greeted his neighbors as he "sauntered...like a murmuring river talking to itself (4,119-120)" accompanied by his faithful terrier. He recalls these walks "with thanks and gratitude and perfect joy of heart (4,134-5)."

He returns to the Lake District to be renewed just as the young Wordsworth, the college student, returned to the Lake District and experienced renewal, a pacification of homesickness in the young student. Wordsworth fetches those good things from his time past in order to shape them into "novelties," stories like Don Quixote or an Arabian Knight tale, to nourish him for difficult times, like the one he is experiencing now.

The meaning or significance of a past experience accumulates when the experience seems to recur again in other forms. The writing of the narratives about these "returns" is itself an act of returning and as such is a meaningful and significant act. The act of returning as a college student, the act of returning as the depressed adult, the act of remembering both returns and narrating them are different acts yet metaphorically similar in that they constitute the essential, synecdochic nature of the act of returning as a significant one in Wordsworth's consciousness. In Friedrich Nietzsche's autobiographical document, *Ecce Homo*, he dwells on this philosophical, theoretical problem of what happens when individuals "eternally return,"[11] through memory, to re-examine their lives and re-discover themselves. Personal consciousness of self, narrative voice and viewpoint, are formed by this eternal return of the memory to past events and other selves in dialogue.

Zarathustra, Nietzsche's fictional alter ego, is the "other" whom he says gives him this idea of the eternal return principle: the continual re-discovery of the self through the cyclical entrance into Nabokov's "transparent abyss" and return to exhilaration. The discovery of Zarathustra, another form of the Wordsworthian creative spirit, is both Nietzsche's and Wordsworth's "highest formula of self-affirmation (95)." This ideal spirit resurrects Nietzsche within himself and the spirits play and laugh innocently together and this resurrection and interaction cause him to forget the struggling selves that had previously occupied him and made him feel so alienated and estranged from himself. Zarathustra invades Nietzsche's soul ever so gradually, in a process of retrogressive, recursive progress as does Wordsworth's creative spirit re-inhabit his soul in this retrogressive/progressive return home. Zarathustra is a metaphoric representation of that essential, comprehensive, stable being who invaded Nietzsche at a particularly unstable, painful time and, in the process of dialogic interaction of voices, changed him. His autobiography is Nietzsche's philosophical reflection on that process of the eternal return of memory and his philosophy of memory contained therein is in fact an autobiographical theory of memoir: an eternal return and metaphoric replacement of voices, perspectives, attitudes.

This process of his own re-discovery through the intervention of his fictional Zarathustra is an example of the eternal return, the repetitive re-discovery of other selves at all kinds of levels. The past is redeemed and transformed in the present return to what seems to be a compulsive repeat of an apparent death-destruction experience in the return to some person, place or activity with which one is obsessed but "turns" to a resurrection-cum-re-creation, a second sight. Nietzsche feels like he dies and resurrects in the re-discovery. Wordsworth felt "dead" and was resurrected in the return to the Lake District.

Nietzsche minimizes any obsessive-compulsive aspect of the return. Each return results in new discoveries. The crisis of the self to purge the alien, befriend the stranger within, fill the void, and breathe freely enough to return to the possession of the healthy self is an instinctual, natural desire against any further estrangement, any return to the abyss, any obsessive compulsivity. Instinct runs from the crisis experience of estrangement, misunderstanding, discontent and emptiness to the memory of comforting, rewarding experiences of past states of Zarathustrian repose, Wordsworthian creativity, a self-consciousness who is not a stranger.

But this memoirist concept of the eternal return involves a repetition of a cycle of healthy self-consciousness to unhealthy, deadly estrangement. Nietzsche says that a person must say "yes" to the one in order to get the other. Through nutrition, climate and pleasant surroundings, the self recuperates in recreative play with the variety of others within (30-41, 48).

The task of a person like Wordsworth is to determine who he is, where the creativity is, in all the apparent chaos of this particular "return." Nietzsche makes it clear that he himself is not any one of his writings nor his experiences, nor a composite of them, but parts of him are discoverable in each and in the stories about the stories. He hears only that which he is given access to hear by the experiences that he is given. He can't hear something about himself if it is as yet absent. He will need to wait for a return in the eternal revolution of the circle again when something new will come to light through the descent into the abyss, the dialogue and the rise to Zarathustrian ecstacy or enlightenment.

When a particular "turn" or re-turn appears to be "just like" (a metaphor) a previous one, Nietzsche says that there is always something new about this particular turn that makes it different, special, representative (synecdochic), if only that it causes a greater sense of integration and wholeness to the self (a metonymy) hence not obsessive-compulsive, irreplaceable. When he takes the various unique, yet similar "turns" and connects them (metonyms), he has a "life story" or a life history as a narrated series of diegetic insights or points made or mimetic experiences and voices re-created in narrative. Just as specific parts of each turn can stand alone as representative, as synecdoches, so they can replace each other as metaphoric representations or serve as connectors (metonyms).

Both Nietzsche and Wordsworth narrate and write from relatively frozen, fixed points in time in that they remember past "turns" and "returns" to past moments of crises and repose. The present time of narration seems to be a suspended, reflective one, like Wordsworth who has lost his creativity and is suspended in a particularly difficult, critical "turn."

Edward Said's theory of history repeating itself, like Nietzsche's eternal return, accents the return and the discovery of something new. History is not a "gratuitous series of occurrences of haphazard events nor a wholly foreordained blueprint,"[12] but an accumulation of meaning as the weight of past experiences return and evidence their similarities and their differences. Reproduction and regeneration of past events in narratives produce not only similarities between them, a strong transmission of likeness, but they also produce unique shadings of difference. Narrative allows a recapitulation that will accent these differences and similarities and the creation of the narrative is itself a form of repeating the experience and discovering the newness, the differences and the similarities with other experiences.

Like the river (9,1 ff.) which knows that it is proceeding toward its end in the "ravenous sea" and tries to turn and "measure back" its course, seeking regions it once crossed, regions which hold the richest memories, Wordsworth "measures back" and returns to the Lake District in an attempt to recapture and re-discover the roots of his creativity in the return to those childhood places and experiences and their attendant memories.

The stealing of the boat, the horseback ride with the servant, and the Christmas experience on the crag are three metaphoric narratives in particular that interlace as one synecdochic narrative expression of Wordsworth's return to creativity. They can be read separately and substituted one for the other as metaphoric exemplifications of Wordsworth's consciousness of the loss and renewal of his creativity. Or they can be read as one synecdochic narrative in keeping with David Fischer's concept of the braided or interlaced narrative as a complex interweave of changing perspectives by a self-conscious mind integrating those perspectives through a process of re-arranging and interrelating the various details.[13]

Wordsworth continues "to muse (4,177-8)" and to pass into "solemn thought (4,190)" as he walks about the Lake District this second time. And after remembering the first return as a student, he remembers the time as a child that he came upon a little boat tied to a tree on the lake (1, 357 ff.). He remembers and sees himself untying the boat, getting in and rowing away. He recalls suddenly being overwhelmed and frightened by a "huge cliff uprearing its head" and he flees back to the shore. The act of stealing the boat may be a metaphor locating the source of his creativity in the young boy who takes risks and seeks adventure. The huge cliff driving him back to the shore in fear may be a metaphor for the loss of the creativity. The act of remembering this event in this way and writing it out in this narrative may be a metaphoric way of explaining the source and loss of the creativity but the conscious act of remembering and writing is itself an act of renewing the creativity.

He then remembers another time when he went out for a horseback ride as a child with one of his father's servants (12, 225 ff.) and in the course of the ride, he became separated from the servant. He remembers finding himself at the bottom of a valley where there was an old, decayed gibbet-mast on which thieves and murderers were once executed. Often, the name of the murderer or thief was carved in the wood of the mast. He recalls fleeing in fear again, as in the boat experience, and he reascends to a "beacon" pool "on a summit" where he meets a girl, struggling against the wind, carrying a water pitcher on her head. The memory of the experience results in the creation of a "radiance more sublime (12,267)" in him. He sees in it a "power...left behind (12, 268-9)" and the narrative becomes a metaphoric explanation for the loss and retrieval of creative power as it shows the creative power in action. After becoming separated from the servant, he comes upon this place of execution in a valley, a metaphor of the loss of the creative spirit. The fleeing in fear and the re-ascension to see the girl carrying the water is a metaphoric action symbolizing the renewal of the creative spirit and can replace the same fleeing and fear in the boat sequence. The narrative act of combining the elements into this narrative is rooted in the creative power of his spirit which has been renewed.

And again, he remembers going out into the fields with his brothers one "tempestuous, dark and wild" Christmas day (12, 287 ff.) and he recalls stopping to rest at the summit of a crag "with a hawthorn on his left and a sheep on his right," each of them surveying the valley below. He recalls feeling good at this experience. Ten days later his father dies and his consciousness connects this joyful experience on the crag and with the death of his father. The "good feeling" experienced and remembered with the hawthorn and the sheep on the crag overlooking the valley metaphorically represent the source of the creative spirit in the feeling associated with the experience. The death of the father ten days later metaphorically represents the loss of the creative spirit and feeling. The conscious act of placing these two experiences together is itself a creative act explaining loss of creativity. The impact of the narrative depends upon the fact that these two events happened and can be mimetically represented and diegetically combined through the creative insight of Wordsworth. Wordsworth's present creative consciousness makes the diegetic connection between the two events which his past consciousness placed in memory and so he writes the narrative with that connection.

There most likely were many other occurrences during those ten days between the experience on the crag and the death of his father which he could have connected. But the depressed Wordsworth identifies most strongly with the depressed boy who lost his father, saw the names of the murderers on the gibbet mast or fled in fear from the mountain. Wordsworth is obviously not interested in the metonymic sequence of every detail in a mimetic narrative. He is interested in a metaphoric, synecdochic sequence of details in a diegetic narrative that is an evaluative comment on his present condition.

These three experiences and their narrative re-creations in *The Prelude* braid together and illustrate Wordsworth's conscious realization that his creative spirit began and was nourished in and by the rivers, lakes and hillsides of "the dear Vale, Beloved Grasmere." They also illustrate his consciousness of the loss of his creativity rooted there in such remembrances as the death of his father, the gibbet-mast and the huge cliff. By connecting these experiences in the narratives, he exercises the very creativity which he thought he had lost. He is back on the crag with the hawthorn and sheep; he sees the girl running up the hill; he takes the chance and steals the boat again. The narratives can be read together as metaphoric replacements for each other or read separately as synecdochic representations or read metonymically as a narrative explanation of Wordsworth's experience in consciousness of the loss and retrieval of his creativity. I am considering them in this chapter as metaphoric narratives because they can replace each other as representative of Wordsworth's diegetic commentary on the loss of his creativity.

The three childhood narratives along with the two narratives of return recapitulate a sequence of events which becomes representative of the larger issue of Wordsworth's creativity and they can replace each other in an explanation of the creativity issue.

In Book 11, he compares his memory to a "nook" which restores for him the "sacred delight of his infant world of play (419-20)." These memories of this place are his "spots of time (12,208)" memories where his life maintained a distinct pre-eminence, virtue and creativity which had come to be depressed by "false opinion and contentious thought (12,211)" but are now revived, voiced and preserved in narrative remembrance. These memories of the experiences in these places nourish and repair his spirit and allow him to return and re-experience them through narrative.

Maxine Hong Kingston

Maxine Hong Kingston's mother had an experience as an adolescent at her girls' boarding school which she apparently repeated to her daughter because it appears in the daughter's memoir as a significant story within that memoir. Maxine's narrative about her mother mythologizes the mother by making her the heroine of this adventure story. The account is as much a biographical statement by Maxine about her mother as it is an autobiographical one about herself and her roots but the distortion, fictionalization and mythologizing that are apparent in the narrative reinforce the fact that when present consciousness examines past consciousness, the chronology, the mimetic sequence of events may be lost, distorted or changed and certain diegetic, mythological, aspects will stand out as representative.

In representing the mother as a heroine, a woman of great strength, Maxine gives her ancestry, her roots, the same heroic stature much like Wordsworth offers his narrative memories of his childhood in the Lake District as the source of his poetic power or Maya Angelou remembers herself as the strong, little girl who survived a rape experience. These are diegetic comments by these autobiographers after reflecting on their mimetic experiences.

The representation of the mother as idealized, heroic, is a diegetic statement by Maxine about her feelings about her mother; Maxine recognizes that mimetic accuracy of detail and factuality may have been sacrificed. Even though there is distortion and idealization caused by distance and repetition, Maxine's personal feelings about herself and her mother as heroines are not lost.

The fact that her mother spent the night with a ghost when she was a student and was the heroine of the student body is itself an interesting story; it invites elaboration, fictionalization and idealization and it is a memory that asks to be preserved. We all have favorite stories about relatives that we enjoy remembering and retelling. Like Edmund Gosse in his *Father and Son*, Maxine functions as both biographer for her mother and autobiographer for herself. Both Maxine and her mother are "women warriors." Both Edmund and his father lose their mother and wife and need also to be "warriors" in the Victorian conflict between faith and doubt that surfaces in their relationship. I will discuss Edmund and his father in greater detail later in this chapter.

In the dormitory where the mother resided as a young student, there seems to have been a "ghost room" that all of the students, except Maxine's mother, were afraid to enter, especially at night. She was willing to show her classmates that there was nothing to be afraid of by volunteering to sleep there one night. This gives her heroic stature in the eyes of her classmates, herself and later her daughter. Maxine portrays her mother in the narrative as having a sobriety and realism about this adventure; she does not have the characteristic fear and apprehension about the room or the ghost that the other students have. In fact, even when she does confront the ghost, she still evidences no panic or fear. This narrative is a way for Maxine not only to idealize her mother but also to memorialize her mother and set her mother up as model for herself. The experience of the ghost also serves as a way for the mother to explain to her daughter how to confront difficult situations.

The legend that there is a ghost in this room in the dormitory is one handed down to the students at this particular school through the generations of students who have attended the school. Stories like these are, of course, not unusual among children and adolescents. Many of us have created imaginary persons, places and things that become objects or situations to conquer which will then make us heroes. We each have some kind of story like this in our past; a story where we participated in an adventure to a mysterious place to conquer a "monster" and become a hero or perform some heroic activity that elevated us in the eyes of our peers. And sometimes we use these stories about ourselves and our family members, like Maxine did about her mother, as ways by which we can remember these people.

When the shaman-mother returns to her classmates in the morning, as the story goes, she tells her classmates that she first needs to participate in a ritual cleansing called an "earlobe touching"[14] by which she assures herself and her classmates that she did not "lose any of herself (84)" in the experience while alone with the ghost in the room. She is concerned that the experience may have caused her to lose some of herself because the experience was so fearful, anxiety-ridden and exhausting.

So, as the mythological priestess, the shaman, she leads her classmates in a ritual exorcism with bucket, alcohol, oil and dog's blood. As priestess, she 'preaches' to them by encouraging them to be unafraid when they meet their own and other ghosts. They return to the "ghost room" together where the mother-high priestess performs the ritual of swinging the lighted bucket overhead and leading the "go home (88)" chant to the ghost.

The mimetic details of the story of the ghost room in the dormitory as told by the mother and handed down to Maxine may have been forgotten, distorted, and so diegetically changed and fictionalized according to Maxine's need to idealize her mother and her roots or her mother's own need to idealize this conversion experience. As the story was repeated and became more removed from its source, it began to be fixed and have a life of its own.

Mimetic/Diegetic Voices in Metaphoric Narratives 111

After the ritual return, the mother narrates what happened in the room and her experience of this ghost sitting on her. This narration of the personal experience of the mother is central to the mother's public persona as heroine and shaman to her classmates and daughter. They know that something happened in that room and they want to hear about it but only Maxine's mother is the one who can tell it.

This narrative unit where she describes what happened in the room, is part of the larger narrative unit called "Shaman" and can stand alone as representative of the mother who gives advice and it is also Maxine's way of coming to a self-understanding about her mother after having compared and contrasted various perspectives about her mother and distilled them in this story.

She says that she was initially surprised to learn that it was going to be a "sitting ghost" whom she manages to overcome. The trial lasted about an hour and she narrates this interior unit as one of personal conversion and trial during which time she experienced "babies crying, relatives and friends screaming in torture, energetic amassings of wind sounds, along with a general malaise and suffering (86)." She says that she "died for awhile (85)" after having her knife wrested from her by the ghost. She lost her way and wandered in an interior chaos where "everything turned to sand." She was determined not to be conquered by this ghost. The ghost was trying to elicit the necessary fear and anger that would allow it to overtake her totally but she refuses to let that happen by allowing herself to experience the ghost as a void, an experience of emptiness or loss, and die for awhile. She talks to it and tells it that it will not win. As a diversion, she chants her school lessons and falls asleep.

This ghost and the room become external objects where an interior crisis and conversion are enacted in Maxine's mother. The narratives are devices by which both Maxine and her mother recapitulate the experience and talk about it. The ghost is that part of the self which Maxine's mother's consciousness had never met, Derrida's "other." The act of consciousness was the act of reconciling the others within her with this new experience of a void. But in becoming reconciled with the other within whom she had never met, she also needs to experience states of consciousness which went from chaos to emptiness. She tells her classmates that this ghost, the ghost being a metaphor for these other selves and voids within, is by no means dead and gone. This was just a particular moment of victory over this particular "sitting ghost (86)." Other selves will appear at other times with different degrees of intensity in different kinds of experiences. She tells her classmates that these other selves are serious ghosts (87); they do not want to be ignored and they will create the chaos and emptiness to force the conscious person's recognition of them. They want the gut, the very life, the surrender of the conscious, controlling self and they will feed off the panic and fear of this conscious, controlling self until it gives up, retreats and in effect dies for awhile so as to allow chaos and void to intervene and then the "other." The fictional myth of the ghost room itself which has come down through tradition to the students is demythologized by the mother for the students.

This narrative unit within the story "Shaman" in Maxine Hong Kingston's autobiographical document is rich in metaphoric, metonymic and synecdochic resonances. This story of her mother is essential to Maxine Hong Kingston's memory of her mother and integral to her memories about her childhood. Maxine's experience of her mother is a significant part (metonym) of her life and this one narrative is representative (synecdoche) of the mother's heroism and can replace (metaphor) other stories where the mother acted equally heroically. By means of the narrative unit within the story itself, where the mother mimetically describes the experience, Maxine diegetically compares and contrasts various experiences of her mother which are empty or other. There may have been interior strengths that her mother should have given to Maxine and didn't for one reason or another and this story about her mother fills those kinds of voids. Similarly, there may be many other "mothers" whom Maxine met in her mother and this story best captures that variety of others.

The narrative becomes a diegetic story about her roots to which Maxine can return and repeat to herself and the memory can be a source of strength to her. Wordsworth does the same thing in his return to Grasmere; he gains strength by returning to his roots and re-telling his own story.

> What though the radiance which was once so bright
> Be now forever taken from my sight,
>   Though nothing can bring back the hour
> Of splendor in the grass, of glory in the flower;
>   We will grieve not, rather find
>   Strength in what remains behind;[15]

Even though these experiences may be distorted and mythologized by the memory and the diegetic voice of the narrator due to time and space distance, some stories like Maxine's and Wordsworth's retain a mimetic clarity in memory even though the facts may be fictionally re-arranged. Maxine Hong Kingston examined, in a series of acts of consciousness, the great mass of mimetic detail which she had stored in memory about her mother and she diegetically bracketed and reduced that material by editing it into this narrative whose mimetic sequence of events co-operates with the diegetic creativity which makes not only a good, fictional, short story but makes a good, non-fictional representation of Maxine's consciousness of her mother.

Arthur Miller

Arthur Miller returns to the memory of his highly publicized marriage to Marilyn Monroe but, unlike Kingston or Wordsworth, who convey the sense of the nietzschean eternal return to discover something or someone new, Miller returns to the memory more like Tom Wingfield or Vladimir Nabokov, as if through the gauze portieres into a transparent abyss, even as if seeing it for the first time. In his life story, which he calls *Timebends*, Miller's narrative, mimetic voice attempts to remember the real, mimetic experience of the writing and filming of the movie *The Misfits* for and with Marilyn but his present, diegetic voice comments on those past memories, apparently real experiences, by comparing and contrasting the memories and the voices.

He says that he has lived for more than half his life, 40 years, in the Connecticut countryside because he thought he could write better there. But he says that he really wanted to be in the city "where everything is happening"[16] so he would always talk about this country home as "temporary" but in retrospect he feels that there is something funny about a "40 year temporary residence (599)." He feels that some "timebends" in life are sacred because they make us aware that the flow of time is supreme and deserves our utmost respect. The flow of time makes him wonder who he really is now, at this present moment of writing and remembering, in relation to whom he was at other times.

He wrote two plays for Marilyn: *After the Fall* and *The Misfits*. They contain fictional representations of Marilyn in the characters of Maggie and Roslyn. But there is a difference between the two. He wrote *The Misfits* and the character of Roslyn expressly, explicitly for her as a factual, real representation of her and as a vehicle through which she could tap her potential as an actress, the "greatness of spirit in her, a crazy kind of nobility that the right role might release, and if that happened she might step out of herself and see her own worth (458)" and this experience would cement their marriage and their professional, working relationship. She, in effect, would be playing herself, as <u>he</u> perceived her, the "real" self that he felt she was unable to find in her own life. He saw the play as therapeutic for her as a person, helpful to her as a professional actress and an expression of their working relationship as professional, married partners.

All of this, of course, backfired. She methodically "studied" Roslyn as a fictional character portrait separate from herself under the tutelage of the method acting of Lee and Paula Strasberg. She actually became less co-operative and professional as an actress. The film almost stopped at many points. And she completely separated from Miller and lived with the Strasbergs.

But Miller admits in retrospect that both he and Marilyn had ideal visions of themselves, their professional lives and their marriage that were impossible to meet. He wanted to be her savior by writing the perfect play for her. She would then, of course, play this part perfectly and in the process re-discover her own true worth and they would live and work together "happily ever after." The vision is as idealistic and unrealistic as it is heroic and mythical and so sets itself up for defeat.

It was her miscarriage, he says, that caused him to feel "an urgency about making something for her (458)." So he began sketching out this screenplay (and the narrative turns out in many ways to be more of a reflection on his process as a writer than his intended narrative of his relationship with Marilyn) and he recalls that Marilyn would laugh delightedly at some of the cowboy's lines but "seemed to withhold full commitment to playing Roslyn (459)."

As the play developed, Miller says his interest became both "technical" as well as "emotional (459)." He was constructing a gift for her at the same time that he was creating a work of art and learning about the making of a movie. He wanted to give her something to make her "feel and experience her own worth" and the best way that he could do that was through the exercise of his own talent as a playwright. He prepared himself to dedicate a year or more of his life to her enhancement as a performer, a person and his wife but he also dedicated a year of his life to the enhancement of his own writing skills in a successful movie. The original desire to write a play for Marilyn also becomes an exercise of his own abilities and talents as a playwright.

This narrative remembrance of the creation of *The Misfits* in *Timebends* is synecdochic in that it is representative of Miller's craft as a writer; his writing process. It is also representative of the tenor of his relationship with Marilyn. It is a metonymic narrative because it captures a five or six year period in Miller's life that was a significant, sequential "timebend" for him. It also grants some access to the consciousness of the writer and the husband. But it is above all a memoirist's metaphoric narrative which can replace many other similar narratives about his relationship with Marilyn and his writer's craft.

He wanted the ideal cast, director and script for his "Eastern Western...about the meaninglessness of our lives and how they become that way (462)," although he doesn't like to rationalize and explain his work. This diegetic statement about the theme of the play takes it outside of his personal life and his relationship with Marilyn into the realm of literature where he offers it as a narrative for and about everyman. The play was not *just* written for Marilyn; it seems that it was also written to make a point to the world about the meaninglessness of our lives generally. But this theme of meaninglessness and the plotting of how our lives become meaningless is representative of the progress of meaninglessness in the life of Marilyn and her marriage to Miller and her acting career.

The illusion, the fictivity of the play, finds a parallel in the reality, the non-fiction, of Arthur Miller's life and perceptions. Miller notes that in the filming of the first scene taken on the bridge overlooking the Truckee stream in Reno into which divorced women customarily threw their wedding rings as a celebration of their freedom (463-4), the character of Roslyn in *The Misfits* had just received her divorce but she doesn't throw her ring in the stream because she is depressed about the failure of the marriage. The real Marilyn Monroe had also been twice divorced at the time of filming and the relationship with Miller was failing and she was depressed about her own failures and the failure of her career as a "legitimate" actress and the real Thelma Ritter and Arthur Miller attempt to cheer the real Marilyn.

In this brief narrative, Arthur Miller re-constructs the voices from the palimpsest of his memory, fact and fiction blend, compare and contrast. He braids the truth about Marilyn and himself with the illusion of Roslyn.

Miller also discovered that his non-fictional "eye" as a writer is different from the fictionalizing "eye" of the camera or the director (485). As a writer, he can control what is foregrounded and backgrounded with image-describing words. The eye of the camera and the director change what the writer wants foregrounded and backgrounded. The situation of *The Misfits* is seen differently in the film as opposed to the written text. Miller also learned by observation that actors and directors often go through the same kind of creative process of interiorization and recapitulation that he goes through as a writer. Each may need to be self-absorbed and distant as each gives boundaries, shape and form to their creations. The creative process is a deeply personal one, whether the creator is a writer, an autobiographer, an actress or a director, and his narrative of how he wrote and participated in the filming of *The Misfits* becomes a metaphoric replacement for other writing projects and for his creative process generally.

In writing this autobiographical document and the narrative unit about *The Misfits*, Arthur Miller distances himself from others and from himself at the time of writing and looks into the transparent abyss in order to tap the memory for the comparisons and contrasts. Contrariwise, he must become "self-absorbed" in the conscious, creative process of shaping and forming a series of narrative representations of himself in an eternal return to the scene.

Arthur Miller's narrative of the writing and filming of *The Misfits* is a narration that is an autobiography as well as a memoir in the sense that it synecdochically unifies his own overriding sense of himself as a writer at the same time that it metaphorically replaces other possible narratives from other writing projects.

He remembers that he wanted the film to end with the girl and the cowboy staying together (as he wanted he and Marilyn to stay together) but he knew that the characters he created had found their own life force and sustenance on the very indeterminacy and uncertainty of their lives. The characters had understandably gone beyond his control and assumed a life of their own and were people who could not stay together; it was their nature and essence to roam freely. When Marilyn herself announces that the characters should separate at the end, Arthur became more determined than ever to keep them together (as he was more determined than ever to keep him and Marilyn together) in the face of the bald, logical truth that, according to the nature of the characters and the natures of both Monroe and Miller, it makes better sense for them to separate (474).

At one point, Marilyn had taken to paraphrasing speeches and omitting words and sentences (476). The director demanded that she get the words right. This becomes an instance where Miller as the artist, the professional writer and Marilyn, the artist, the professional actress, are at odds with each other. Marilyn said that it was the emotion behind the words that mattered, not the words themselves. The words, then, of Miller, as writer, were undermined in favor of the vocal expression and dramatic ability of Monroe, the actress.

Miller asserts that he is a professional writer and, as a professional writer, he must insist on the importance of using the exact words of the writer. He felt very strongly that the spontaneity and freshness of feeling, the depth of emotional impact and power comes *through* the words of the writer not *despite* them. Marilyn's foray into creative improvisation and oral interpretation based upon the Strasberg's method acting may have been a good exercise for her as an aspiring dramatic actress but not as part of a finished text in an actual performance.

Marilyn may or may not have been trying to upset Arthur but these two incidents (the separation of Roslyn and Langland and the text change) with relation to the movie bear strong resemblance and significance to two real incidents with Arthur and Marilyn. She wants Roslyn and Langland to separate at the end. Miller does not. She wants professional freedom in interpretation of the author's text. Miller does not want his text changed. The two incidents accent the two major areas of the marital and the professional relationship. He wanted the film to unite these and the film actually served to divide them.

He admits, in retrospect, and as part of the comparing and contrasting of his memories about this, that he despaired at his presumption, his stupidity, that he could ever 'save' her or protect her in any way with this play and film. He became just as exhausted and hopeless as she. He became a reminder to her, by his personal presence as her husband and by his presence in the script as her writer, that she could not pull herself out of her old life even when she did at last truly love someone. Neither Arthur, her husband, nor his script, treated her like the Strasbergs did, like a star and a good actress. Arthur and the director and the script treated Marilyn as a fallible, weak, sensitive human being who needed to be corrected when she made mistakes. She preferred the infallibility and untouchability of "stardom (483)." She lived in that reflected glory and not in the endless soul searching discovery for her real self that Arthur asked of her as her husband and writer.

And it was at about this time, that an event happened, which he includes in the memoir for the sake of metaphoric contrast, but which became for him a central, synecdochic insight (483-4). He was asked to write a screenplay based on the Albert Camus novella, *The Fall*. He was not interested in writing the screenplay but the story of *The Fall* paralleled his own story with regard to this filming of *The Misfits* and raised crucial questions for him about his relationship with Marilyn as husband and writer which may have occurred to him at the time but he articulates in the memoir as an important consideration. The mimetic voices within him which dictated that he help Marilyn, save their marriage and her professional life, gave way to a diegetic voice which made him realize how wrong he was and caused him to add a synecdochic 'narrative within the narrative' of *The Misfits* filming.

He attempted to use a fictional character and story to reach her as a person, wife and actress and it was at this same time that he realizes in retrospect that he saw himself in the fictional character and story of *The Fall* much like DeQuincey remembers the visit to the Whispering Gallery and connects this visit with the day that he left Manchester but makes the connections some 35 years after the events which events themselves were years apart.

He realized that the key to Marilyn's salvation, however much he may have cared for her and loved her, was not with him. His own vanity as a writer was interlaced with his love as husband. If an act of love for someone else, he says, is really a disguised self-love and vanity, isn't the love for the someone else nullified (484)? Can anyone save or help anyone else unless the one who needs to be saved feels that need? How does one person bring another person to this desire, this recognition of the need to be saved?

Marilyn neither felt the need nor the desire for what Arthur was bringing her. He was bringing her something that would detract from the glory of her stardom and she didn't want that. The key insight that he got from *The Fall* was that he realized that he would feel the same way if someone tried to bring him something, to show him something about himself that would take him away from his writing. He could not bear the thought of not being a writer so, like Marilyn, he would reject anyone who tried to negate or underplay that talent. The central, synecdochic reality for Arthur Miller is that he is a writer first and foremost. His writing *The Misfits* for Marilyn was a metaphoric replacement, another version of the central reality about him which was writing. His marriage and relationship with Marilyn, as he narrates it throughout *Timebends*, is done in fragmented, metonymic bits and pieces.

Miller closes his memoir by addressing what Jay Martin calls the central autobiographical question of the twentieth century: *Who Am I This Time?* Who was I then? What I am trying to do now? What was I trying to do then? Miller addresses these questions on the last page of *Timebends* with the poignant narrative of himself as "grandfather" which dovetails with the narrative at the beginning of the book about his own grandfather. In this last narrative, he experiences himself at this particular "bend" in time, the present time, when he is writing this life story, his "memoirs", as a grandfather. When he hears this word "grandpa" over the phone from one of his son's three children, he resists it as "not him---My God, I had hardly begun (598)!" He wonders who these small persons are sitting on his lap lovingly repeating this "terrible accusation with all its finality (598)." They "confidently imagine (599)" him to be grandpa and this makes him wonder who he is. He is aware of a pleasure he is experiencing in being called grandpa and a pleasure he experiences in being able to articulate the word himself over the phone when he calls his grandchildren and he remembers the pleasure he experienced with his own grandfather. The warmth of feeling, the depth of consciousness and personality in Arthur Miller find expression in the articulation of these interlaced roles of the grandfather and grandchild, metaphors of his self, the husband of Marilyn

Monroe, a metonym for his self, and the playwright, a synecdoche for his self.

He closes his memoir by shedding the metonymic fictions, the metaphoric non-fictions and the synecdochic roles narrated in the 600 pages and acknowledges the overriding great mystery of the self, which I suppose is just another metaphor. Just as others may wonder who we are, so do we wonder at ourselves. He remembers himself in a particular role and wonders what he was doing there. Identity certainly is a mystery but the one truth about which he feels sure is that "we are all connected, watching one another...trying to figure each other out, figure life out and understand the mystery (599)."

At one particular "timebend," he is a 40 year "temporary" resident of a Connecticut town and a grandfather and at another he is sitting in fear at a religious service with his own grandfather and at another he is the husband of the mythical Marilyn Monroe. There are 600 pages of such memories and narrations which compare and contrast with memories, perceptions, voices and roles from other "timebends," other experiences, other relationships and roles.

Edmund Gosse

Edmund Gosse narrates the story of the sickness and death of his mother when he was seven and his subsequent baptism at ten in his book, *Father and Son: The Clash of Two Temperaments*. The narrative of the death of the mother contrasts the relationship of the father and son while the narrative of the baptism contrasts the son's interior state of doubt versus faith. Gosse originally intended to portray the voice of his father's temperament but ended up portraying the voices of both temperaments in comparison and contrast and ultimately the clash of faith and doubt in his own interior voice.

The death of the mother sequence which begins with the announcement of her cancer is perceived in retrospect as a "tragedy...which altered the whole course of our family existence"[17] because her death foretells and foregrounds the relationship and clash between the father and son and the relationship and clash of faith and doubt in the son himself.

Gosse remembers the night that his mother arrived back from the doctor with the announcement that she had cancer. His father had put him to bed that night which event itself was "noteworthy" since his father rarely did that and it contributed to the young Gosse's memory of the evening. His "crib" was in the same room as his parents "four-poster." He recalls awakening to see his father writing at his desk by candlelight. The adult Edmund attempts to narrate mimetically the voice and consciousness of the seven year old. He recalls that his mother entered the room and his father arose; the mother announced that she had cancer and they folded into a "long, silent embrace" and "sank to their knees" out of the boy's sight where the "father lifted his voice in prayer (69)." The seven year old boy went back to sleep. They did not know he was awake. This section focuses more on the relationship between the husband and wife than the son. Gosse remembers his parents as being visibly "loving" and "prayerful" in this moment of crisis.

But the next morning at breakfast, the son is highlighted in the narrative and presumably in the reality. He recalls that as he sat at breakfast, the scenario from the night before was in his mind and he asked what cancer was because obviously it was something bad since his parents embraced and prayed. It is at this time at the breakfast that the parents realized the boy was awake and overheard them talking and they "gazed" at each other with "lamentable eyes (69)."

There is a sense that the boy knew that he was saying something significant because he said it while looking down at his plate and looked up only after he did not get a response. The adult autobiographer recalls that as the seven year old boy, he felt "conscious of the presence of an incommunicable mystery (69-70)." Although "tortured with curiosity," he "kept silent and never repeated his inquiry (70)" about the cancer.

This narrative, I believe, begins the diegetic focus of the clash of two temperaments of the father and son because the mother will soon be absent and the faith and doubt in the son will surface. The fact of the mother's cancer drew the mother to the husband as wife and separated them both from the son, although they were keenly aware of the effect that this would have on the son. The husband would be losing his wife and he would need to become both mother and father to the boy. The fact that they were going to be drawn so closely together as father and son highlights the clash that will result.

At the deathbed scene, the little child is pushed forward at the mother's request and she insists that the father raise the child in faith. Edmund, in retrospect, recalls this "dedication (81)" where the seeds of the clash take root. The father will now feel the responsibility to be true to the wife's deathbed request that he raise his son in faith and the insistence will only divide them from each other and enhance the clash because the father may only be responding to the last wishes of the wife.

It is also at this time that Edmund begins to have the seeds of doubt and questioning, the clash of two temperaments in himself. This sudden death of his mother at such a young age causes him to wonder why a good God would do this not only to the young mother but to both him and his father. There may be this clash of faith and doubt within the consciousness of both the father and the son so that they have no choice but to clash with each other and the Victorian clash of faith and doubt itself predominates the scene for both of their interior lives.

The father's sense of responsibility to be faithful to his dead wife's last wishes and raise their son in religion finds it climax in what Edmund, as synecdochist, calls a "central event in his whole childhood (156)," his "public baptism" in Chapter 8 but as the memoirist, he merely illustrates the many examples of the clash of faith and doubt in himself. His mother's illness and death altered the course of his life because it made him question what place faith had in a seemingly uncaring universe. And his father's insistence that he study and be baptized further exacerbated the clash in himself and between the two of them. The memoirist comparison and contrast of states of consciousness called doubt and faith, father and son, which Edmund Gosse records, give way to a synecdochic to a synecdochic unification of his consciousness of himself represented in the baptism sequence.

The baptism occurred 3 weeks after Edmund's tenth birthday, October 12, and he remembers it as an event that was "dazzling beyond words, inexpressibly exciting, an initiation to every kind of publicity and glory (157)." He and his father and Miss Marks and Mary Grace were received at the "Room (156)," as he calls it, in an adjoining town, for the baptism "amidst a blaze of lights, pressure of hands, murmur of voices, ejaculations, tears and unspeakable emotion (157)" and they were escorted to "places of honor (157)" in the front. Again, the boy Gosse is as central as he was in the mother's death sequence but he is also as divided in temperament. He "was the acknowledged hero of the hour (157)" principally because he had learned all that he needed to know about baptism in order to be baptized but he had learned everything so quickly and thoroughly and at such a young age, indicating his above-average intellectual ability. The news of this "remarkable ceremony (157)" where a little 10 year old boy was immersed and baptized like an adult was a newsworthy fact that spread far and wide so that the chapel was crowded to the ceiling on this night and the crowd came "as every soft murmur assured me---to see *me* (158)," even though some of them didn't appear to be all that interested, "sitting perfectly listless, looking at nothing...(158)." He was more proud of the fact that he had done something that was drawing so much attention than he was of being baptized.

The small swimming pool in the center of the chapel floor was surrounded by the tiered seats in which the congregation was gathered; the equally impressive, "hieratic (158)" figure of the clergyman stood to address them and begin the service. There was suddenly this great splash and a "tall young woman (158)" leapt into the pool, her arms waving about, her ballooned crinoline keeping her afloat. This was followed by interminable cries and shrieks from the crowd and more cries and shrieks demanding silence. The young woman was subsequently removed and it was learned that she wanted to be baptized but such baptism was forbidden by her parents.

The contrast between the pure faith of this woman and the "performance" by the precocious Edmund is what makes the narrative representative, synecdochic. The woman was not intellectually able to learn the dogma and rules but she certainly had the interior desire and conviction to be baptized. Edmund was only interested in being baptized because his father wanted him to be baptized and he would get a lot of attention.

Some people at the scene maintained that this young woman fell into the pool by accident while others said that even though her parents opposed her baptism, God must have wanted her baptized. Edmund's legalist father proffered that she could not have been baptized because her head was not immersed and she must have been deliberately pushed or jumped herself because her head was not wet and if she had been pushed or jumped herself, her head would have gotten wet. He approaches the question of this woman's baptism from a totally intellectual-legal point of view. She is not baptized because her head was not immersed but Edmund, from his knowledge of theology, would also offer that she is not baptized because the words of baptism were not said. Both of which facts are beside the point for Edmund because he does not care about baptism anyway.

Mr. Gosse would have loved his son to have had the same "spirit" as the young woman but the son doesn't. The fact of the woman's head being wet or not depending on whether she was pushed or not is trivial. She quite simply believes and wants to be baptized and she knows from watching other baptisms that she has to jump into the water to do this. Edmund does not believe but he knows all the rules and is able to be baptized.

Edmund was motivated to write about the nature of his personal conflict between faith and doubt and to represent that conflict in the relationship with his father. The consciousness of the father was one represented as dedicated and religious in contrast to Edmund's which was critical and skeptical. The love and affection between them as father and son did not suffer. The purported clash between the two temperaments of father and son was actually a way for Edmund to voice the clash between faith and doubt as two states of consciousness in himself.

Mary McCarthy

In Mary McCarthy's "tin butterfly" episode, she tells the story of how her little brother was awarded this prize butterfly from a Cracker Jack box. The butterfly subsequently disappeared and Mary was accused of stealing it, which she denied, until it was discovered pinned under her placemat at the dinner table. She says that her uncle put it there because he disliked her and wanted to blackmail her but as she tells the story she admits that there may have been other motivations going on.

The first half of the story establishes her dislike for this Uncle Myers who favors the little brother Sheridan by giving him the butterfly. Mary's first memory of "the punitive Uncle Myers" was "the violence of the whipping"[18] she got after defacing the wallpaper in her bedroom which she says that she did out of boredom.

She explains that he seemed to dislike children generally because he himself was "childless and middle-aged (56)" and "not the gentleman" that her deceased father was. He was also a German and a Lutheran which meant that he was "very outside grace (58)." He ate different meals from the ones that the children were forced to eat. Aunt Margaret insisted that the children have a particular diet and regimen, a program that was meant to keep them happy and in good health but was actually a way for Aunt Margaret, according to Mary, to destroy any privacy for the children (70). She could not understand why her Aunt Margaret, three years older than Myers, ever married him. They seemed to be so different, from different backgrounds. But Mary soon discovered that Uncle Myers "liked to keep smart, military discipline" and exercise his power over both Margaret and the children (59).

Mary won an essay contest in grade school and Uncle Myers "beat her with the razor strap---to teach her a lesson,...lest she become stuck-up" and the "usual tribute" was paid to him by the others as a man of "great discernment."

Mary says that they were beaten "all the time (64)" as a matter of course, it seemed. She says that she felt like she was in a Dickens novel (64). These punishments were generally administered as "preventive medicine (64)" and she was whipped more frequently than her brothers because of her "seniority," and for not setting a "better example" for her brothers.

Her uncle's "impartial application of punishment...did nothing for discipline, since we had no incentive to behave well, not knowing when we might be punished for something we had not done or even something that by ordinary standards would be considered good (65)." Out of fear, Mary says that she became a "problem liar" in those years in order to avoid punishment.

And so the stage is set for the tin butterfly episode (72 ff.). Uncle Myers, during an outing in the park, bought little Sheridan a box of the highly-coveted Cracker Jack from which he "fished out the painted tin butterfly with a little pin on it at the bottom (72)." This became the "immediate cherished possession" of the six-year old Sheridan. Uncle Myers relished Sheridan's performance and Mary was "disgusted" by the whole display. This was a first toy, or object that belonged "privately to one individual" and so it was coveted but Mary "held herself stubbornly apart" from the "excited passion" about this butterfly.

Mary's "holding herself apart" thus sets her aside as a prime suspect when the butterfly mysteriously disappears. Mary's aunt insists that the little girl help look for the lost butterfly which Sheridan had apparently mislaid or had become bored with. Mary's "lackadaisical indifference" manifested itself in the search and Aunt Margaret was furious with her until it was finally revealed that "Uncle Myers thinks you took it (75)." Her aunt warned her that if she knows anything about this butterfly and is hiding it, her uncle will punish her. Mary says she "insists with full self-righteousness" that she doesn't know anything about the lost butterfly and this is one time that she will not be punished.

At dinner, Mary was "exultant" because she was saved from punishment. Her brothers wondered how she avoided punishment and Uncle Myers sat with his "cunning look, as though events would prove him right," which they did, when the butterfly was discovered pinned to Mary's place under the tablecloth (76).

This was "grimly conclusive" and after each brother was questioned by Uncle Myers and the girl who set the table before dinner testified that it was not there when she set the table, Mary's "judges" concluded that the person "slipped it under the tablecloth at dinner (76)." Even Mary wonders how anybody could be so stupid as to imagine that she would hide it at her own place where it was sure to be found.

After the questioning, and all eyes looked to Mary as guilty, she was taken to the lavatory to be beaten by Uncle Myers. Even Aunt Margaret joined in the beating in an attempt to get Mary to admit that she did it. In exasperation, she finally admitted it and was taken before her uncle but couldn't admit it to him and was taken for another beating for disobeying the pact she made with her aunt to tell Meyers that she did it.

She says that she fell into bed with a "crazy sense of an inner victory, ...for not having recanted...(78)." She awoke with her "feeling of triumph abated" and she still walked about "on air, incredulously, ...pompously, seeing myself as a figure from legend: my strength was *as* the strength of ten because my *heart* was pure!" She was beaten again and the question of the butterfly was closed forever in that house.

In a first postscript, still part of the original story, the diegetic voice "connects the butterfly incident with the subsequent rescue by the Protestant grandfather the next year (78)." The lawyer who transferred the children to the grandfather did so on the basis of his interview with them during which time it was not so much the story of the tin butterfly as the fact that Mary did not have her glasses on as a punishment for breaking them in a fall in the playground. This so enraged the lawyer that he arranged to have her out of Myers custody.

In a second postscript, still part of the original story, Mary says that "six or seven years later," she stopped to see her brothers and Preston told her then that he saw Uncle Myers "steal into the dining room from the den and lift the tablecloth, with the tin butterfly in his hand (80)."

In a final, italicized postscript, she reveals that she since learned that Uncle Myers did in fact have a job then, given him by the family, soliciting grain shipments on the road (81) but she still wonders why she remembers him as being "home all the time (82)" as does her brother, Kevin.

The key insight in this final postscript is Mary's realization and admission that, after reading the story over, she remembered that she started to write a play about this subject in college. She wonders in the postscript:

> Could the idea that Uncle Myers put the butterfly at my place have been suggested to me by my teacher? I can almost hear her voice saying to me excitedly: "Your uncle must have done it!" ...And I can visualize a stage scene, with Uncle Myers tiptoeing in and pinning the butterfly to the silence pad (82-83).

After this insight, Mary called Kevin to consult with him about it. He remembers the incident with the butterfly and the terrible whipping but he does not remember Preston's comment that Myer's put it there. So Mary called Preston who remembers neither saying that nor seeing it. She concludes that Preston was only seven at the time and it "would be unlikely, therefore, to have preserved such a clear and *dramatic* recollection (83)."

Mary then thinks that she may have suggested her teacher's theory to Preston who may have agreed with it and even "have thought, for the moment, he remembered, once the idea was suggested to him." Mary says that she cannot remember if she took the course in playwriting before or after the night that they all got together and discussed it. Mary concludes that she has "fused the two memories:" the discussion on the porch with the brothers and the teacher's comment. Her diegetic postscripts are actually a series of voiced perspectives which alter the original perspective and they can replace each other as metaphors in the representation of the incident.

She still wonders who put the butterfly there and concludes that it could have been Uncle Myers after all because he did have a motive and an opportunity and she wants him to have put it there because she dislikes him so strongly.

Conclusion

I have chosen the foregoing pieces of writing in this chapter because they contain narrative units which support my thesis (even though the pieces themselves my not be admittedly autobiographical nor memoirs) that a memoir is a type of autobiographical writing in which the writer attempts to compare and contrast the varieties of voices and perspectives surrounding particular incidents and these varieties of voices and perspectives serve as metaphoric replacements for each other.

Each of these writers perceived inconsistencies, gaps and contradictions that each tried to reconcile or explain. Some of them experienced themselves and their voice at particular times as empty and silent and at other times as multiple, confused and disorganized.

The autobiographers in Chapter One, on the other hand, experienced themselves, their perspective and voice, as predominantly unified and integrated around a particular, highly significant, synecdochic, awareness.

The fictional memoir pieces accent the mimetic chaos in the narrator's memory which elements the narrator's consciousness then attempts to separate, organize, compare and contrast. Vladimir wants to narrate a unified story of a day in his life but Pozzo and Estragon point out to him the contradictions and loopholes in his memories. Tom Wingfield attempts to justify and explain the reasons why he left home.

The non-fictional pieces focus on a mimetic reality which had become distorted with time and the writer attempts to clarify the distortions in the narrative. Gosse, Kingston and Wordsworth return to their childhood situations and significant persons there in an attempt to decipher, separate and understand. Arthur Miller returns to a particularly significant relationship and connects it with his vocation as a writer.

In the next chapter, I will interpret the confessions of writers who will place the diegetic focus more on the revelation of and explanation of the mimetic voices and experiences in terms of both the interlaced diversity of comparisons and contrasts that the memoirist attempts and the unified, synecdochic portrait of the autobiographer. The confessor focuses on voices and perspectives in particular events which have been hitherto unrecognized, underdeveloped, unconnected. The memoirist attempts to retrieve the events through comparisons and contrasts; the autobiographer attempts to retrieve the self by representing a highly significant, synecdochic event; the confessor attempts to retrieve the perspective by making a significant connection that is essential to understanding the event. For the memoirist, the retrieval is the recognition of elements that may have been buried and now serve as new metaphors for the experience; for the autobiographer, the retrieval is the recognition that this event or experience is singular in the life of the writer; for the confessor the retrieval is the recognition of some new voice, fact or perspective in a particular event which gives it a renewed integration.

> Each succession has seemed to bury all the before. And yet, in reality, not one has been extinguished...[19]

Notes

1. Thomas DeQuincey, *Tales and Prose Phantasies*, Volume XIII, *The Collected Writings of Thomas DeQuincey*, ed. David Masson (Edinburgh: Adam and Charles Black, 1890), 346.

2. James Goodwin, "Narcissus and Autobiography," (*Genre*, Volume 12, Spring, 1979), 78.

3. Robert Langbaum, *The Mysteries of Identity: A Theme in Modern Literature* (New York: Oxford University Press, 1977), 3.

4. Steven Marcus, "The Psychoanalytic Self," (*Southern Review*, Volume 22, #2, April, 1986), 318 ff.

5. Jacques Derrida, *The Ear of the Other: Otobiography, Transference, Translation*, trans. Peggy Kamuf, ed. Christie McDonald, (New York: Schocken Books, 1985), 45, 57-58, 157.

6. John Sturrock, "The New Model Autobiography," (*New Literary History*, 9, 1, 1977), 62.

7. Samuel Beckett, *Waiting for Godot*, (New York: Grove Press, Inc., 1954), 39. All further references will be to this edition.

8. Tennessee Williams, *The Glass Menagerie*, (New York: A Signet Book of the New American Library, 1945), 19. All further references will be to this edition.

9. Vladimir Nabokov, *Speak, Memory: An Autobiography Revisited*, (New York: G.P. Putnam's Sons, 1947, 1948, 1949, 1950, 1960, 1966), 73. All further references will be to this edition.

10. William Wordsworth, *The Fourteen Book Prelude*, edited by W.J.B. Owen, (Cornell University Press, 1985), Book 2, lines 325-327. All further references will be to this edition.

11 Friedrich Wilhelm Nietzsche, *Ecce Homo* and *The Birth of Tragedy*, (New York: The Modern Library, Inc., 1927), 69, 95, 107. All further references will be to this edition.

12 Edward W. Said, "On Repetition," in *The Literature of Fact: Selected Essays from the English Institute*, edited by Angus Fletcher, (New York: Columbia University Press, 1976), 138.

13 David Fischer, "The Braided Narrative: Substance and Form in Social History," in *The Literature of Fact*, edited by Angus Fletcher, (New York: Columbia University Press, 1976), 120.

14 Maxine Hong Kingston, *The Woman Warrior: Memoirs of a Girlhood Among Ghosts*, (New York: Vintage Books, A Division of Random House, 1977), 84. All further references will be to this edition.

15 William Wordsworth, "Ode: Intimations of Immortality from Recollections of Early Childhood," in *The Norton Anthology of English Literature*, Volume Two, fourth edition, edited by M.H. Abrams, E. Talbot Donaldson, Hallett Smith, Robert M. Adams, Samuel Holt Monk, Lawrence Lipking, George H. Ford, David Daiches, (New York: W.W. Norton and Company, 1962, 1968, 1974, 1978), p. 217, lines 176-181.

16 Arthur Miller, *Timebends: A Life* (New York: Grove Press, 1987), 599. All further references will be to this edition.

17 Edmund Gosse, *Father and Son: A Study of Two Temperaments*, edited by Peter Abbs (New York: Penguin Books, 1983), 68. All further references will be to this edition.

18 Mary McCarthy, "A Tin Butterfly," in *Memories of a Catholic Girlhood*, (New York: Harcourt Brace Jovanovich Publishers, 1957), 56. All further references will be to this edition.

19 DeQuincey, 346.

Chapter Three

A Confession Reveals Mimetic/Diegetic Voices in Metonymic Narratives

Yes, reader, countless are the mysterious handwritings of grief and joy which have inscribed themselves successively upon the palimpsest of your brain;[1]

Introduction

The diegetic narrative voice, narrating in the present time, in a confession, reveals various motivations and intentions which constituted the mimetic voice in the execution of a past act. A piece of autobiographical writing is called "confessional" when the mimetic, narrating voice comments diegetically on a past act by representing the voice and activity of the self in that past act but revealing in the present, narrating voice, voices and elements which were omitted in earlier re-tellings. A confession fills in the gaps, confusions and inconsistencies. The diegetic voice narrating the confession reveals, explains and metonymically connects the various behaviors of the narrating protagonist. Specific voices and incidents within the narrative as well as the narrative itself are rhetorically metonyms when the piece of writing is autobiographically confessional.

In a memoir, voices and events are compared, contrasted and are generally configured and juxtaposed metaphors for each other.

In an autobiography, narrative voice and perspective about past voices, events and perspectives are united and become synecdoches, significant unique moments, for the writer. But in a confession, the narrative voice and perspective is one which attempts to reveal and explain voices and perspectives in past events which give the past event a logic and coherence. The past event and voice of the protagonist do not make sense for one reason or another and a confession reveals some of those reasons and so connects metonymically the narrative. The added, diegetic explanations and revelations in a confessional narrative become metonyms which serve to connect the experience.

In Appendix G of his *Apologia* on "Lying and Equivocation," Cardinal Newman discusses the interior conditions of a person who would intentionally tell a lie. He distinguishes between the formal, internal intention, disposition or motivation to lie and the external, material act of uttering the particular words of the lie itself. Newman says that the particular external words or actions are secondary when they are viewed as the means or tools to other more important, primary ends, other words or actions, but he says that those secondary words and behaviors, the lies, must be at least "equal in value" to the more important, primary word or action which is at the end.

Correlatively, the particular internal dispositions and motivations must be placed on a similar scale of value in relation to each other. In other words, an individual intends to tell a lie but also intends to protect someone's reputation. The intention to protect the reputation is of greater value than the lie so it takes precedence. One particular intention or motivation becomes secondary to the achievement or recognition of another more significant one. He says that it is acceptable to utter the words of a lie if someone else's reputation will be preserved.[2] He also says that it is acceptable to "equivocate,"[3] that is, allow a lie spoken by someone else to stand as true, if the primary end is still to protect someone's good name. He also says that a person may avoid answering certain questions, "evading," if the answers will hurt someone's reputation.

Besides the lying example, Newman also uses the example of accidental murder to explain the difference between formal, interior intentions and material, external acts. The actual murder occurred but there was no formal intention to do so. Similarly an actual lie may have been told but there may have been no formal intention to do so. There is a material act of murder or the material words of the lie but there may not be the formal, constituting act of intending to lie or to murder. The formal, constitutive intention was to protect oneself or someone else's life and reputation which "material" act was executed by pairing it with the "formal" intention." The lie or murder are accidental, "immaterial," because the formal, constitutive act of intending is absent.

My point in using Newman here is to illustrate the fact that there may be a great variety and hierarchy of internal dispositions, motivations and intentions which can be randomly selected and paired with any number of external words or behaviors which pairing itself then requires explanation in a confessional narrative.

Kenneth Burke takes issue with this kind of reasoning. He says that if a murder was committed, whether accidental or not, the "intention to murder" must be considered as a part of the internal gestalt of intentions. The "intention to murder" is to be sure not primary on the scale of interior intentions but Burke wants it to be admitted that it may have been there, albeit unconsciously, preconsciously, subconsciously.

The same holds true of the lie, equivocation or evasion. The person must intend to utter the words of the lie as well as protect the reputation of the self or the other. The protection of the reputation is higher on the person's scale of values but the fact of the matter is that the intention to utter the words of the lie is still present on the scale.

Burke is arguing with the casuistry that can justify a particular act, of lying or murder, for example, by randomly pairing it with a particular good intention. He wants the individual to admit that the words of the lie or the act of murder were intended whether they were the direct, primary intentions or not.

Burke discusses this in his article "Directing the Intention" in *A Rhetoric of Motives* and his appendix on the "Four Major Tropes" in *A Grammar of Motives*. When the particular, formal intentions, attitudes and motivations combine with the particular external, material acts of particular words and behaviors and are categorized and classified according to value, neither the external nor the internal gestalts must be paired randomly; one action cannot pick a particular intention as its director. The multiplicity must be acknowledged and respected. There is a gestalt of "perspective among perspectives"[4] in both the internal intentional structure and the external situation of the words and behaviors. Both the internal and external forums need to be analyzed carefully.

Goram Hemeren points out that speech act theory's discussion of illocutionary activity encourages this exploration of the different kinds and levels of intention and their distinctions. The crucial question is: is information about intention relevant to the act committed? Hemeren agrees with Burke in that intentions and motivations are important and how they are expressed is just as important.

Hemeren supports Burke's idea of a perspective among perspectives with an articulation of a literary hierarchy, taxonomy or classification of linguistic conventions and structures which point to intention and motivation. Literary signals like exaggeration, circumstance, internal clashes, disharmonies, gaps, ironies, paradoxes, figures of speech, symbols, traditions, contexts are the elements from which intentions and motivations can be deduced. Literature and writing can be ways to access Burke's conception of a dramatistic, behavioral pentad where intentions, motivations, attitudes and dispositions are accessed.

Gordon Allport also refers to Burke's "perspective of perspectives" and Hemeren's "taxonomy"[5] as a "gross anatomy of motives"[6] underlying words and behaviors. David Fischer's conceptualization of the "braided narrative" (which I referred to in Chapter Two in relation to Wordsworth) encompasses this idea of a gestalt or taxonomy of motives.

An autobiographical narrative, particularly one which calls itself confessional, is one which is sufficiently complex as to allow both interior life and exterior words and behaviors to be represented. The "plethoric, heterogenous multitude"[7] of external facts blends with a similar multitude in the interior life of individuals. Fischer points out that narratives are often not merely linear sequences of chronological causes and effects because there are circular, interlaced narratives of voices and perspectives; a braided, paradoxical, ironic interplay of opposites. Many autobiographical documents and their narrative units, following the lead of the "new historicism," attempt to combine the autobiographer's mimetic voice which remembers and recounts intentions, motivations and attitudes in the narrative units with the autobiographer's diegetic voice as the historical analyst who places intentions in an interlaced gestalt with the linear, cause and effect sequencing of events.

Many autobiographical documents and narratives have contributed importantly to an understanding of the nature of the confessional narrative as opposed to the memoir or autobiography, principally because they have called themselves "confessions" or have in some way indicated and invited the revelation and explanation of motives and intentions. For this chapter, I have selected Edward Albee's fictional narrative *Who's Afraid of Virginia Woolf?* which I will use as a point of departure to discuss Thomas DeQuincey's non-fictional *Confessions of an English Opium-Eater*, Norman Mailer's *Armies of the Night*, Andrew Greeley's *Confessions of a Parish Priest*, and Perry Edward Smith's autobiographical statement to the court psychiatrist in Truman Capote's "non-fiction novel" *In Cold Blood*.

Edward Albee, like Samuel Beckett and Eugene Ionesco, mimetically portrays characters in a stage drama who not only perform for an audience behaviors where motivations are in question but he also portrays characters who are also authors and narrators telling mimetic stories about particular past events and experiences and their narratives are accompanied by this confessional questioning and clarifying of motives and intentions with regard to the past event being narrated. A diegetic voice comments on and explains the words and behaviors of the mimetic voice and event being narrated. These narratives in this drama are confessional to the extent that they suggest that motivations and intentions in particular events and experiences of the particular characters are as multiple as the remembered details of the events themselves and can be juggled by whomever is narrating. The voices and perspectives are determined by narrator, protagonist and author--each of whom can be a separate person or can be the same person exploring the three points of view and voices in the self.

Thomas DeQuincey gives voice and perspective to the thoughts and feelings that he had on the morning that he left Manchester. He arrives at certain diegetic convictions based upon his examination and remembrance of the particular mimetic voices and experiences surrounding the event of his leaving Manchester. His retrospective, diegetic conviction is that "once a word is uttered (or a behavior performed), it is irrevocable."[8] The words or behaviors are irrevocable because they are intimately tied to, constituted in, this gestalt of intentions and attitudes that motivated them and are revealed in the autobiographical narrative that is confessional and such revelation gives the words or behaviors a metonymic coherence.

Norman Mailer reveals and explains his personal reasons for participating in a Viet Nam war protest. He gives voice to his own particular mimetic words and behaviors during the protest and diegetically comments on them as he narrates, giving the narrative of the protest a metonymic vigor.

Andrew Greeley reveals the nature of his own mimetic voice as priest, sociologist, and novelist by diegetically explaining how they are linked. He connects three apparently disconnected professions.

Perry Edward Smith writes an autobiographical statement for a court psychiatrist in an attempt to explain and defend his life such that the court will understand why he murdered the Clutter family. His is a diegetic explanation of why he mimetically acted and spoke as he did. Truman Capote prints this statement in his "non-fiction novel" *In Cold Blood* in which Capote purports to have thoroughly investigated the case for five years with a view to explaining it coherently. It is a murder with no apparent motive; it does not make sense. Capote's non-fiction narrative is an attempt to metonymically connect the event and the autobiographical statement by the murderer is one metonym in the puzzle.

I will now discuss these narratives in more detail to support and illustrate my theoretical perspective that confessional writing reveals, explains and connects voices and behaviors and so these narratives and their parts function rhetorically as metonyms.

PART ONE: FICTIONAL CONFESSIONS

George, Martha, Nick and Honey

When George and Nick are left alone together in Act One of Edward Albee's *Who's Afraid of Virginia Woolf?*, there are two confessions: Nick confesses to the circumstances under which he met and married his wife and George tells a story about a young boy he once knew who accidentally killed both of his parents under separate circumstances. Later, both Martha and George narrate (in a different voice) the story of the birth and upbringing of their son who is supposed to return home for his eighteenth birthday. Finally, Martha narrates diegetically the story of a boxing match between herself and George during which narration George gets a fake gun with which he pretends to shoot Martha after her narration.

These narratives represent a mimetic sequence of external events in the drama itself accompanied by a mimetic sequence of internal attitudes, motivations and intentions surrounding the marriages, the accidents, and the boy as well as the boxing match and the shooting. The sequence of external diegetic/mimetic voices and behaviors in these narratives braid with a sequence of internal diegetic/mimetic voices articulating intentions and motivations in perspective around the events and mimetic details and circumstances of the marriages, the accidents, the boy, the boxing match and the shooting.

Nick's story of the circumstances of his marriage is re-told later in the play by George but both George's and Honey's diegetic additions as commentators, observers and narrators change Nick's gestalt of intentions and motivations in his narration. George's narrative of the young boy who accidentally killed his parents is first re-told by George and then re-told by Martha and the diegetic additions of both George and Martha change the gestalt of intentions and motivations in this boy and the story. George and Martha's illusory, mimetic narrative of their fictional son is also diegetically expanded later in such a way that the gestalt of intentions and motivations which accompany the raising of the son are changed. I will illustrate how Martha's story of the boxing match and George's pretending to shoot her during her narration interlace with the other three narratives and with his actual attempt to strangle her at one point.

George and Nick have their discussion of Nick's marriage at a late-night, after-faculty-party visit, amidst much drinking, at George and Martha's house. They banter casually about interests, likes, and dislikes.[9] George compares his "40 something (35)" year old physique to Nick's twenty-eight year old physique and suggests that they play handball together (35). Martha has made it clear up to this point that George is not "running" the history department (38) like Nick will be "running" the Biology department when he's "40 something" years old. George is highly attuned to his sense of his own inadequacy and lack of success in his job; he sees that Nick is in a position to become highly successful and adequate. George sees that Nick is at that stage in his life where he will begin to climb the ladder and achieve success which George can no longer do but George sees climbing ladders and achieving successes diegetically, retrospectively as things which are "historical inevitabilities (112, 114, 144)" that have little to do with the person's intention or motivation to do so. People who are successful often say that they were altruistically motivated and intended to achieve as they did but George says that there are other motives and intentions which are unknown and unrecognized as part of any journey towards apparent success. The person will participate in certain activities, like "plowing pertinent wives (112)," and will justify those activities by pairing them with the heroic desire to succeed and achieve recognition and status.

George's non-fictional narrative about the young boy who accidentally killed his parents became the fictional subject matter of his first novel which was rejected by publishers and represents his one failed attempt at success. George sees himself in the young Nick who is beginning his career (a kind of "eternal return" for George) and George knows that this young Nick may do just about anything to achieve success because George "did just about anything" to get that novel published when he had to admit in his own voice that the fictional boy who accidentally killed his parents was really himself. The rejection not only turned into a professional rejection of his work, his writing, but it turned into a personal confession and rejection of himself. He wants Nick to realize that as he strives for professional success, some personal values may have to be sacrificed and he may have to say and do things that he wished he had never said and done like telling George the circumstances of his marriage.

George is visibly angered and insulted by Nick's lack of sympathy and his "smug, self-righteous, scientific distance (92)" about the fact that Martha is embarrassing him and humiliating him in front of them. The natural reaction, it seems to George, would be one of sympathy. George wants to elicit some pity, some compassion, some involvement, from Nick but all he gets is this "pragmatic idealism (92)" that is "impressed" with George and Martha's repartee----comparing them to two professional boxers in the ring (92); Nick admires their "method." He admires something that he would rather not participate in: flagellation is not his idea of a good time but he does admire good, professional flagellators, like George or Martha (93).

This boxing metaphor recurs, of course, in Martha's story of her actual boxing match with George at a faculty party given by her father. Her father wanted George to put on the gloves and fight but George was not interested and while the father was trying to cajole George into putting the gloves on, Martha put them on, and called to George, who turned, and Martha took a swing at him and knocked him out. The truth is that she knocked him out absolutely unintentionally, humorously. It was a joke at which she laughs hysterically, not only at the time that it actually happened but in the re-telling. But the truth might also be that there were some secondary, possibly unconscious/subconscious desires to knock him out, embarrass him, impress her father.

Her narrative of this boxing incident is followed immediately by the fake gun sequence where, as Martha is telling the story of the boxing match, she is gloating quite gleefully in her knocking the poor George into the bushes, and George has gone to get a double-barrelled shot-gun. He re-enters the room and points it at the back of her head at which time Honey and Nick both scream in genuine fear and shock. He fires the gun and an American flag pops out. They all sigh with relief and laugh at this wonderful trick, this illusion. "I really thought you were going to shoot her (58)!"

The truth is that its a phony gun and he was just playing a joke, like Martha was with the boxing gloves. He had no intention of shooting Martha as she had none of knocking him out. But there may also be the unconscious/subconscious truth, especially in the context of the boxing story, that he really does want to kill her and she really does want to knock him out. Instead of actually killing each other, they figuratively do so by killing each other's most cherished feelings and attitudes, shattering each other's illusions, flagellating each others' desires. George kills Martha by not only killing her fictional son but by also killing her non-fictional desire to have had a child. He kills Nick and Honey by revealing hidden, non-fictional motives and intentions in their marriage relationship in a fictional narrative re-telling that he creates. Martha kills George by revealing hidden intentions and motivations behind his "first novel." The boxing match and the gun sequence are metaphoric versions of the same intention and each incident connects the whole to such an extent that Nick himself, with the reader and audience, can say at the end of the play "I think I understand what's going on here!"

George tells Nick that his so-called polite, pseudo-detached non-involvement, in the name of scientific advancement and research which examines external, material words and behaviors as entities separate from interior, formal motivations and intentions is the nadir of hypocrisy. There are internal, formal intentions and motivations that succeed each other, one after another, as historical inevitabilities in life that can't be scientifically categorized and researched, they don't fit into the gestalt of the words and behaviors that accompany them. The intention to be successful and have a good life does not fit with the intention of "plowing pertinent wives" along the way.

George wonders if Nick and Honey have any children and or if they intend to have any (40-41) and Nick reveals to George that he had to marry his wife because she was pregnant. This confession of this external behavior naturally invites further conversation and questioning from George about the internal feelings and attitudes associated with the behavior. This first pregnancy turned out to be "hysterical (94)." She did not conceive then nor has she conceived since. She is a younger version of Martha as Nick is of George.

Nick does not want to leave the bare, scientific facts of his confession in a gestalt by itself without some explanation of the justifying details and the explanatory interlace of interior motivations and attitudes. He wants to choose particular intentions and motivations and pair them with the behaviors to justify them. The fact that they had to get married coupled with the fact that she was not really pregnant is joined by Nick's diegetic commentary that there was never really any "passion (105)" between them and that there were "compensating factors (103)," other motivations. They knew each other since early childhood, played "doctor" together (104) and were always "expected" to be together in marriage by their families (105). George suspects that there may have been money involved (102) so Nick adds the story of his wife's minister-father who made a lot of money for himself, his family, and God by building hospitals, churches, "mercy" ships (108). The father-in-law was called to preach, baptize and save when he was "pretty young" and so he became "pretty famous" and made a lot of money.

George says that he thinks this story is "nice (109)" but he will not re-tell it "nicely" later in the play. He will re-arrange the gestalt and re-pair the interior motivations and intentions with the external circumstances in an attempt to shatter Nick's illusions about himself. Nick says that he was motivated to marry his wife because she was pregnant and because they had always known each other and were expected to be together. Nick voices his motivations and intentions as relatively honorable and straightforward. He suggests that he married out of love and that his intentions were and still are in the right place and he wants to do the right things. George wants him to recognize that there may be other intentions and Nick may have to compromise some of his most cherished beliefs, like George did with his first novel.

George situates his re-telling of Nick's story in two contexts: The first is that George has just been humiliated by Martha with her story which he entitles "Humiliate the Host."   Martha has re-told George's story of the boy who accidentally killed his parents. George's story about the young boy who accidentally killed his parents is told by him as a observer-narrator. He is one of a group of boys who knew the boy. They were the same age and went to the same Prep school and at the end of the school year, the bunch of them would go to this "gin-mill owned by the gangster-father of one of us (94)" and drink with the "grown-ups" and listen to jazz. They all knew that the boy had accidentally shot his mother "some years before (94)" and at this one school year's end, this boy happened to go with them drinking. He was "blond and had the face of a cherub (95)" and he ordered bergin and water which made everyone laugh. The waiter who took the order passed the word on to other tables about the laughter until the whole place was laughing, including the boy, and everyone was ordering bergin. The ordering of bergin and the laughter continued through the evening and the next day each of them had a "grown-up's" headache but George remembers the evening, synecdochically, diegetically, as the "grandest day of my youth."

Nick wonders what happened to the boy and George tells him that the following summer, the boy was learning to drive on a country road with his father and he swerved to avoid a porcupine and drove straight into a large tree. He was not killed but his father was and when he awoke in the hospital and was told what happened, he started to laugh until he needed to be sedated. When he recovered from his injuries, he was placed in an asylum and has been there these 30 years and has not uttered one sound.

George claims that the boy's earlier shooting of the mother was certainly quite "accidental, without even an unconscious motivation (94)" as was the car accident. Nick, who is supposed to be so scientifically detached, sympathizes with this young boy who experienced such tragedy and lost not only his parents but his sanity.

George narrates the story from a distance. He observed the boy and he participated in the evening of drinking and there is not much in the way of his intentions or motivations as author, except to write a good novel that will sell. George thinks that this is a good story, worthy of publication, if only evidenced by the emotional involvement and concern of the hitherto scientifically detached Nick.

This story is also very important to George because it is his own. When Martha reveals this information later, George's physical attack and attempted strangulation of her is a diegetic behavior which testifies to the apparent truth of what she is saying. The fact that this was the subject matter of his first novel and the fact that some of it was apparently autobiographical and the fact that this information was mocked by Martha and rejected by the publishers are facts which, when connected, elicit this diegetic confession from George in the form of the strangulation attempt.

This is now not just an interesting, sad story of a boy who accidentally killed both his parents and is now in an insane asylum. Parts of it come from George's real experience and attitudes. He wants people to read it, like it and buy it. Nick's story is also not merely a "nice" story of a young couple. It indicates motivations, intentions and attitudes which are important to Nick and are not so easily explained.

George wants revenge for having his identity in his novel revealed by Martha so he takes Nick's story and reveals other intentions and motivations in another story, his "second novel," which he calls "Get the Guests (140)." He says that this second novel is a pleasant "bucolic allegory...in straight, cozy prose...about a nice young couple who come out of the middle west (142)." The hero is about 30, blond, a scientist and a teacher and his "mouse is a wifey little type who gargles brandy all the time (142)." The reader/listener now knows, along with Nick, that this second "allegorical novel" has characters in it who are drawn from real life. Nick is now aware that "sneaky" George is making his not-so-ineffectual attack. The diction George chooses as narrator influences the tone of the story and riddles it with sarcasm and cynicism and changes the entire perspective of Nick's original story. Nick's voice and perspective are represented quite differently by George. George's re-telling is unsympathetic.

> This couple got together when they was only teensie little types, and they used to get under the vanity table and poke around, and....Mousie's father was a holy man...who ran a sort of traveling clip joint based on Christ and all those girls and he took all the faithful....(142)

Honey now begins to recognize the story in spite of George's "artistry;" it sounds familiar to her (142); she feels that she's heard it before and that she knows these people but George has couched the story in all sorts of negative, descriptive terms that she's not sure. His rhetoric distorts, re-arranges and so confuses her a bit.

Nick, Honey, George and Martha do not tell their own stories negatively. They attribute motivations and intentions which justify their behavior. But the re-tellings by other narrators from other points of view change the rhetoric, the voice, and hence the point of view and the power behind the voice.

> Mousie's papa died and they opened him up and all sorts of Jesus and Mary money came out. So Blondie and his frau leave their "plain" states with all their money and settle in New Carthage.

Nick does not want George to continue with this story but Honey likes "familiar-sounding" stories (144).

"Blondie comes to New Carthage 'disguised' as a teacher and a scientist because he knows that his 'ticket' has "bigger things written on it....It's an historical inevitability (144)" that he will rise to great heights of success and recognition. But George says his wife is now part of his "disguise," some "extra baggage," that he needs to carry. He needed her father's money to help him get those "bigger things" and everybody wondered why he was so solicitous of this

Mimetic/Diegetic Voices in Metonymic Narratives 149

"brandy swilling upchucker." People wondered why he ever married her.

He obviously married her for the money her father had made as a minister so that he could advance himself without having to worry about money and when he had finished climbing the ladder, he could dump the wife. *She* won *him* by pretending to be pregnant. The detached scientist has external, material goals to achieve and he will perform certain behaviors and say certain words in order to meet those goals. He justifies the certain not-so-good means (the father's money, the pregnancy) because his goal of success and recognition is more important. Rather than admit that he may not really have loved his wife, that he married her because she was pregnant, he may instead focus on the fact that he did an honorable, heroic thing by marrying her. Rather than admit that he may have wanted her father's money or that he was more interested in job success, he may instead focus on the fact that he and his wife were always expected to be together and he has always wanted to be a scientist. The not-so-honorable intention would have been to admit the mistake, the possible duplicity.

Kenneth Burke suggests that the interior intention and motivation to perform each and every action is somehow, somewhere present. Nick intends both the not-so-good means as well as the admirable ends. Although he may not want to admit it, he will "plow pertinent" wives and "insinuate" himself in the right circles of people with the intention of achieving. Cardinal Newman, on the other hand, would suggest that marrying the girl because she was pregnant would be pairing an internal good intention with an external unfortunate act. The internal, formal intention was not to get pregnant outside of marriage; the internal, formal intention is to show love for one another; when that intention is paired with the external behavior of sexual intercourse, pregnancy, and hence, marriage may result. The formal, internal intention is to show love for someone else and this is paired with the external, behavioral act of sexual intercourse. There is no formal, internal intention to have children or marry. The expression of love is limited to sexual intercourse and so may be distorted and considered more appropriately as an expression of lust, concupiscence.

When George makes reference to the hysterical pregnancy in his story, Honey realizes "with outlandish horror (147)" that Nick has told them "her" story. She now hears herself being clearly revealed, however negatively, in George's "novel" which he created from facts gathered earlier. George makes her aware that there may have been other, less altruistic, motives and intentions for her as well (146-7). She may have had the internal, formal intention to marry; her desire to marry and have a family may have been so strong that she participated in sexual relations and became hysterically pregnant based on that interior desire. The less altruistic, questionable part about Honey's intentions and desires is that Nick may have little to do with them. She would take any man who would marry her and she would become hysterically pregnant to achieve that end.

Honey rushes out to be sick, her typical response, which George calls another example of historical inevitability, the pattern of history. Honey has no control over her getting sick; as she likely had no control over the hysterical pregnancy; the pattern is inevitable because it is unconscious, unrecognized, like Nick's so-called rise to greatness will be an inevitable pattern outside of his control and, like history, according to George, itself inevitably proceeds according to an uncontrollable succession of non-stop events, accompanied by unrecognized motivations and intentions.

Honey's reaction is itself her diegetic commentary, an addition to the story, like George's attack on Martha after the additions to his story, that indicates unrevealed, probably unrecognized, intentions and motivations. This marriage and the pregnancy are very important, central, and deeply personal issues in the forefront of Honey's consciousness. It was extremely important to her that she be married and have children and when confronted with the fact that her marriage may be loveless and that she may have no children, she is being confronted with real facts that contradict her real desires both of which are supremely, continually present to her consciousness. Another woman may not be bothered by these facts at all be-

Mimetic/Diegetic Voices in Metonymic Narratives 151

cause her interior gestalt of desire is different. Ironically, paradoxically, Honey's very real, non-fictional desires and motivations created the fiction of the hysterical pregnancy. Martha's very real desire to have had a child also resulted in the fictional story of the son who is about to visit on his 18th birthday. George's very real desire to be a successful writer resulted in the very real production of a novel but that novel, the fiction contained therein, is based on non-fictional material from George's real life. Nick's story follows a similar interlace. It is my point in using Albee's play here as point of departure to illustrate the dovetail of fiction and non-fiction, particularly with regard to confessional material. Voices, perspectives, attitudes and various testimonies about nonfictional events can be fictionally juxtaposed.

Nick curses George for his "viciousness and cruelty (148)" for which he says he "will be sorry (149)." George's narrative is vicious and cruel because it exposes an interior state of intentions and motivations which are at odds with other, very important intentions and motivations to both Honey and Nick. The fact that their marriage may be loveless or that they can never have children is coupled with the overwhelmingly central desire to have love and children. It is "vicious and cruel" to destroy Honey's desire for a loving marriage and a family when she is faced with the reality that these may not happen. It is equally "cruel and vicious" to suggest to Nick that his real motivations are to walk all over everyone else because he desires personal success, fame and achievement. According to George, Nick needs to face reality and re-align his motives. George forces Nick to do what he himself had to do many years ago when his novel was rejected and his personal life was revealed. He lost self-esteem because he compromised values. He used facts from his personal life, deeply personal facts, as a way to achieve success in publishing and it backfired on him. He is telling Nick: make sure you recognize the ulterior, not-so-good motives so that you're not too shocked when everything backfires and they are revealed. Make sure you realize that you may not have loved your wife; you may have married her for money and you are out to achieve success and you may say and do things that really go against your conscience.

George's desire for anonymity in his story and his desire for success in writing are overwhelmingly central desires in George's life and he compromised those by revealing the facts about his personal life and that he used these facts as a way to achieve success and lost both.

George warned Nick earlier that he (Nick) would be sorry later when he hears this story and now Nick warns George that he will be sorry later when Nick *finishes* George's "second allegorical novel." George has taken the facts and construed them in such a way that he has "created" a gestalt of fictional intentions and motivations for both Nick and Honey. Nick takes George's creation and says that he will finish it as George has predicted it. He will "be what you say I am (150)." Nick's nonfictional story becomes a fiction in George's mouth and Nick takes the fiction and makes it non-fiction. George says that he (George) will no doubt regret what he has done by creating this fictional set of intentions and motivations in this way because they will now become real but he hates hypocrisy (148) and he wants Nick to know that these that he has created may not be so fictional and to stop kidding himself and others.

Similarly, Martha revealed George's other intentions and methodologies and when intentions and methods are revealed, perspectives change. Nick will now have to re-arrange his alliances (149), his interior life, and make the best of things now that other aspects of his intentions have been exposed. He will have to go to his wife, for starters, pick up the pieces and create another game plan by which he can save his marriage and re-start his climb to the top.

Earlier in the play, Nick "joked" that he would indeed insinuate himself generally, play around with the right people, find the weak spots, "shore 'em up" and put his name plate on them (112). George says that this is not a joke. It really, inevitably, will happen even though Nick makes a "joke" out of it. The irony is that Nick will really do what he so flippantly jokes about but with a complete lack of awareness of intentions and motivations. He will say: "I am achieving the success I have set out to achieve (the first and most important motive) by "plowing pertinent wives" (a secondary and less important and unrecognized motive). He will become an established fact on the campus or, as George would say, a recognized fact, an historical inevitability; "he always seems to have been here." His rise to recognition is inevitable and in the process of the rise, he will get caught in the whirlwind of climbing and pleasing, playing around, and insinuating that he won't even recognize the intentions and motivations that George says are there and with which he creates this "second allegorical novel."

George says that he is trying to teach Nick a lesson about the recognition and formation of intentions and motivations. George wants both Nick and Honey to face the fact that things happen, people get promoted and marriages succeed and fail not because people intend the promotion, the success or the failure, nor because people are aware of their motivations and intentions but precisely because they are *not* aware. They allow "the stars" and the "wheel of fate" to control their lives. Things happen to people as inevitable consequences of unrecognized intentions and motivations. Nick, the biologist, would rather think that he has this scientific control and objective detachment, that he married his wife out of love and continues to love her but George, as historian, sees that the scientific detachment of a controlled methodology sinks into the quicksand of historical inevitability. Nick is too smug, self-righteous and self-assured to admit the possibility of any duplicity or hypocrisy of motivation like marrying his wife because she was pregnant or because her father had money; but the quicksand of unrecognized motivations will still suck (115) him in whether he intends it or not.

George assures Nick that everything does not work out if "played by ear." We must be conscious of the gestalt of intentions and motivations, the unspoken agenda, otherwise life is just a continual sucking us into the quicksand of these unrecognized intentions and motivations. George says that he tried to make contact with Nick, to communicate with him, to touch him emotionally, spiritually, interiorly by putting him in touch with a possible perspective of intentions and motivations which he may not have recognized. But the contact was never made because either Nick resisted or George misread.

Similarly when Martha pointed out that George's story about the boy who accidentally killed his parents was really about George and was the subject of his first novel, George's involvement in the story changed significantly. He was reminded of his darker side, another array of intentions and motivations which she brought into view.

The story of both Honey's and Martha's fictional children which runs through the entire play fits into the same frame. George and Martha speak as if they really have a son, complete with mimetic details and diegetic commentary about him until which time, it is revealed by George that there is no son and Nick, in an apparent flash of insight, says that he thinks he understand what's going on here. George adds the diegetic comment that all this business about the son is fictional. He destroys the fiction for Martha by means of a mimetic narrative of the boy dying in a car crash on his way home for his eighteenth birthday by swerving to avoid a porcupine, reminiscent of George's own story about himself.

The motivation and intention to have had a child is as high on Martha's scale of desires as it is on Honey's. She wants so badly to have had a child, that she in effect creates one and a story to go with it. The confessional narrative is the revelation of the metonymic facts that there are no children and that they were unable to have any. The confessional narrative also involves the revelation of the equally metonymic fact that Martha's desire, her intention and desire, to have a child never went away. She has always had that desire and always will. Both Martha and Honey desire and intend to have a child and the desire and intention are their "stories." Martha creates the external, mimetic narrative, the fiction, the illusion, as a fulfillment of her very real, nonfictional desire and as Honey listens to Martha's story, the same nonfictional desire for a child is re-kindled in her.

George desires to have been a good, successful writer who published many books and he created a story to meet that desire. The story failed but the desire remains. His "confession" is the metonymic revelation of his unfulfilled desire. Nick's story of his meeting and marriage to Honey and the hysterical pregnancy contain no particular intentions and motivations. George diegetically tells Nick, through the mimetic re-telling, that his real desire, like his own, is for success and achievement and he may do anything to get it. Nick's "insight" at the end of the play when he realizes that he thinks he understands what's going on here receives the skeptical response from George: "Do you?"

"What's going on here" is the dovetail between illusion and reality, fiction and nonfiction. Both Martha and George and then Nick have lost the ability to distinguish between the two. Martha tells George a number of times in the play: "Truth or illusion, George; you don't know the difference." And when Nick asks them at the end of the play "was this after you killed them," both George and Martha respond "maybe (nonfiction)....and then again maybe not (fiction)," suggesting that they either may not know, they have lost control, or they have not decided what fiction to create yet. But it is in the creations of these fictions that their motivations and intentions, desires and interests have been lost. New connections and distinctions need to be made; especially the distinction between what is fictional and what is nonfictional.

Narratives can be constructed which give voice to motivations, intentions and desires behind particular words and behaviors but voices and points of view in narratives can also be constructed which have no real constitution in any real person's interior life. The words and behaviors about the raising of the son are illusory and fictional but the motivations and desires are not. The words and behaviors about Nick and Honey's marriage are true but some motivations and desires are omitted. My point is that there are very often two stories that need to be read and interpreted in a confession: the internal story of the personal motivations, intentions and desires and the external story of the words and behaviors of a particular protagonist. As Kenneth Burke says, both gestalts of the words and behaviors and the intentions and motivations can be arranged in any variety of perspectives and the two can also be arranged in another gestalt. Newman says that motivations and intentions can be paired with particular controversial words and behaviors, like his examples of murder or lying, as a way to justify them. Conversely, fictional words and behaviors, like having a child, or the creation of any fictional set of behaviors and words, can be paired with the motivations and desires that would accompany them. The important point with regard to confessional narratives is that the gestalt of external words and behaviors be a coherent network, a sequence of cause and effect; easy to follow and understand; objectively provable and witnessed. But added to this would be the gestalt of internal motivations and desires in a similar coherent network, a sequence of cause and effect. Once the metonymic relations are established in each of these worlds, the question of fiction and nonfiction can be addressed to each. For example, Honey and Martha both desire children (internal) and both of them have no children (external). The point is that in the gestalt of their interior lives, the desire to have children is so central, synecdochic, and pervasive that it defines the whole nature of the gestalt and influences the external gestalt. The synecdochic desire to have children becomes the key, the metonym which explains the behavior. The desire to have children is unfulfilled, an absence, a gap, and the fictional narrative fills it. They pretend that they have a child so the desire is fulfilled.

PART TWO: NON-FICTIONAL CONFESSIONS

Thomas Dequincey

Thomas DeQuincey's "impassioned prose captures a purer subjectivity, a purer illocutionary act"[10] says Elizabeth Bruss. His "constitutional determination to reverie (102)" is that interior place where the activity of intention and attitude formation in consciousness occurs which motivates DeQuincey. DeQuincey has learned throughout his life that once a word is uttered as a locutionary act or performed in a behavior, it is irrevocable because it is empowered by a stronger, interior, illocutionary act or force in consciousness and he incorporates that lesson as a major theme in his *Confessions*. DeQuincey views his life in the *Confessions* in overview but focuses on specific moments where he made decisions and "uttered those irrevocable words" and performed those irrevocable behaviors. His desire to leave Manchester and his formation of the intention to do so are two parts of one decision that once made could not be revoked. DeQuincey diegetically analyzes and gives narrative voice to the mimetic state of consciousness that establishes certain intentions and motivations for itself.

"That I would elope from Manchester---this was the resolution (65)." He wonders where the intensity of this desire comes from and he asks if it is the "first born [child] of resolution" or was the resolution the first born child of the desire, the hope. He concludes that the two go indivisibly together, "like thunder and lightning." A hope, a desire to do or say something consubstantiates the subsequent resolution to do it. The actual saying or doing it are what Cardinal Newman called the "material" manifestations of the "formal," interior act of forming the desires and hopes into resolutions. Kenneth Burke distinguishes the functions of the various hopes, desires, and attitudes in the formation of intention.

> So to go was settled. But *when* and *whither*? (66)...My plan had been to travel northwards to the region of the English Lakes....(68) in the dream of presenting myself to Wordsworth (71) who was the attraction that drew me so strongly to the Lakes (70)...[Until] at length all was ready...arrangements...had been finished (76).

Nothing remained to be done and yet he "lingered as under some sense of dim perplexity (77)." When he realizes that the particular day on which he was to leave had arrived, there was a "sadness of heart" that prevailed. A "secret sense of farewell or a testamentary act [a synecdoche] is carried into every word and deed of the memorable day (77)." And so DeQuincey recounts the details of the "morning which would launch him into the world."

He tells the story of this morning in retrospect, 19 years later, and as he gathers the memories and recollections before setting them into writing, he is moved, like Helen Keller was, by the synecdochic realization of how important this decision and day were and what an impact they had on his life. But I am including this story in my discussion of metonymic confessions rather than synecdochic autobiographies because in his re-telling the story of the day he left Manchester, he also communicates the significant, confessional insight which he had learned from experience that particular desires, intentions and attitudes formed in consciousness are those which unite and form the force behind words and actions and are their genesis. And this is the root of a confessional narrative. A confessional narrative reveals those desires, intentions, attitudes and feelings which motivated a particular behavior.

He narrates this sequence of events of this morning that he left Manchester as an interior monologue, a sequence of thoughts and feelings, motivations and perceptions, his mimetic voice standing in the room on the morning that he was to leave which blends with the diegetic voice of the commentator, the evaluator, narrator, writing thirty years later. The narrative then is a way for DeQuincey to bracket or frame this particular experience as a detachable mental state which he could apply to other states. It is a significant, synecdochic event that is also confessional. It is a representative confessional event.

His "whole succeeding life has in many points taken its coloring (83)," from that morning which was to launch him into the world and the many consequences of that world. He "was firm and immovable in purpose, but agitated by anticipation of uncertain danger and troubles" to which the "deep peace" and silence of the early morning presented a contrast.

He dressed and lingered in this room that had been his "pensive citadel" of study for nearly a year and a half. He remembers this time as composed of "happy hours" and he fears that he may never see their like again. He almost "receded from his plan" but "no retreat" was now open and "in this condition, this distracted view," he was thrown into despondency for one-half hour and he "dreamed, wrapped in a sort of trance, a frost of some death-like revelation" which he recalls as a "hateful remembrance derived from a moment left behind." His focus on the time-sequence of the experience accents the mimetic elements of the narrative.

He remembers that, on this morning as he was to leave, as he was standing in his room, he remembered a visit with a friend to the Whispering Gallery at St. Paul's Cathedral two years earlier. The present construction of the narration of this experience by the autobiographer, the remembering and the writing the narrative of the day he left Manchester, includes in it another past experience, remembering a visit to Saint Paul's Cathedral, which remembering became part of the morning of leaving.

The Whispering Gallery of Saint Paul's Cathedral is a place of distinction because of its acoustic ability to echo back a sound with great clarity and his visit to it plays an important part in this narrative. DeQuincey is conscious of the fact that a word or question uttered at one end of the gallery "in the gentlest of whispers, is reverberated at the other end in peals of thunder." This act of leaving Manchester is an act which may reverberate loudly at the end of his lifetime as a mistake.

Before he and his friend entered the Cathedral, they paused "beneath the dome...on the very spot where rather more than five years subsequently Lord Nelson was buried" and where "flags captured" from France, Holland and Spain "floated." These "solemn trophies of chance and change amongst mighty nations" occasioned another moment of dreamlike reverie in him during which he was "persecuted by a thought" based upon the great, biblical, Roman warning: *Nescit vox missa reverti* (that a word once uttered is irrevocable), accompanied by the thought that "fatality must often attend an evil choice (85)." The flags of the conquered nations and the tomb of Lord Nelson remind him that they made a wrong choice in their decision to do battle because they met with the "fatality" of being conquered.

He then personalizes the insight with regard to his own decisions and choices that seem to have contributed to personal fatalities; thus the document becomes confessional when he has insights which give metonymic connection to personal fatalities in his own life. These personal fatalities are not necessarily synecdochic, so they are not autobiography *per se* but "confessional."

The conscious decision to leave Manchester results in the arrival of the day on which he will actually do so. The arrival of the day and the act of leaving occasion this memory of the previous act of visiting Saint Paul's Cathedral and the conscious examination of that visit and its attendant thoughts and insights. The key, synecdochic insight is that some acts do result in fatalities because they are prefaced by inadequately formed intentions, motivations and attitudes to substantiate and connect them. The formation of the intentions, attitudes and motivations constituting irrevocable decisions, words and behaviors is the root of the problem when a decision, word or behavior goes awry.

He was "already at fifteen...deeply ashamed of judgments ...pronounced, of idle hopes...,false admirations or contempts... (85)" Standing there under the dome of St. Paul's, he concludes that there have been and would continue to be acts and decisions which he would never really feel quite sure about and the "doubts" would never really "wither" with the successions of years because the "principles," the intentions and motivations, upon which the decisions were based and the "inevitable results," the consequent fatalities, of these decisions were at the root of the doubt.

Decisions and actions are based upon the formation and recognition of a hierarchy of intentions, attitudes and motivations. The degree to which there are doubts and questions about particular motivations and intentions, or the degree to which they outweigh the consequences because they are not equal in value to the consequences, and the intensity of those doubts and questions with regard to the sincerity and honesty of the decision and action to be taken is the degree to which the doubts, questions and reservations will echo loudly in and through the course of the inevitable, sometimes fatal consequences. The presence of these doubts and questions about motivations and intentions means that there are gaps in the logical sequence, the explanation. The confessional explanation attempts to fill these gaps, explain the doubts and questions and give the narrative of the event a metonymic coherence.

These "sentiments" cause DeQuincey to "recoil from any word or deed" which would recall and reawaken in him the slightest twinge of doubt. And this sentiment was re-confirmed as he and his friend proceeded to walk into the Cathedral and to the Whispering Gallery where his friend "softly" whispered "a solemn but not acceptable truth," which "ran the walls of the gallery,...and reached me as a deafening menace in tempestuous uproar." If a word is uttered or a decision enacted with great solemnity and it is not equal in value and solemnity to the intentions that motivated it, then the word uttered will reverberate as a tempestuous roar and a deafening menace because it is not constituted in an intention and motivation that is equally strong and solemn. Decisions based on the formation of a recognized, metonymic gestalt of synecdochic attitudes, motivations and intentions minimize subsequent doubts, questions and fatalities because the intentions, attitudes and motivations will return to the person with their "original crispness and clarity," re-constituting the decision.

The conscious act of remembering the visit to St. Paul's returns "ominously" to him as he stands in that room on the morning that he was to leave and the words "once you leave this house and a Rubicon is placed between thee and all possibility of return (86)" echo in his mind. His consciousness, after having accumulated a wealth of perceptions and intuitions, feelings and thoughts while standing in that room, brackets this raw material into an act of consciousness which tells him that what he is about to do may not be "altogether approved in thy secret heart:...At the other end of thy life-long gallery that same conscience will speak to thee in volleying thunders."

The fact is that this is a "once for all" decision, an act which distinguishes itself 19 years later and again thirty years after that, "at the other end of his life," when he is writing and re-writing his *Confessions*. The scene emerges with a metonymic clarity and synecdochic significance as a confession. His realizes that most of the mistakes in his life were made because of inadequate formation of intentions and motivations, inadequate reflection, inadequate coherence.

A noise on the stairs broke his reverie and the "dangerous hours were now drawing near" so he "prepared for a hasty farewell." In the narrative, the diegetic voice says that he could see this moment of 19 years earlier "as if it were yesterday,..." especially that last moment, as he left the room and fixed his parting gaze, the natural standpoint of consciousness and his most natural, realistic memory, on the picture of a lovely lady which hung over the mantelpiece, a portrait from which he had a thousand times gained consolation as if from some patron saint, her countenance so radiant with divine tranquillity. As he gazed, he recalled that the clock outside struck six. He began this morning reverie at 3:30 by gazing at the same church tower that was now tolling the hour of six A.M.

This autobiographical narrative is a mimetic sequence of interior voices representing various points of view which are reflecting on the importance of the recognition of and the formation of intentions and motivations. DeQuincey uses the mimetic voice to represent the interior monologue, occurring for the two and one-half hours that he stood in the room, along with his own diegetic commentary at the 19 and then 30 years distance. A diegetic voice, as part of the mimetic one narrating many years later, not part of the mimetic one in the room, represents the series of acts of consciousness which remember, comment upon and evaluate a visit to the Whispering Gallery of Saint Paul's Cathedral. Another diegetic voice represents the series of acts of consciousness which remember and comment upon the entire morning. I believe that this confessional narrative of DeQuincey reveals and explains how motivations and intentions are formed and the intentions and motivations are the key, metonymic elements that need to be revealed in a confessional narrative.

Leaving Manchester, visiting the Whispering Gallery, seeing Lord Nelson's tomb and the flags were significant actions, events, in DeQuincey's life to the extent that they caused him to focus on his own hierarchy of attitudes and intentions, their formation and execution, and their effects in his life.

The utterance of these words in this autobiographical narrative are constituted in 19 years and then 30 years of decisions and actions based upon formations of degrees of sincerity and honesty and hierarchies of intentions and motivations. Leaving Manchester, visiting the Gallery and the tomb, and later, taking opium, are synecdoches representing DeQuincey's life and the point he is making in this narrative unit in his *Confessions*, based upon his personal experience and his moral-ethical realizations, is that "once a word is uttered, it is irrevocable." Utterance of the words "to leave Manchester or to fight or to take opium" is constituted in the formation of sincere and honest intentions, based on a gestalt of attitudes and motives, hierarchized and categorized, and the words uttered will return to confirm those intentions, attitudes and motivations. The degree of strength of motivation, sincerity and honesty and the hierarchy of equally valuable intentions testifies to the accompanying degree of failure, doubt, "fatality" or success, surety and productivity because the interior act of consciousness which forms, hierarchizes and evaluates is the formation of the intention that constitutes the exterior words and actions.

Norman Mailer

Norman Mailer begins his confessional *Armies of the Night* with the one page article from *Time* magazine which portrays him as the drunken, incoherent "publicity hound." Mailer proceeds with his own 300 page defense with the somewhat cynical words: "now we may leave *Time* in order to find out what happened."[11]

Hierarchies of personal intentions and motivations can be distorted and re-arranged in any number of ways. For the writer of the *Time* magazine article, Norman Mailer was a drunken publicity hound. This synecdochic image is used as the metonymic glue to explain Mailer's behavior at the protest.

> The papers distorted one's actions and that was painful enough, but they wrenched and garbled and twisted and broke one's words and sentences until a good author always sounded like an incoherent overcharged idiot in

newsprint...the motive for their action was distorted and their words were tortured (80);

So Mailer situates his words, actions and motives in his own gestalt of synecdochic images because "if we are not loyal to our own unendurable and exigent inner light, then some day we may burn (54)." Norman Mailer's *Armies of the Night* becomes a confessional narrative in which Mailer attempts to answer the distortions of the press by sequencing his own mimetic voice and diegetic commentary in a metonymic narrative that explains his behavior and so is confessional.

In his book, *The Rhetoric of the Other Literature*, Ross Winterowd examines Norman Mailer's *Armies of the Night* as a "confession." He places Mailer with DeQuincey, Rousseau, and Augustine in terms of the "semantic intention," to reveal the self (or a persona, and in principle it makes no difference...) with a candor that "confesses" to great ability, to genius, as well as to baseness."[12] Winterowd compares Rousseau's candor to Mailer's honesty and DeQuincey's addiction to Mailer's "dipsomania (28)."

> In the confession, the focus is sharply on the author *in propria persona* as he or she goes through a central experience (of conversion, disillusionment, enlightenment etc) (29).

I would like to elaborate briefly Professor Winterowd's accompanying distinction that "autobiography can be impersonal; a confession cannot." Autobiography is "impersonal" in the sense that it can unify and idealize particular apparently heroic states of consciousness, representative events; the autobiographer narrates a story about the self as heroic other in a wondrous activity; whereas the confession can never be impersonal because it reveals and explains motives, intentions, attitudes and desires which may not be so heroic about behaviors and events which may not be so heroic.

The *Time* magazine article portrays the predominant impression of Mailer as the "drinker, stumbling and spewing obscenities (14)" and gives only those parts of his speech at the protest in which the article intimates that Mailer participated because he is a "publicity

Mimetic/Diegetic Voices in Metonymic Narratives 165

hound (13)." Mailer will address these personal questions of his drinking, the obscenity and his desire for publicity as he proceeds to examine his motives in greater detail.

He admits at the outset that he was not "particularly pleased" about "standing in a large meadow listening to other men make speeches (19)" but he "warily accepted" the invitation to speak at what he felt would be a "wasted weekend (20)."

> --but wit or no, grace or grace failing, it was bitter rue to have to root up one's occupations of the day, the week, the weekend and trot down to Washington for idiot mass manifestations which could only drench one in the most ineradicable kind of mucked-up publicity...He wondered if he would burn or surrender his own draft card if he were young enough to own one and he did not really know the answer. How then could he advise others to take the action, or even associate his name? Still, he was going to be there....he could hear the sound of his own voice and it offended him. It seemed weak, plaintive,...phony (30,32).

Clearly, there is an honesty about his lack of enthusiasm for this event. But the thought of a "captive audience" who would "titter and rise" appealed to his "showman's instinct" and so he supports the press belief that he may indeed be somewhat of a publicity hound (39), although he prefers the word "showman."

He became very involved in the drama of the event, the staging. At one point, as he waited in line and someone started shouting to hurry up and get moving, Mailer reflected that the voice was not right, it didn't have the right "ring" to it and the unsettled, wrangling dialogue of the marchers to "hurry up" was "wrong." Mailer wanted to re-write the script of the march (129) so as to make some kind of deeply felt intentional-motivational consciousness ring from the protestors mouths.

> He was fond of speaking in public because it was thus near to writing. An extravagant analogy? Consider that a good half of writing consists of being sufficiently sensitive to the moment to reach for the next promise which is usually hidden in some word or phrase just a shift to the side of one's conscious intent (40).

Mailer was concerned about what he would say and how he would look and he has varieties of speculations about himself as a "fair country orator (49)" or a "frustrated actor (65)." He jokingly talks about himself as being as "full of shit as Lyndon Johnson (63)" and then in the privacy of the confession, he admits quietly that "that is probably exactly what you are at this moment (63)." He admits at the beginning of his book that he is writing the history of an event as a person who was not central to the event which he says brings "competence and honorability of motive into question (67)" and he resolves to "look at his mind," the intentions and motivations therein.

Mailer detested the thought of getting through the oncoming hours. Under the best of these circumstances the nature of these heroics was too dry, too dignified, too obviously severed from bravura to make the Novelist happy (69-70).

He admits that he is "sufficiently devil-ridden to need a little action from time to time (83)." He reflects on the fact that he, "Lowell, and MacDonald are liberal academics...certainly not suited for jail...and aware of how their careers may be diverted and impeded...but they were each attempting in some way to break the mold of their own security (92)."

He also wanted to get back to New York in time for a dinner party on Saturday night and didn't want to risk an arrest that might inconveniently carry over into Sunday or Monday (100). He indeed did not want to risk anything more than a few days. He was "secretly afraid that too much would happen or too little" but he was sure that he had "one decent motive" and that was to give "good example to others and excite others to further effort (137-8)."

> One did not march on the Pentagon and look to get arrested as a link in some master scheme to take over the bastions of the Republic step by step, no, that sort of sound-as-brickwork logic was left to the FBI. Rather, one marched on the Pentagon because...because...and here the reasons became so many and so curious and so vague, so political and so primitive, that there was no need, or perhaps no possibility to talk about it yet, one could only ruminate over the morning coffee (102-103).

Using the mimetic device of dialogue between himself and a reporter, he states his intentions and motivations followed by a paragraph of diegetic commentary:

> "Why were you arrested, Mr. Mailer?"..."I was arrested for transgressing a police line."..."I am guilty," Mailer went on. "It was an act of protest to the war in Vietnam."
>
> "Are you hurt in any way?" asked the reporter.
>
> "No. The arrest was correct."
>
> He felt as if he were being confirmed. (After twenty years of radical opinionism he was finally under arrest for a real cause.)....now he felt important in a new way. He felt as if he were a solid embodiment of bone, muscle, flesh and vested substance,... (157)

This excerpt illustrates my point that a mimetic narrative, complete with dialogue and direct quotation may also be accompanied by a diegetic voice who comments on the mimetic. In a confessional narrative, the mimetic/diegetic voices seek to explain and connect, as this one does in Mailer's case. However, the use of mimetic/diegetic voices in narratives can also be representative of heroic, significant events or events which are similar, metaphoric.

Another significant fact about Mailer's motivations lies in the very title of the book itself. He had this fantasy that "before he was done, he would lead an army (107)." Ironically, they are protesting armies and war and they become an army themselves. But this revelation makes a significant connection in explaining Mailer's behavior.

His speech upon release from prison is motivated by a desire to say the right thing because the media is there, the world is listening, history is being made and he wants to say something important, significant, and persuasive against this war. He _is_ the publicity hound that _Time_ magazine says he is but he has other motives as well which take precedence over the public recognition.

He feels that one of the most effective ways to make a point about the horror of this war is to make some reference to religion and the religious life of the nation. He intends to say something significant to the media and contribute to the end of the war and he feels that a religious frame would win the hearts of his listeners. This is a metonymic, confessional revelation explaining a particular behavior within the protest itself.

But the fact of the matter is that Mailer is admittedly not very religious nor has he shown any interest in religion. He decides to mention that his wife is Christian which fact should give him a right to talk about Christianity. It does not matter that he is not a Christian nor that he knows little about his own wife's Christianity. The references will serve his final goals (publicity, end the war) so they are of use. His motivation is as follows:

> A protest movement which does not grow loses power every day, since protest movements depend upon the interest they arouse in the mass media. But the mass media are interested only in processes which are expanding dramatically or collapsing. Active civil disobedience was therefore essential to give glamour and publicity to the demonstration--a page-one story for Washington must instead become a page-one story for the world (259).

Therefore, how can Mailer get a page-one story out to the world? What could he say to have that kind of impact? Maybe by making reference to Christianity based upon the fact that this is Sunday and most people are in church praying and loving each other while we are "burning the body of Christ apart in Vietnam" (239, 240) might be a good opener. The country is basically built on Christian ethics and values, "the foundation of this Republic, which is the love and trust of Christ (239)."

There are a hierarchy of values and goals here and a hierarchy of intentions and motivations about those goals. His first priority is to contribute to an end of the war in Vietnam by participation in this protest. He is motivated to participate in the protest and risk being jailed or having his reputation ruined. He hopes that an occasion will arise when he can give a speech and make a significant statement that would make front page, world wide news. He himself admits that there is something strange about his reference to Christianity and bringing his wife into the speech, especially since he never really talked to her about her Christianity. He admits this by ending his speech with the editorial, diegetic comment: "He was silent. Wow. And Boyle gave him a sidelong look, as if to say, "Watch it, old buddy, they put junior reverends in the cuckoo house for carrying on (239)."

According to Cardinal Newman's distinction between formal intention and material execution of intention, Mailer's formal intention is to end the war and make a significant statement that will get in the newspapers and will directly influence the ending of the war. So he materially executes that formal intention by making reference to Christianity and religion. He uses the rhetoric of religion as an external, material way to further a formal, interior goal of his own. The rhetoric of religion is paired with two interior intentions: maybe it will help to get my statement into the newspaper and maybe it will help to end the war.

According to Kenneth Burke, these formal, interior intentions and material, external execution of them must not be conveniently, nor randomly paired with each other. For Burke, there is a gestalt of external, material activities taking place at this protect in Washington and there is a gestalt of internal, formal activities taking place in Mailer. They are both concerned about ending the war in Vietnam but Mailer has other intentions, feelings, motivations of his own which he brings to this common cause.

My point in using Mailer is that the media may cause the reader to see Mailer as the drunkard, the publicity hound and the manipulator. His confessional narrative does not necessarily remove these, it just develops them, explains them and connects them more clearly than the media does. His narrative voice puts them into a different, a Burkean perspective, and makes the reader more sympathetic to Mailer than does the bare, factual statement of selected, brute facts by the media.

Norman Mailer speaks in his own voice. He re-presents his own voice as he remembers hearing it in the protest. He comments on the voice and the motivations and intentions of the protestor behind the voice. He tells what his acts and states of consciousness were at the time in the face of newspapers and magazines who were telling the world what they thought they were. His autobiographical document is a confessional defense which reveals (mimetically) and explains (diegetically) motives and intentions in a metonymic narrative.

Andrew Greeley

Andrew Greeley entitles his autobiographical document *Confessions of a Parish Priest* which document mimetically and diegetically explores and metonymically explains and connects the various voices which accompany the synecdochic unification in one person of three metaphoric vocations of priest-novelist-sociologist. He explains diegetically how the voice appropriate to a parish priest mixes with the apparently contradictory voices of the so-called "dirty" novelist and sociological researcher. He diegetically attempts in a mimetic, narrating voice to put the past metaphoric/synecdochic voices and experiences, which seem to be contradictory and incompatible, into a confessional narrative that will metonymically link the different voices and perspectives into a hierarchy, a gestalt, that will satisfactorily explain them. In some cases, he follows Newman's pairing of particular formal, interior intentions and motivations with specific, selected, material goals and ends. In other cases, he follows Burke's gestalt of perspectives among perspectives, most notably the complex, controversial gestalt of priest-sociologist-dirty novelist.

He states near the beginning that he is first and foremost the parish priest to which the novelist and sociologist are subordinate/complementary roles. The parish priest then becomes a synecdoche and the novelist and sociologist become metaphoric replacements of equal value. But the matter for confessional revelation is that apparently the successful novelist or sociologist often take synecdochic preference over the priest. His metonymic link is his professing to be a storyteller.

> I'm a priest. Not a priest-sociologist or a priest-journalist, or a priest-novelist, or any multiple variations of these hyphenates. I'm a priest, a parish priest. The other things I do in life: sociological research, journalistic writing, storytelling, are merely ways of being a priest. I decided I wanted to be a

priest in second grade, have never changed my mind, and have never had any doubts....Only the innocent or the ignorant will deny that priests have been artists, scholars, storytellers, writers, journalists, tentmakers, fishermen, kings, architects, stained-glass makers and virtually everything else that is human in the course of Christian history.[13]

He proceeds to explain the consciousness of the priest who writes dirty novels and the priest who conducts sociological research which research will upset the church hierarchy and who was apparently "out to get Cardinal Cody (410)."

He says that "the sheer raw vividness and power of his memories are what constrain him to turn to fiction writing (15)." The so-called "steamy" novels are not dirty or pornographic, they are just an expression of the "imaginative dimension of his personality (87)," his vision of God, life, the church, on which his memories feed. He devotes an entire chapter to a study by a Professor Ingrid Shafer and a sociological study he himself did on his own work to find out what his readers really feel.

He correlates the secular storytelling of the novelist with the religious storytelling of the priest by saying that religion itself finds its origin in storytelling and the use of this raw power of imagination and memory to transmit heritage (87).

Quoting the theologian James Dunn, Greeley "defends" himself as a novelist:

> ...the life of the Christian Church can go forward only when each generation is creatively able to reinterpret the gospel and common life out of its own experience of Spirit and word which first called Christianity into existence. (Dunn) (317)....To understand how a parish priest became a novelist as part of being a parish priest, you have to realize what twenty years of reflection on the sociological approach to religion did to my thought processes, my perspectives, my imagination, my prayer life. I was trained in the seminary to reflect on religion from the top down---from dogma and theology down to practical programs---and learned in Christ the King [parish] to work with religion from the bottom up---from human problems and needs to religious responses. Sociology taught me to reflect on religion from a yet third perspective---from the empirical evidence of the sacred to the articulations, imaginative and propositional, by which we try to share our experiences with others and to represent them to ourselves (317).

Sociology, religion, memory and imagination, feed his novel writing. The sociological research taught him to re-think his religious life, especially the function of storytelling in that life. He predicts that storytelling in novels and screenplays will soon come into alignment with church ministry and evangelism as valid ways of proclaiming the good news (231).

The social sciences were a new way for him to reflect religiously upon the idea of the sacramentality of the created world. Jesus is the "sacrament of God" and Jesus' parables, his stories, are the best insights into his person, his consciousness, the divine and human natures. Greeley says that he learned from Mircea Eliade that myths were not fictions but stories purported to tell about the Really Real, the essentials (225). Greeley sees himself as a Catholic presence, a sacrament of the created world in the created world, in the secular academy through his sociological research and his novels. He is intense about his community and institutional loyalties even though institutions and communities have marginalized him.

There is then a variety of intersections of states of consciousness: the priest-sociologist-novelist triad interacts with his perception of himself as marginal to each of those communities. He says that he is "marginal" simply because he is this "odd blend" of priest-sociologist-novelist. "My canonical status was moving me to the fringes of the institutional church at the same time that my professional standards and intellectual concerns were pushing me to the margins of the priesthood (249)." He considers those "blessed" who are on the margin as he is (419) and with his appointment to the University of Arizona and the Diocese of Tuscon, he perceives himself as a marginal member of different communities and cities. The important fact about this "marginal" idea is that it makes each experience and each voice a metaphoric replacement for the other. No one voice, no one vocation, stands out as central, synecdochic because they are all marginal voices in that particular community of voices. The synecdochic voice of the priest then becomes a metaphoric one when it is heard as marginal in the community of priests.

There came the time then when his "energetic, self-confident intelligence" indicated to the seminary and church officials that he was "up to something (156)." People became suspicious of him; he became more and more marginal and he had to defend himself. There were questions about his behaviors that needed explaining, connecting. In retrospect, he is impressed with how naive, unsophisticated and youthful his early books are but he still stands by them as right (161-2). He had things to say then and he wanted them said.

Greeley feels that there are myths that have been propagated about him and this autobiographical piece of writing is in many ways a defense, as much as it is a memoir, an autobiography, or a confession, where he reveals and explains the intentional structure from which came the voices of priest-sociologist-novelist and from which came the "myths" about each of these. His sociological writings and studies and his novels are acts of consciousness themselves which attempt to clarify points of view taken which he felt were important (174). "This volume (his *Confessions*) is primarily an articulation of my own spiritual development and self-awareness" and priest, sociologist, novelist are significant aspects of himself even though he feels marginalized in these communities.

He takes all the negative criticisms and myths about himself and turns them around not only by quoting Mircea Eliade's definition of myth but also Oscar Wilde who said that myth and caricature are the compliments that mediocrity pays to the genius, the marginal man (195). In other words, for Greeley, being a priest-novelist-sociologist are three central, significant aspects of his personality. But the communities of priests, sociologists and novelists have either ostracized or marginalized or mythologized him and his work in these areas. The church gets angry at his sociological research and insights and his dirty novels. Literary critics wonder why a priest writes such novels.

The basic thrust of his chapter on "The Unmaking of a Cardinal" is of course to clarify the myth that he had a poor relationship with Cody and was "out to get him." "We were both out to get each other," he says. And of course if the story is a myth, then there must be some grain of truth to it. His relationship with Cody was not "mediocre" to be sure. But the point is that Greeley was demanding a confession from Cody and he here confesses that he demanded this confession.

> Are you not ashamed of what you did to Cardinal Cody? I'm frequently asked....Can't you leave the cardinal alone now that he's dead? Haven't you done enough to harm him already?
> My intent is not to do anything to the cardinal. It never was. My intent was and is to tell the truth, not because it will have any immediate practical consequences, but so that it will be on the historical record (407).

His directed intention is to "set the record straight and tell the truth" not to "do anything to the cardinal." If he is going to set the record straight and tell the truth, there will have to be some defamation of the cardinal's character. He (and the *Chicago Sun-Times*) gathered all of their information about the Cardinal--poor administrator, unpopular, racist--and got a Federal Grand Jury Investigation going during which time, not surprisingly, the cardinal died and the case was dropped.

Interestingly, Greeley still does not want it dropped because this "monumental antisocial character" has "harmed the church in Chicago (419)" to such an extent that it will take "long after the end of this century (419)" to repair and the "bland mediocrity" of the present administration has "buried it (the Cody scandal) in cement."

At the same time that Andrew Greeley feels as strongly as he does about this anti-social man who destroyed 'his' Chicago, he also wants to redeem himself of any implications that he set out to "get" Cardinal Cody. He wants to get rid of the myth that he did have something to do with it. But his own story in his own autobiography confesses that there was some degree of this motivation evidenced in his private papers marked "Personal and Confidential." And his own admission about the value of storytelling is that where there is myth, there is some truth. His love for his hometown of Chicago motivates him to pursue Cody. He is pairing an honorable motivation with a not-so-honorable material execution of that motivation.

The details of the Cody myth go like this (416 ff.), according to Greeley: A staff member from the Notre Dame alumni magazine asked if he could do an article on Greeley for the magazine. Greeley consented to week long interviews and then allowed the staff member to return to Rosary College and gave him permission to look at the manuscripts of his books. It seems that the writer also looked at his diaries and personal papers marked "Personal and Confidential" from which the news writer gathered his information about a "plot" by Greeley to "get" Cody. Greeley phoned Rosary College and asked why this writer was given permission to see his personal and confidential papers and diaries. The answer he was given by the librarian suggested to him that *she* was "out to get *him* (417)." Greeley requested the return of his property which the writer denied.

The writer then produced a 100 page document linking Greeley with a plot to get Cody but it was never published. No link has ever been made, and "none was or can be (418)," asserts Greeley. Greeley says that the editor of the Notre Dame magazine and this writer violated his trust but I say there was obviously something in those personal papers, letters and diaries which indicate that Greeley would have been highly motivated to "get" the Cardinal even though no proof can be supplied that he made any efforts in that direction. The very language used and the general sentiment of this chapter on "The Unmaking of a Cardinal" indicates Greeley's deeply-felt hostility towards the man for "destroying" his home town. Greeley is the villain "on the margin" in this chapter on Cardinal Cody in which he makes Cody the apparent villain-protagonist, who, also unconsciously is made a marginal man and a kind of tragic hero whose flaw may have been his anti-social character defect and Andrew Greeley's tragic flaw may be his need to have the last word, "be right," and save Chicago.

My point is that Greeley's unsympathetic attitude belies the desire, if not the actual machinations, of a plot to get the cardinal. One marginal man is out to get another. He may have intended to free himself from implication in a plot to get Cardinal Cody but in many ways he freed Cody himself from the myth that Cody himself was so tyrannical. Besides having varieties of intentions where some of the less honorable ones serve the more honorable ones, Greeley also has intentions about which he is unaware. He asserts so strongly and confidently, with great sobriety, rationalism and logic, that the church, especially the church in Chicago, needs to be re-vamped and run in very particular ways. He offers legitimate criticism of Vatican II and it's implementation, the procedure for the election of popes (since he experienced three popes in one year, and two elections) and Cody.

I think that the myth of Greeley and Cody is set in fact and as much as Greeley may have tried to diffuse it, the fact underlying the myth remains that Greeley certainly would have liked "to get" Cody, as Mary McCarthy would have liked to get her mean uncle Myers. And his guidelines for running the church are all indeed wonderful, well-thought out, "sociological," but I think there is not enough accent on the faith and trust that is willing to give oneself over to a fallible, human system as it is and not as one wishes it to be or predicts that it will be or demands that it should be in the light of Vatican II. Like the King in his own parable with which he ends the book, Greeley wants to take a little bit of his own little kingdom with him.

Perry Edward Smith

Truman Capote braids into his non-fiction novel, *In Cold Blood*, a number of autobiographical pieces by Perry Edward Smith among which is Smith's own written statement to the court psychiatrist in which he attempts to explain his life so as to explain his criminal act. The statement is a metonymic narrative in which Perry's present, mimetic, narrating voice seeks to present his past mimetic voice in various representative situations which he will diegetically comment upon as a way to explain this murder with no apparent motive.

Part of Capote's activity in the novel is not only to give a "true account of a multiple murder and its consequences" but also to investigate the state of a consciousness that would murder "in cold blood." Capote interlaces the pieces of writing by Perry with direct quotations by Perry taken from Capote's interviews with him and other documents not included in the novel like the pile of letters written to Capote by Smith over the 5 year jail period before Smith's execution and a final 100 page document written by Perry about the philosophy of George Santayana.

Capote gives voice to a formation of and hierarchy of motivations and intentions underlying Perry's criminal act and his criminal state of consciousness. The nature of the criminal consciousness seems to rest with the criminal's life experience of rejection and hatred which distorts his desires, motives and intentions. Because of Capote's five-year personal relationship with Perry, he is able to show other sides of his consciousness, other motives and intentions, which are at odds with the criminal acts and motives. The inclusion of various documents and quotations is to "create an impression of character rather than narrate an event."[14] Capote suspends the mimetic narrative ordering of events surrounding the murder so that he can diegetically expose the "depth and complexity of the character of Perry Smith" through autobiographical materials and quotes. Capote "characterizes Perry in depth," at the same time and "inseparable from" his revelation of Perry's violent actions in the Clutter home.[15] The "strongest element in the book" is the "extraordinary access"[16] that Capote gained to the criminals' minds represented in the many viewpoints given about Perry. Capote exemplifies in Perry Kenneth Burke's "perspective among perspectives" idea. Capote selects certain primary source materials, documents actually written and saved by Perry himself, and in so doing captures fragmentary aspects of Perry's mimetic voice that Capote diegetically connects with the murder.

Perry is the most interesting character in the book because Capote "always had a feeling for the loner, the lost one, the unloved, the fatherless"[17] based upon his own unhappy childhood.

> Perry Smith is perfectly, patly, and in almost every detail a spooky embodiment of Capote's earlier fictional creations. He has all the right characteris-

tics: a rich and childish imagination, his dreams... his physical deformity...his sensitivity...even his family background."[18]

In the light of Capote's earlier work, Smith is "the total symbol of exile, the alienated human being, the grotesque, the outsider, the quester after love, the sometimes sapient, sometimes innocent, sometimes evil child."[19] Capote admittedly agreed in an interview that "Perry was a character that was also in my imagination...[he] could absolutely...[have stepped] right out of one of my stories."[20]

> He presents a premeditated murder performed in cold blood...as an unpremeditated murder performed in a fit of insanity...by imparting conscience and compassion to Perry...inner sensitivity, poetry and a final posture of contrition in his hero.[21]

> [But] the presence of the Clutters and their brutal murder within the same pages as the men who so vagrantly murdered them denies us, or should, recourse to sentimentality...to any special call on our tenderness towards them ...Perry Smith's life story is "so casebook as to be a cliche"...[22]

Capote's predominant attitude towards Perry is that he is indeed one of the world's poor unfortunates who was "unloved, unaccepted and had a hard life" and so developed into a criminal whose consciousness then told him never to submit to anyone because no one loved or accepted him. The criminal consciousness required that Perry fight for attention, acceptance and love achieved through the anti-social, criminal behavior.

Perry supplements a narrative that his father submitted with his reminiscence that before his father was able to bring him home, a series of Catholic orphanages became homes for him where he was beaten for bed-wetting and for being an Indian (his mother was an Indian). These autobiographical testimonies obtained by Capote in interviews with Perry contribute again to Capote's contention that the criminal consciousness is formed by continued experiences of being unloved and rejected resulting in the compulsive need to be one's own boss and the equally compulsive need to work for acceptance and love but to work for this acceptance and love in radically anti-social ways. He kills the Clutters because they were there and he could vent all of the pent up anger.[23] He kills the Clutters in an act that in and of itself says, "I am not well; I need help; I don't know how to ask for and accept love and recognition."

Perry remembers his father as someone who was perceived by others as strange and the father remembers Perry as being strange. There is the emotional affinity of father for son but there is also an emotional distance caused by the fact that they were afraid of each other's "strangeness" and their needs to be their own bosses.

Perry seems to have always seen himself as the prisoner and criminal. In his autobiographical statement to the court psychiatrist, Perry recalls being "frightfully scared (308)" when his father beat his mother or he was pushed away by his brother as being "too small" to shoot a B.B. gun. He testifies that incidents like these only contributed to the keen insight he has about himself that his "mounting anger (308)" finally vented itself on the innocent Clutters. The "mounting anger" is the result of these years of rejection and hatred. He is angry because he has spent his life working compulsively for a love and acceptance which most people come by naturally in the family unit.

When a person does not receive love and acceptance, as when she doesn't get food, clothing and shelter, she will fight for them and work for them because she needs them. Most healthy people give and take love and acceptance naturally, freely. When there has never been this free, natural give and take, then the compulsive, unnatural give and take of the criminal is an alternative, a solution. Perry behaves compulsively, unnaturally and he knows it because he feels it and so the "anger mounts." His overall point of view towards his own life is based on his experience of it as "a hard one." The mood of his autobiographical statement, its tone, is intended to elicit pity and mercy from the court for a person who "knew not what he was doing." He was acting compulsively. His autobiographical statement is reliable in that it expresses as closely as possible what he feels generally about his life and because it was written at this very significant, critical, self-interested moment. Perry takes the facts as he remembers them and compares and contrasts them around a unified, synecdochic perception of his life as "hard, difficult." He intends these memoirist comparisons and contrasts and these syneocdochic insights about himself to be the metonymic glue in his confessional narrative about the murders.

He is a man who has been formed into one who wants to "do something" to "all people who made fun of him (310)." He demolished a Japanese cafe, stole a Japanese taxicab and had "many violent outbursts of anger (310)" while in the service. These are metaphors of his interior life. The mass murder of the Clutter family is *the* synecdochic representation of his accumulated anger. And Capote's book and Perry's autobiographical statements in the book are metonymic fragments that connect the metaphors into a confessional narrative. He ends his statement by saying that he has much more that he would like to tell the psychiatrist but the statement needs to be concluded. Truman Capote supplements the "much more" about Perry in his non-fiction novel.

Capote permits the reader to experience Perry as a person who was unable to form intentions and motivations, who did not know his own consciousness, except the compulsive motivation to be loved and accepted, obsessively intended and obtained. He merely acted and reacted compulsively and it was only during his five years in prison that he examined his motivations and intentions, his life story, in a retrospective attempt to integrate and connect it.

Capote selects other little memorabilia articles which build his inferred point of view about Perry. They are the metonymic fragments of this confessional narrative. He includes an interesting segment based upon this theme of "few people really knowing him" during which Perry told Capote what he would say if called upon to give a speech.

The text of Perry's "spontaneous" speech begins with the assertion that he would pretend that he forgot what he was going to say when in fact it was written down and prepared long ago. This is another example of a dovetail between fiction and nonfiction, illusion and reality, within the real itself. And this is exactly the interesting, ironic interplay here. He has written out a speech for a celebration that would honor him which he has memorized and he will then pretend to speak it spontaneously when he is called upon to "give a speech" at this fictional dinner in his honor.

This nonfictional speech paired with this fictional group of people who love and care for him and are honoring him at a dinner is in ironic contrast to the fact that there is no such group of people who love him and care for him; there are actually groups of people who want to execute him, get rid of him. Perry diegetically imagines what the mimetic circumstances surrounding a spontaneous moment of speech-giving at a dinner in his honor would be and structures that spontaneous moment in his imagination. This is a voice within him that has never been heard in a circumstance that has never existed.

The overriding, predominant feeling of the speech is that he is "very, very glad at this wonderful, rare moment for which so many people are responsible (170)." In terms of point of view, this anecdote is indicative of a consciousness that wished it was otherwise than it was; he wished that people knew him and loved him; he wished that he could make himself known and lovable; he fantasized that many people did know and love him because he had this speech prepared and written in which he thanked these people for their love and honor. The actual, real point of view of Perry Smith the criminal is that no one loves him or honors him and he is prepared only for that spontaneous hate which erupts in words and actions of hate, ultimately this mass murder.

On the other hand, the consciousness that prepares a speech to be given at a banquet in his honor by people who love and respect him is the obvious complementary, healthy point of view of one who feels that he is lovable and can love others in "spontaneity" and freedom. In one place, Perry remarks that "few people actually know him" and in another place he points out that he is capable of "being known" and is capable off a "rare and wonderful moment" in his honor. His point of view that "few people actually know him" is complemented by the fact that Capote knew him and loved him and allowed him to speak spontaneously and freely for five years.

The narration of a set of facts about a particular experience or person from a particular point of view is what makes up the narrative voice with its variety of intentions, motivations and desires. These autobiographical documents selected by Capote for his book are part of a precious group of autobiographical memorabilia, a "bulky, messy, assorted archive" which was an "apologia and a guarantee of identity for this man," and it was difficult not only for Capote but for Perry himself to try to decide what to throw out and leave behind---books, maps, letters, songs, poems, souvenirs---"the stuff of which Perry feels he is made and the stuff of which biographies and autobiographies are written....the stuff always set his emotions racing---self-pity, love, hate and released unwanted memories of his childhood (152)."

Truman Capote, over the five to six year period that he spent researching this novel, developed a love and respect for, a relationship with, Perry Smith that was reciprocated. His point of view towards Perry was influenced not only by his investigative research but also by his personal experience of and feelings for Perry. Capote apparently intended to make a diegetic statement about the nature of the criminal consciousness at the same time that he made a mimetic statement about his relationship with the real Perry Edward Smith. Like Norman Mailer, Capote's book gives narrative voice to Perry Edward Smith in a way that the newspapers and courts didn't and couldn't. I argue that Truman Capote *proves* that Perry Smith *is* capable of a submissive-loving relationship with him as the novelist. He proves that Perry was able to submit to him and form a relationship based on love, acceptance and affection where the need for criminal, anti-social behavior recedes into the background and a co-operative Perry Smith emerges. Perry worked together with Capote in the writing of this novel and some limited experience of love, acceptance and happiness were the by-products for both of them.

Conclusion

The confessional mode of autobiographical writing is the most stimulating and attractive to readers because their curiosities are excited by the prospect of a confession in which answers, revelations and explanations are expected. If a writer contracts a personal "confession," an autobiographical document, in the title in some way, then readers, expect to hear these clarifications and connections about intentions and motivations behind particular words and behaviors. These are principally metonyms as opposed to replaceable metaphors in memoirs or significant synecdoches in autobiographies. The autobiographical piece of writing is confessional when the present narrative voice mimetically reveals as best as it possibly can the actually experience, the series of voices and acts in the past experience, and when the present narrating voice diegetically comments on, evaluates and explains the accuracy of that mimetic voice. These diegetic comments serve as metonyms connecting the experience into an integrated whole.

Edward Albee's fictional piece focuses on the multiplicity and complexity of connections and interlaces in the palimpsest of the confessional consciousness. The mimetic interaction of George, Martha, Nick and Honey in the drama itself consists of their personal narrations of other mimetic interactions and diegetic commentaries on those interactions of intentions and motives in those narrations.

The non-fictional pieces of course focus on the real confessions of real people and their real lives but, as Albee shows in his play, reality and illusion blend, fiction and nonfiction mix. Andrew Greeley attempts to diegetically justify the unhappy, mimetic alliance of the metaphoric priest/novelist/sociologist. Norman Mailer defends himself and his involvement in a war protest against the inaccuracies in the newspaper reports. Thomas DeQuincey explains the state of consciousness that would lead to a need to justify, defend, apologize for or confess to and Perry Edward Smith, through and with Truman Capote, obviously tries to explain why he murdered the Clutters "in cold blood."

In each case, new traces and connections are revealed in the gestalt of the narrative voices. The feeling is that some aspect of the person's consciousness, some voice, was asleep at the time and they were acting under some other predominant voice or impulse and the confession seeks to reveal and explain the gestalt of these buried or sleeping acts and states of consciousness underlying a particular behavior. A confessional narrative focuses on the fact that a particular voice, a particular perspective, may have been the predominant, synecdochic one at one particular time in an individual's life and that voice may have caused questionable behaviors. The confessional narrative seeks to connect that voice with other buried voices which could have tempered it at the time.

In my final chapter, I will interpret Cardinal Newman's autobiographical writings as confessions where he justifies and defends his conversion, autobiographies where he portrays himself as the student and scholar, and memoirs where he compares and contrasts perspectives in his attempt to come to certitude about his beliefs. Newman's mimetic voices interlace with his diegetic voice in a variety of narratives which are synecdochic, metaphoric and metonymic. The *Apologia* is that synecdochic document which not only seeks to represent his most significant self but it is also a document which contains a variety of narratives which are metaphors for Newman but ultimately, intentionally, it is a document which seeks to explain, confess to and defend his controversial conversion to Roman Catholicism and in so doing is rhetorically a metonymic narrative, containing lesser, metonymic narrative units, which give his life a connectedness, an integration, a wholeness.

"They are not dead but sleeping."[24]

Notes

1 Thomas DeQuincey, *Tales and Prose Phantasies*, Volume XIII, *The Collected Writings of Thomas DeQuincey*, ed. David Masson, (Edinburgh: Adam and Charles Black, 1890), 346.

2 John Henry Newman, *Apologia Pro Vita Sua*, ed. David DeLaura, (New York: W.W. Norton and Company, 1968), 261. All further references to the *Apologia* will be to this edition.

3 Kenneth Burke, "The Four Master Tropes," in *A Grammar of Motives*, (Los Angeles: The University of Southern California, 1969), 503.

4 Kenneth Burke, "The Four Master Tropes," in *A Grammar of Motives*, (Los Angeles: The University of California Press, 1969), 503.

5 Goran Hemeren, "Intention and Interpretation in Literary Criticism, " (*New Literary History* 7, 1, 1975), 72-73.

6 Burton Pike, "Time in Autobiography," *Comparative Literature*, 28 (1976). 326.

7 Angus Fletcher, "Forward," *The Literature of Fact: Selected Essays from the English Institute*, edited by Angus Fletcher, (Columbia University Press, 1976), xxii.

8 Thomas DeQuincey, *Confessions of an English Opium Eater*, Volume I of *The Works of Thomas DeQuincey*, (London: The New Universal Library: George Routledge and Sons, Limited), 85. All further references will be to this edition.

9 Edward Albee, *Who's Afraid of Virginia Woolf?* (New York: Atheneum Press, 1975), 31. Al further references will be to this edition.

10 Elizabeth Bruss, *Autobiographical Acts: The Changing Situation of a Literary Genre* (Baltimore: The Johns Hopkins University Press, 1976), 94.

11 Norman Mailer, *The Armies of the Night* (A Signet Book from New American Library, 1968), 14. All further references will be to this edition.

12 W. Ross Winterowd, *The Rhetoric of the Other Literature*, (forthcoming, the University of Southern Illinois Press, 1990), Chapter 3, page 27.

13 Andrew Greeley, *Confessions of a Parish Priest: An Autobiography* (New York: Simon and Shuster, 1986), 32, 72. All further references will be to this edition.

14 Donald Pizer, "Documentary Narratives as Art: William Manchester and Truman Capote," *Journal of Modern Literature*, (2: 105-118), 114.

15 ---, 116.

16 Jane Howard, "Horror Spawns a Masterpiece," *Life*, 60, (January 7, 1966, 58-76), 70.

17 Tony Tanner, "Death in Kansas," in *Truman Capote's In Cold Blood: A Critical Handbook*, edited by Irving Malin, Belmont, California: Wadsworth Publishing Company, Inc., 1968, pp. 98-102. (Reprinted from *The Spectator*, CCVIII, March 18, 1966, 331-332), 100.

18 George Garrett, "Crime and Punishment in Kansas: Truman Capote's *In Cold Blood*," in *Truman Capote's In Cold Blood: A Critical Handbook*, edited by Irving Malin, Belmont, California: Wadsworth Publishing Company, Inc., 1968, pp. 81-91. (Reprinted from *The Hollins Critic*, III, February, 1966, 1-12), 86-87.

19 Garrett, 90.

20 Jack DeBellis, "Visions and Revisions: Truman Capote's *In Cold Blood*, (*Journal of Modern Literature*, 7, 519-536), 533.

21 Phillip Tompkins, "In Cold Fact," in *Truman Capote's In Cold Blood: A Critical Handbook*, edited by Irving Malin, Belmont, California: Wadsworth Publishing Company, Inc., 1968, pp. 44-58. (Reprinted from *Esquire*, LXV, June, 1966, pp. 125,7,166-171), 57.

22 Diana Trilling, "Capote's Crime and Punishment," in *Truman Capote's In Cold Blood: A Critical Handbook*, edited by Irving Malin, Belmont, California: Wadsworth Publishing Company, Inc., 1968, pp. 107-113. (Reprinted from *Partisan Review*, XXXIII, Spring, 1966, 252-259), 109, 111.

23 Truman Capote, *In Cold Blood: A True Account of a Multiple Murder and Its Consequences* (A Signet Book: New American Library, 1965), 69. 326, 338.

24 DeQuincey, 346.

Chapter Four

John Henry Newman: Autobiographer, Memoirist, Confessor

> I shall be telling this with a sigh
> Somewhere ages and ages hence:
> Two roads diverged in a wood,[1]

I call him an autobiographer, memoirist, confessor to illustrate at the outset the connection between the fiction and the nonfiction, the reality and the illusion of his life. His writing contains synecdochic narratives which put forth an ideal self-portrait. They also contain metaphoric narratives which portray less significant versions of himself and he is classically remembered for his *Apologia* which is a metonymic narrative which portrays an integrated, connected self. His novel, *Loss and Gain*, is a fictional portrait of one Charles Reding and a fictional representation of his nonfiction; an imaginative creation of what really happened to Newman.

I will select certain illustrative sections from three pieces of Newman's autobiographical writing: The *Apologia Pro Vita Sua*, his novel *Loss and Gain: The Story of a Convert*, and Henry Tristram's compilation of some lesser known, shorter pieces of Newman's autobiographical writings.

My point in devoting a single chapter to a single author is to illustrate that one particular autobiographical document of one particular author, whether it be an edition of letters, journals or diary entries or a volume that the writer publishes as a "memoir," "confession," "autobiography," or "novel" will contain varieties of synecdochic, metonymic, metaphoric narrative units whose mimetic/diegetic voices will attempt to unify and balance the consciousness of the writer, or compare and contrast different voices and perspectives of the writer or will reveal, explain or defend particular voices and activities.

In other words, just because the *Apologia* is an admitted defense, a confession, of Newman's conversion and may apparently fit quite neatly into the "confession" category, there are other narrative units and subsections which also contain a synecdochic unification and balancing of consciousness proper to autobiography as well as a metaphoric comparison and contrast of various states proper to a memoir. I will point out similar stresses in the other two documents. Just because *Loss and Gain* is a novel, a fiction, does not mean that there may not be some dovetailing with the nonfiction, the reality and so will contain narrative fictions and voices which will be synecdochic, metaphoric, or metonymic versions and representations of a real self, a real person. Similarly, just because the *Apologia* and Henry Tristram's compilation of some of Newman's lesser known autobiographical documents are considered nonfiction, the real, does not mean that there is not some interlace with fiction, the illusion, and so will contain some synecdochic, metaphoric, metonymic narrative versions and voices which are not real, and are the individual's self-creation.

I will be using certain sections from each of these volumes to indicate where Newman is portraying a unified self-consciousness, where he is comparing and contrasting states and where he is confessing and defending. The *Autobiographical Writings* compiled by Fr. Henry Tristram were pieces that Newman wrote late in his life for his biographer. It contains his narrative of the story of his illness in Sicily which is a synecdochic, representative narrative, which Newman separates as significant. He also narrates in Father Tristram's compilation the story of his invitation to found and govern a university in Ireland, which story is similarly synecdochic. Finally, throughout these short pieces for his biographer, he draws attention to the fact that the single, most significant quality of his life and person was his vocation to be a student and scholar. The conversion to Roman Catholicism is hardly mentioned.

In these shorter documents that Newman wrote for his biographer and which Father Tristram published, he talks about the "change in his state of mind (about himself as a student and scholar) that took place in him in the autumn of 1821," and he says that he described his own feelings at that time in the following passage of his novel *Loss and Gain*,

> He (Charles Reding) recollected with what awe and transport he had at first come to the University, as to some sacred shrine; and how from time to time hopes had come over him that some day or other he should have gained a title to residence on one of its old foundations. One night, in particular, came across his memory, how a friend and he had ascended to the top of one of its many towers with a purpose of making observations on the stars; and how, while his friend was busily engaged with the pointers, he, earthly-minded youth, had been looking down into the deep, gas-lit, dark-shadowed quadrangles, and wondering if he should ever be Fellow of this or that College, which he singled out from the mass of academical buildings.[2]

Newman diegetically expresses his unified sense of his own consciousness of himself as a student at Oriel through his own writings to his biographer as well as through passages like the above from *Loss and Gain*. He unifies his own fictional Charles Reding with himself.

His Synecdochic Self: Student and Scholar

He says in his advice to his biographer and in his writings for his biographer that from the time that he took the stage as the acknowledged leader of the Tractarian Movement, he carefully preserved his correspondence and diaries as the raw material for his biography. He wanted his personal history to be narrated through the medium of his letters. He envisaged his biographer as an editor whose function it would be to arrange the letters in their temporal sequence and furnish them with a simple narrative for coherence and intelligibility (Tristram, 23, 145). This was his idea of an ideal biography. And the *Apologia* is his idea of an ideal confessional defense because he followed the same procedure there that he recommends to his biographer.

Although he wrote the *Apologia* according to the same method, that is, by reviewing, summarizing and quoting from his letters, he sees this document, this biography, as quite different from the *Apologia*. He did not want his biography to be a "panegyric, which would be sickening, but a real, fair, downright account of me according to the best ability and judgement of the writer (Tristram, 24)." His idea was that this volume should be "brief and should consist of the Memoir amplified by family letters (Tristram, 26)."

His attempt to control the writing of his biography was thoroughgoing. He had a series of school exercise books which he labelled "Personal and Most Private." These consisted of recollections of thoughts and feelings on religious subjects from boyhood which he afterwards re-read and destroyed, transcribing some into another book while preserving only the covers of the originals. He was very concerned about who would read and interpret them and he wrote that he wanted them destroyed; he wanted "whoever found them" to burn them without reading them, as the finder would desire in the fulfillment of any wish of his own, concerning earthly matters after his death (Tristram, 145)." Obviously, then, one wonders what Newman wrote in these pages that would be so personal, private and secret that he would wish no one to read them. There seems then to be an autobiographical ideal self, the unwanted panegyric, that Newman wants in the biography by the fact that he is hiding some things as so personal and secret.

In the shorter documents written for his biographer, he indicates that he wants himself portrayed as the student and scholar, the founder of the university and leader of the Tractarian movement. These are diegetic summations indicating the unified consciousness found in an autobiography. He wants himself portrayed as the student whose "heart boils over with vainglorious anticipations of success (Tristram, 59)." He says that he "devoted himself to the sordid ambition of success (Tristram, 58)."

His one desire was to get into Oriel College and "obtain a prize for his Essay." He portrays himself as a "good classical scholar...in mind and powers of composition, in taste and knowledge, decidedly superior to competitors (Tristram, 64)."

In his "Memorandum: The Catholic University," he portrays himself, using the words of Dr. Cullen, as "an accomplished scholar and profound divine of our age who has been persecuted and deserves our sympathy and support (Tristram, 64)" and should be appointed the first Rector of this new Irish university. His reminiscence of "My Illness in Sicily" also portrays this balanced, unified view of self as one for whom "God still had work to do (Tristram, 123, 136)." He felt that this illness had a remarkable effect on his life story since it occurred at such a crucial point, just before his return to England and the beginning of the Tractarian Movement in which he played such an important role and from which questions about his later conversion arose. The illness in Sicily is then seen diegetically, retrospectively by him as a synecdoche. It was one event in his life that he separates as significant and representative of his importance.

The founding of a university and the leader of the Tractarian Movement are equal in value and both depend on the recovery from the illness. They are metaphorical then in the sense that they can replace each other as representative of his life but the predominant, synecdochic image overriding and constituting the two metaphoric ones is his perception of himself as student and scholar.

Newman interprets the illness as a time when "God was overpowering his self-will" and he experiences his own "hollowness." He felt little love for others and was unwilling to deny himself. He had come to his intellectual conclusions and convictions based upon one or two truths and no one would sway him from these. He acknowledges that he was rightfully accused of preaching himself and putting forth his own peculiarities as high excellences. Like his reminiscence of his early days as a student and the days when he started the university in Ireland, these days of his illness in Sicily are also remembered and interpreted in terms of this unified portrait of himself which continues in the *Apologia* where he portrays himself as one who is an intellectual leader able to reach certitude about his faith and conversion based upon deduction from rational probabilities and his right to make such deductions for his own life.

These kinds of narratives are at odds with the subsections in the *Apologia* and *Loss and Gain*. *Loss and Gain* is his fictional representation of the conversion process and it contains sections that portray Charles Reding, the protagonist, as having a unified, balanced self-consciousness as well as an awareness of the multiplicity of points of view which are compared, contrasted and commented upon but neither of these writings, the *Apologia* nor *Loss and Gain*, focus on his illness in Sicily nor his founding of the university. Both of them, though, are mimetic re-enactments of his diegetic assertion that he was called to be a student and scholar. His conversion is based upon his perception of himself as a student and scholar and his representation of Charles Reding is predominantly as a student and scholar.

I will be using parallel passages from *Loss and Gain* to support my points about Newman so I need first to clarify his relationship with this novel and its protagonist.

> The following tale is not intended as a work of controversy in behalf of the Catholic religion, but as a description of what is understood by few, viz.,the course of thought and state of mind,--or rather one such course and state,-- which issues in conviction of its Divine origin.
>
> Nor is it founded on fact, to use a common phrase. It is not the history of any individual mind among recent converts to the Catholic Church. The principal characters are imaginary, and the writer wishes to disclaim any personal allusion to any.[3]

This preface indicates that this fictional representation in *Loss and Gain* will be a memoir, an autobiography and a confessional defense of Charles Reding since it will describe the "one course and state" of one mind which mind will discover in its course a unified voice consisting of comparative and contrastive voices and metonymic voices which connect the comparisons and contrasts. In other words, Charles Reding's story is similar but quite different from Newman's. Newman acknowledges the obvious similarities:

> ...it is impossible that the ideal representation should not more or less coincide, in spite of the author's endeavor, or even without his recognition, with its existing instances or champions (*Loss*, 2).

And Alan Hill contributes the following helpful information in his "Introduction" to the 1986 Oxford University Press edition of *Loss and Gain*:

> Newman's own relationship with his fictional hero will always remain something of an enigma. This indeed is part of the fascination of the novel. To what extent is it autobiographical? Charles Reding certainly has much in common with his creator...ascetic ideal,...tastes in music and literature,...Romantic temperament---...Reding belongs to a younger generation ...arrival at Oxford in 1840...totally different stage of development from what Newman had by then reached. The chronology of the novel,...1840 to autumn 1846, is carefully worked out to correspond with the period of Newman's abandonment of the Anglican *Via Media* to the aftermath of his conversion, and Reding's development has been simplified and speeded up to fit into this six-year period.
>
> The novel is not exactly a trial run for the *Apologia*. Nor can Charles Reding be taken as a "portrait" of Newman,..., Some incidents are pure invention...In other places, however, he relies almost entirely on memory and introspection (*Loss*, xiv-xv).

His Metaphoric Selves: The Quest for Certitude

Certitude gained from accumulated probabilities is a doctrine that runs through both *Loss and Gain* and the *Apologia* and contributes to a unification of his consciousness. Absolute certitude, a synecdochic surety and self-concept, according to Newman, results from the assemblage of concurring and converging possibilities, metaphoric selves, cumulative forces and voices which take the possibilities, the metaphors, the voices, perspectives and experiences, one by one in an attempt to see them as isolated probabilities, voices and perspectives, which together constitute the synecdochic self, the mind and will of the person.[4]

Certitude is a "divinely intended (*Apologia*, 157)" habit of mind and a point reached where multiple propositions, a procession of a series of possible doubts, unfolds into a perspective, a point of view, a unified consciousness, that gives the person a sense of confidence and surety that what is said in fact is what is right for the person (*Apologia*, 157). This theory receives full treatment in

Newman's discussion of the ilative sense in the *Grammar of Assent*. For Newman, this "certitude" was a psychological condition, a "constitution of the mind," while "certainty" was a quality of the various propositions, tautologies, empirical arguments, metaphoric selves, used to arrive at certitude,[5] at synecdochic unity of self-perception. The certainty that unites consciousness of the self in autobiography comes from the comparison and contrast of multiple points of view, metaphoric selves, in the memoir and both serve Newman's revelation and explanation in the confessional defense.

Newman's consciousness of himself is as of one who can shape himself and his church by logical arguments into an intelligible, unified, consistent system (*Apologia*, 64). Sound judgement, patient thought, discrimination, a comprehensive mind and an abstinence from private fancies, caprices and personal tastes give him this divinely intended wisdom and certitude of soul (*Apologia*, 64). He bases his conversion on this confidence in this somewhat fictional surety that he can have such clearness and firmness of intellectual conviction. This interior motivation to be sure, to be certain, to prove that his conversion was right for him creates the illusion that he is indeed certain and can scientifically prove it; but he is fully aware, as he proceeds through the *Apologia*, that such proof is virtually impossible. He realizes that he will need to discuss the various circumstances and contexts, hierarchies and perspectives, in an attempt to situate his conversion but he is plagued by this ideal that he can have certainty, that he "know that he knows (*Apologia*, 176)." He denies any influence of memory or emotion, any conviction due to whim or caprice, that would upset an idealized, consistent system with which he can convince his opponents.

His fictional Charles Reding in *Loss and Gain* follows the same process. Individual creeds of different churches are the consequence of historical interpretation and development, as apostles succeed apostles, popes succeed popes, heresies and schisms break off and form new churches, new creedal interpretations develop. Antiquity, the first apostles and fathers of the early church, did not have a creed, argues Charles, they had "principles" contained in the Scriptures by which they lived the Christian lifestyle.

Loss and Gain allows Newman to extrapolate differently than he does in the *Apologia*. The *Apologia* was written quickly and explicitly to counter the accusation made by Kingsley that "truth was not a virtue with Newman."[6] He researches his correspondence at the time of his conversion and writes a retrospective philosophical exposition and theological treatise some twenty years later explaining his position and defending his integrity. *Loss and Gain* allows him to employ a plot line, a mimetic sequence of events, focusing on a particular character. The general pattern of each chapter in *Loss and Gain* is the presentation of a opening gambit, an issue to be treated, followed by a dialogue about that issue by the characters.

Charles argues the ideal, unified vision in *Loss and Gain* that there is one visible church and the Anglican and Roman communions are parts of that one Church. A kingdom may be divided and distracted by parties, dissensions, heresies, sects but it is still a kingdom, a church. The external, received creeds of particular churches are cumulative interpretations of revealed doctrine based upon accumulated probabilities leading to reasonable certitude regarding dogmatic assertions.

Charles is convinced that common sense tells him that when a particular system is consistent, it does not condemn itself. If a system or person intends to deceive, it defeats its own ends. Charles looks at the Anglican and Roman Catholic systems as consistent, probable systems and Charles looks at himself and the system of his own mind as consistent, based upon common sense and rational probability.

The fictional idea that persons like Newman and Reding can be considered unified "systems" in themselves is the one that gives the *Apologia* and *Loss and Gain* their synecdochic impact. Newman is motivated to examine his consciousness as a synecdochic unity and bracket each multiple, metaphoric part into its place and so give his conversion a metonymic force. He has synthesized, organized and constructed his defense so it will be a convincing portrait of an integrated, sincere person. The gaps, inconsistencies and conflicts are not left to stand; they are reconciled and harmonized in some way. His intention to portray himself this way is the overriding motivation behind the *Apologia*.

Newman re-plays his defense through the mimetic voice of his fictional Reding in *Loss and Gain* when he has Reding say that his decision to convert is based upon the fact that he believes that Christianity does not reside in a particular creed but in the principles contained in Scripture. Creeds, sects, are the result of historical development, interpretation of Scripture by scholars, popes, theologians and the development of dogma through successive ages. But in antiquity, for the apostles and early church fathers, there were no creeds; they based their life and reflections on the principles contained in scripture (*Loss*, 87). There was then (and still is) one visible church. The English and Romish churches are parts of the whole (*Loss*, 209). The distractions of parties, dissensions, factions, and heresies throughout history do not deny a unity at the beginning. It is when groups align themselves with a particular preacher or dogmatic/moral stance that religion becomes "party-like" and political. The unified autobiographical consciousness vies with the comparative-contrastive consciousness of the memoirist. These are parallel passages found in the *Apologia* and *Loss and Gain*.

Newman, through Reding, argues that we must allow the fact that there are many metaphoric, interlaced, comparative-contrastive branches to the one church and to one consciousness. The autobiographer focuses on the synecdochic oneness, the memoirist focuses on the metaphoric divisions and the confessor focuses on the metonymic glue, the transitional selves. The church is in fact *divided* but he also says that we need to maintain the *doctrine* or theory that the church is, should be and will once again be one (*Loss*, 211). Individual consciousness is also divided, multiple and inconsistent but such division is organically interrelated, connected, united, however irreconcilably at times.

The variety of dogmatic statements, rules and theories that a particular church group lays down is based upon that particular group's interpretation of scripture. Another group may disagree and so break off and become its own church with its own interpretation. The "whole word" in scripture, at its beginning, is given to a whole church for interpretation but the "whole" church consists of many parts and sects, each offering its own interpretation (*Loss*, 261). The external received creed of a particular church is a cumulation of revealed doctrine, a cumulative wisdom and experience of the fathers, the founders, of that church, built upon probabilities which caused those fathers to believe that they were "reasonably certain (*Loss*, 263)" that their dogmatic pronouncements were correct. Scripture itself as a unified document, the word of God, a consistent system, comes from a variety of sources from different communities of authors.

Through Charles Reding in *Loss and Gain*, Newman again asserts his primary belief that the Church is one from the time of Christ, the apostles and the fathers. The word was handed to them and has been handed down through the centuries resulting in the creation of metaphoric sub-sects, "parties," other churches and it is the job of historians to supply the metonymic glue and not accent the metaphoric diversity.

The unified consciousness discovers a certitude, a finality, a coherent system through a comparative-contrastive analysis of probabilities. But in the course of this examination of probabilities, there is the realization that there is a core, a center, that is unreachable and surrounded by voids and others. Newman can never construct the clear, coherent, organized system of himself that he would like so what he defends in the confession is his right to have this blank space, this incoherence, which he calls his right to that inexplicable personal judgement, a right to privacy. Historians discover that as they research particular moments in history, there is always that missing piece, that metonym, which will connect and make sense of the whole.

I wish to look at two other parallel passages in the *Apologia* and *Loss and Gain*: one where Newman recounts a brief history of dogmatic conflicts in the church in the *Apologia* and another where he has the many different visitors from the different sects visit Charles in *Loss and Gain*. Then I wish to look at the public opinion about Charles Reding's conversion and the public opinion about Newman's conversion as representative of multiple, metaphoric perspectives out of proportion. The public comparisons and contrasts made both Newman and Reding stand out as aberrant and separate perspectives. Newman's point in the recounting of church history is that the nature of a comparison and contrast is that one or more perspectives will stand out of proportion to the others but especially to the publicly accepted one at a particular time in history.

The historical summary in the *Apologia* is predominantly his diegetic comment which compares and contrasts various voices and points of view which came into conflict in church history. The conflicts in church history parallel the conflicts an individual might participate in while attempting to reconcile two or three contrasting voices and perspectives, each trying to dominate the other.

The microcosmic Newman or Reding compare their histories with the macrocosmic church. Each conflict can replace the other as metaphors for doctrinal conflict generally. On the other hand, the dogmatic declaration of infallibility at Vatican Council I is a synecdochic event to the extent that it stands alone as representative of a significant moment. The various conflicts and crises that led to both Newman's and Reding's conversions are similarly metaphoric and replaceable but the conversion itself is a synecdochic, significant event for each of them.

In *Loss and Gain*, Newman uses the mimetic voices of Charles and the various visitors as his own diegetic representation and commentary on the different voices and perspectives as they compare and contrast with each other.

By means of these analogous passages, he links past church conflicts with his present state of affairs. The brief history of dogmatic conflicts in the church and the section in *Loss and Gain* where the different visitors from different sects visit Charles serve as part of Newman's own plea for tolerance, acceptance and understanding when diversity, conflict and multiple perspectives emerge.

In the one case, the "whole" idea or concept of a church unified from antiquity through scripture braids with Newman's own desire for personal unity in his decision. He recalls conflicts in the life of the one church where heresies were countered and new sects were founded and compares and contrasts them in a perspective, a frame, a horizon of relationships, however conflictual. In *Loss and Gain*, the "whole" idea of Charles' unity of consciousness about his conversion is juxtaposed with the series of visitors representing different sects who try to make him convert to their sect.

Newman feels that the problem of the unity of one church from the beginning, rooted in scripture and the church fathers, and the development of various dogmas, creeds, and heresies throughout history, revolves around the fact that individuals are first of all free to think, inquire and theologically speculate and interpret and he asserts that the one church represented by Rome has always allowed such freedom in exploration of issues. There is no *one and only* way until as many probable avenues as possible have been explored. Similarly, Newman comes to a certitude in his decision to convert based upon his personal freedom to explore probabilities and possibilities in his own personal consciousness.

In the *Apologia* (203), Newman points out how St. Augustine formed the intellect of Christian Europe and brought Latin ideas to Africa from which ideas the heterodox Tertullian arose. Origen in the East was influenced by Rome and he in turn influenced the Roman Hilary and Ambrose. The independent mind of the Scripture scholar Jerome enriched the understanding of Scripture through his commentaries. Malchion met and refuted the heretic Petrarch at the Council of Antioch and St. Athanasius intervened at Nicea from which council came the Nicene Creed. St. Anselm set himself against the Greeks at another Council and Bonaventure had an important effect on the development of the dogmatic statements at Trent. Newman himself was invited to Vatican I as an observer. As a good historian, he attempts to metonymically connect the various metaphoric points of view into a synecdochic unity of perspective. The historian, and the autobiographer, can focus on the synecdochic unity, the metaphoric diversity or the particular points where the metonymic glue is revealed.

Church authorities are slow to intervene and force infallible, final statements with regard to dogma and morality. Propositions, controversies and probabilities are allowed to ferment in healthy conversation. Priests, professors, and lay persons dialogue at various levels and stages of learning. Theology faculties at universities consider the questions. The issues are well-ventilated and turned over before reaching Rome for any decision and then that decision may be put off for many years which postponement encourages further dialogue and clarification. Pope Zosimus treated Pelagius and Celestius with extreme forbearance; St. Gregory was equally indulgent with Berengarius; John Paul II, in our own day, has been equally tolerant and patient with the moral theologian-priest, Charles Curran, and the arch-conservative Archbishop LeFebvre, who wants to break off from the Roman Catholic Church and return to the church as it was before Vatican II with himself as Pope and the theologian of papal infallibility, Hans Kung has been allowed to write freely.

Newman's brief historical overview in the *Apologia* parallels his own personal dialogue with himself as he came to his decision. He views the whole problem of the unity of the church in terms of its history, citing the various councils and figures, and he views his own problem of conversion and the unity of his consciousness in terms of his own personal history, citing various letters and relationships. The comparing and contrasting of the parts of consciousness (of the church) contribute to the unification of the whole of one's consciousness (of the church.)

Charles Reding's voice emerges in contrast to and comparison with other voices of other sects who are trying to get him to join their group (*Loss*, 277 ff.). The first visitors are Irvingites who want Charles to join their group so that he can restore the church to its true scriptural state by developing his own dogmas. They know what he wants and they offer it to him. Charles tells the Irvingites that if they are really interested in staying as close to Christian roots as possible, the Roman Catholic Church is the church that *they* should join. The next visitor is a young lady from an unnamed sect who also invites Charles to join and develop and define his own doctrines and dogmas. Then a newspaper reporter arrives for an interview but is actually a convert to Judaism who believes that Judaism was the first religion, not Christianity, which he diegetically considers to be an "episode in history." Mr. Batts arrives as a member of a society devoted to extend to all classes of society the pursuit of truth and they voted to have Charles join them when they heard about his desire to seek the truth. But Charles does not care to align himself with Emperor Julian who appears on the group's crest. Mr. Batts defends Julian as one who followed the truth as he thought and conceived it; the important point being that he pursued truth. Finally, Dr. Kitchen arrives with his Spiritual Elixir, a document, when read, that is sure to cure all spiritual ills. Kitchen invites Reding to write his own such document, start his own denomination and cure the spiritual ills of society.

Both passages fictionally give that sense of the multiplicity of voices and the variety of points of view but the novel does so with a Shandyesque sense of absurdity and humor. Each voice contrasts strongly with what Charles wants to do and believe in but they also compare favorably in that they offer Charles what he wants.

Newman summarizes dogmatic conflicts in history and gives them perspective just as he goes through his own "history of his religious opinions" and gives them perspective. Reding is reminded by all of his visitors of the issues and controversies in his Victorian England and situates his own voice among them.

But each voice, each perspective, at one time was separate, unique and controversial. Both Newman and Reding, along with each of the figures in the historical narrative in the *Apologia* and the fictional one in *Loss and Gain*, have their perspectives magnified and distorted for a time because they appear to be so conflictual and inconsistent. The paradox is that underneath any apparent synecdochic unity to history or to self is merely a metaphoric replacement of various periods or selves and these periods or selves replace each other during a metonymic moment or self. This metonymic or connecting moment or self then becomes synecdochic because it reveals an important connection. And so, with Frank Kermode, I assert that an individual's life, as well as history itself, are a series of metonymic, transitional moments and selves.

Both Newman and Reding have close friends who love and respect them but can't understand their extremist conclusions (*Loss*, 251). The question on everybody's lips, started by Charles Kingsley, was "What exactly does Dr. Newman Mean?"[7] Charles is also confronted with the same conflict with his personal friends and acquaintances. He confesses that he, like Newman, is acting after "great deliberation and over a year or two (*Loss*, 252)." The only real motive to justify this conversion is that "one's salvation depends upon it (*Loss*, 252)." But they both still became marked men by their friends and the public and "stray remarks that he made were treasured up against him such that people seemed to know more about him than he knew about himself."

> Charles Reding was considered by the Vice-Principal of the University to be a young man of promise, ability and morals who should not be guilty of so great an evasion of the authoritative documents of the Church, an outrage to common sense...clear proof that his mind was perverted, debauched, sophistic, subtly Jesuitical (*Loss*, 167-68).

The newspaper account of Charles' conversion is given as follows:

> DEFECTION FROM THE CHURCH: --We understand that another victim has been added to the list of those whose venom the Tractarian principles has precipitated into the bosom of the Sorceress Rome. Mr. Reding,...the son of a respectable clergyman of the Establishment, deceased, after eating the bread of the Church all his life, has at length avowed himself the subject and slave of an Italian bishop. Disappointment in the schools is said to have been the determining cause of this infatuated act (*Loss*, 246).

Charles then had to carry this secret around within him but he realized that some day he would have to tell (*Loss*, 175) and face the fact that he may not be understood and accepted even though he may be able to supply every convincing reason and logical argument (*Loss*, 178). Logical arguments are misconstrued and either mis-interpreted or re-interpreted and come to sound as absurd to Charles as do the newspaper reports when they are juxtaposed with the strength of his interior convictions and feelings (*Loss*, 191). He knows full well the misery he is causing, the ties he is breaking, the loss of esteem, sympathy and friendship, the invitation to exile (*Loss*, 235). His friends warn him of the Becket-complex of doing the right thing for the wrong reason:[8] "The greatness of the sacrifice (and like Norman Mailer, the greatness of the publicity), stimulates you; you do it because it is so much to do."

Newman goes through the same kind of public scrutiny at the pen of Charles Kingsley who analyzes his language with such care and detail that one begins to wonder what Kingsley's motives are. In the midst of the suspicions circulating about him, Newman's Anglican bishop (unlike Charles' Vice-President) writes him a letter in which he expresses his confidence in Newman's personal integrity and Newman includes part of this letter in the *Apologia*:

> So many of the charges against yourself and your friends which I have seen in the public journals have been, within my knowledge false and calumnious, that I am not apt to pay much attention to what is asserted with respect to you in the newspapers....therefore I at once exonerate you from the accusation brought against you in the newspapers (267-68).

The flurry of public attention gives both Newman's and Reding's conversions a notoriety that does not allow them to be a "perspective among perspectives." Newman's historical narrative summary in the *Apologia* and his fictional narrative of the visitors in *Loss and Gain* show how memory may either allow a particular perspective to be placed in a comparative-contrastive position, a gestalt, among other multiple, diverse perspectives or how memory may fictionalize and idealize ('synecdoch-ize') a particular stance by placing it in sharp contrast to others. The narratives show that one particular perspective or stance, like Newman's or Reding's conversions or some particular heresy in church history, may be seen as entirely out of proportion and perspective. The memoirist attempts to juggle and juxtapose these into a coherent, metonymic unity that might capture a truly representative, synecdochic (but not idealized) self or period. Newman admits that the recollections and reminiscences which he wrote for his biographer are only "irregular glimpses (Tristram, 130)" which seem to vanish in the haze. He experiences a "dreamy confusion" when trying to interrelate his memories into a unified consciousness. He says that during his illness, the events of his life came "thick" before him such that he could not recollect the "state of things (Tristram, 134)," that is, he could not give them any autobiographical order or coherence nor could he put them in perspective in memory. He was so ill from the continual pain that many of the memories appear now as "absurdities" and "fantastic dreams (Tristram, 134)." He is amazed that he cannot even remember *how* he got sick; he only remembers the sickness as significant in retrospect in terms of the rest of his life.

Where he admits that there is a fuzziness and distortion to the memories about his illness in Sicily as well as his early school days and the later days of the founding of the university in Ireland, there is at once a clarity of self-concept, an idealized portrait that Newman gives to himself as student, leader of the Tractarians and first Rector of the university. As the memoirist, he may juggle perspectives and admit confusion but as the autobiographer, he emerges with an absolute consciousness of himself as student, writer and educator. As the confessor, he clearly and adamantly defends his right to private judgement and decision.

His Metonymic Self: The Right to Private Judgement

I would like to situate Newman and Reding in my theory that a piece of autobiographical writing is confessional when it's voices and perspectives are metonymic to the extent that they reveal, explain or describe a past voice or act by giving it a connectedness, a unity, an integration. These metonymic voices and perspectives which both Newman and Reding enlist to support their conversions from Anglicanism to Roman Catholicism are revealed, explained and described in the *Apologia* and in *Loss and Gain*.

Newman's most insightful, crucial, metonymic moment was his realization that he has a right to make a private judgment and decision in and about his own life and he uses the parable of the Pharisee and Publican from the gospels[9] to help him make his point. A similarly crucial moment occurs for Charles Reding when he confronts the multiplicity in his own heart in an interior monologue which functions as a metonymic connector or explainer.

In the *Apologia Pro Vita Sua*, the theme of the value and respect for private judgement rings through the defense as a subtext. Newman defends the fact that at one time he argued against Liberalism in the Anglican Church during the Oxford Movement; he "denounced and abjured (*Apologia*, 306)" the "right to private judgement (*Apologia*, 223, 308)" with regard to Anglican law and practice but then uses the same principle to defend his own right to seek his own point of view, to act according to his own beliefs, based on private judgement.

Charles Reding is called "too viewy (15)" by his critics because he won't reveal the central reasoning that undergirds his private decision; they say that he just continually examines probabilities and possibilities and seems to make a random, haphazard decision; and Newman uses the parable of the Pharisee and the Publican and his own parable of a poor beggar woman to indicate that externals do not reveal the heart. Ultimately, amidst all the perspectives and probabilities, there is that place, that center, the core, the heart, which is inexpressible. In the *Apologia*, Newman is attempting to convince his friends and the public that he is doing the right thing but he comes to the ultimate realization that he can't do it. There is that private place in the interior of one's consciousness, a center, that can never be put into language. So he ends up defending his right to have that private place and confessing that he has done his best to explain his position.

The confessional, apologetic voice is of course the strongest one in Newman's autobiographical writings. He is most noted for his *Apologia*. He is motivated to defend his right to private judgement against all the rumors and gossip about him and his judgments. The autobiographical writing that unites and balances various voices and perspectives or compares and contrasts them is left aside here as Newman seeks to defend his right to private judgments and feelings which means that he is free *not* to reveal, confess and explain possibly because he is not able to satisfactorily do so; he can't find the one or two metonyms that will make his argument cohere. He has learned the importance of "weighing words and being cautious about statements (*Apologia*, 20)." People's faults and failings always draw the attention and excitement of the public (*Apologia*, 46). The accused are then called to defend themselves. Newman wonders why he has been called to reveal and explain his private decisions publicly (*Apologia*, 138,140) especially when he feels that those private actions and decisions are his own, "deeply personal (*Apologia*, 140)" and none of anyone's business (*Apologia*, 13).

This is the key, metonymic point in the *Apologia*; it is not so much a revelation and explanation of the journey to conversion as it is a defense of his right to keep such explanations and revelations to himself. Newman says that there are many things that a man may hold which the public has no right to know and which, in fact, the man has no business telling (*Apologia*, 158).

Newman proposes his *Apologia* precisely to prove that the accusation of theological treason is a violation of his own selfhood, "...an invasion of privacy."[10] These reasons, in keeping with his appendix on "Lying and Equivocation," which I discussed in Chapter Three, are obviously an evasion, an avoidance of the central issue that the conversion is inconsistent with earlier behaviors and beliefs and his silence or his defense still leaves the obvious fact that he acted inconsistently. This is the key point in any piece of autobiographical writing where fictionalizing may begin; the writer realizes that there is an inconsistency or gap and so creates the metonym that will connect the narrative.

He himself knows that when he says that no one else can enter his mind and heart but himself that this is obviously an evasion. And part of the confession is the admission that even he can't totally enter his own mind and heart; only God knows him completely.

This issue of private judgement and personal privacy is the key paradox in Newman's position which makes his confession most significant. He categorizes his own intentions and motivations and those in favor of the Anglican church, that were valuable at one time, but are not as valuable now over against his newer feelings, intentions and motivations about the Roman Catholic church. It is as if, according to Sydney Mendel, each man, before going to bed, needs to determine whether his church is in good standing with God...

> Newman wants to be guided by reason, not imagination, duty, not feeling, but what is one man's reason but a private judgement and how can one know one's duty without exercising private judgement?[11]

Newman compares his situation to that of the publican and pharisee in the bible where Jesus warns his listeners that harlots and publicans are entering the kingdom of heaven before scribes and pharisees and this parable points up this central issue of respect for interior life and convictions (*Apologia*, 191). The sheeplike heart of the publican or prostitute is helpless in the face of their sin. They appear to be condemned sinners, rejected by God, but Jesus is saying that no one knows their hearts where there is the inexplicable possibility of change. The wolflike heart of the scribe or pharisee seeks to pile up religious acts so as not to appear sinful. They appear justified before God but Jesus is saying that no one knows their hearts where there may be no possibility of change.

In Newman's own terms, the formal, interior, constitutive act of the Scribe or Pharisee is that which says that the external, material act of accumulating religious acts for others (and God) to see will win interior justification and reward. The Pharisees take the exterior, material acts of following the details of the laws of their religion and put those acts together with the interior, formal intention. The external acts constitute their interior lives. Whereas, Jesus' point throughout the gospels is that it is the interior life, the interior intentions and motivations, that constitute behaviors and laws. The formal, interior, constitutive act, on the other hand, of the harlot or publican or sinner is that which admits to the external, material act of sin. They do not necessarily pair the sin with any particular motivation to intention. Their interior lives do in fact *not* constitute the acts of sin.

There is no interior conversion activity in the scribe or pharisee who says that the conversion activity takes place in the obedience to external laws. The interior state of the sinner is one that is helpless and defenseless in the face of the external behavior, the sin. The interior state of helplessness and defenselessness is the state of "wisdom and innocence"[12] (the title of his controversial sermon)[13] that motivates change. Jesus' point is that individuals' external activities need to be constituted in this wise and innocent state of helplessness, dependence and defenselessness. The scribes and pharisees external activities were constituted in an internal disposition that was dependent and helpless but dependent on a book of written laws and helpless in the execution of that book of laws. They knew nothing else. Jesus own posture of helplessness and defenseless took him to the cross. Newman's own helplessness and defenseless brought him to the realization that he will be unable to fully, satisfactorily explain his conversion because some of it was rooted in that very personal, helpless, defenseless place which says "I really don't know why I am doing this." The recognition of the interior, formal state of helplessness and defenselessness, an openness to movement and change, results in a change in the exterior, material behavior. Both the harlot and the pharisee are sinners then to the extent that they are interiorly dependent on one sort of behavior.

Newman also gives his own example of the "lazy, ragged, filthy, story-telling beggar woman, who, if chaste, sober, cheerful, and religious, had a prospect of heaven, such as was absolutely closed to an accomplished statesman, lawyer or noble, be he ever so just, upright, generous and honorable, and conscientious...(*Apologia*, 191)." Newman compares himself and his conversion to these people. He stopped being an Anglican because he experienced within himself that helplessness and poverty that lets go of a long-held tradition and retreats to silent contemplation and confusion, a searching of that interior poverty to find his real point of view, his real intentions from which and by which he can re-constitute himself, his beliefs and religious practice.

When he enters the experience of silent submission and withdrawal from Saint Mary's for two years, he realizes that all the scribal proofs and Pharisaical defenses and logically consistent treatises and certitudes will convince neither God nor his accusers that he is doing what is right for him. The root lies in the very private, personal, interior awareness of his own helplessness where preverbal, preconscious, unconscious judgments form the center of his conversion and this root, this center, is certainly unable to be articulated and in effect is inaccessible. I shall discuss this inability to articulate and access in my conclusion in relation to Derrida.

Newman admits that his behavior had that "mixture of fierceness and sport...it gave offense (*Apologia*, 48)" and he says he does not intend to defend it or explain it away in the *Apologia*. His duplicit, confusing behaviors did indeed happen but he is at least going to tell the story from his point of view, even if it does not all fit neatly together. And so he sets out in the *Apologia* not to create controversy about any particular church or theological stance but to "relate things as they happened to him in the course of his conversion (118)." His complaint is that he does not want to be forced to feel guilty about things he said in the past or retract his words now that he is a Roman Catholic (*Apologia*, 161). He meant them at the time and they stand now for that time.

He says that in leaving a church that one so wholeheartedly loved and defended demands an immense and painful soul-searching and the ultimate decision to change rests with private judgement. He needed to come to some conviction about his beliefs in retreat (*Apologia*, 147). The "springs of his conversion" began in intellectual investigation and rational study (*Apologia*, 191), a need for certitude about the evidence, but this ultimately gave way to the need to make a decision, take a stand, state his convictions, and convert. His synecdochic need for intellectual certainty kept quelling the metonymic "driving force" of his conscience, his private judgement, the personal, confessional voice of his heart with new metaphors, new arguments, voices and diversions until which time he came to realize that the synecdochic metonym in his defense was his personal salvation, his relationship with God, and they depended on this decision.

He says that the greater the truth, the greater reality, that is involved, the greater the act to be done (like this change of churches), means then that there is a greater risk of gossip, libel, slander and misinterpretation (*Apologia*, 158) because to reach and express the core is impossible. He might pretend to convert because he thought that his career would do better in the Roman Church. The Roman Catholic Church will have better opportunities than in the Anglican. He might pride himself on the fact that he was able to defend so clearly and logically his decision as if there were no presence of mystery involved.

The newspapers reported Newman's intentions to convert, especially when he left St. Mary's. His silence and retreat merely caused more mystery and question about what he was doing and what he meant and the road was open to gossip, prejudice and misunderstanding (*Apologia*, 169). They remember his strong devotion and defense of the Anglican church against the Liberalism of the time and his involvement in its defense in his writings of the Tracts of the Times. They remember that he said that people needed to listen to the Anglican church authorities and not depend on their own private judgement. The point Newman is making is that his external acts always came from interior belief and conviction.

Newman portrays his fictional Charles Reding in *Loss and Gain* as one who was perceived by his fellows as "too viewy (*Loss*, 15)." Charles was always critical and impatient to reduce things to logical, clear systems. He was too fond of argument and did not lay very much to heart. Charles is unable to take his final examinations at Oxford because all the opinions and arguments had caused him to doubt the Thirty-nine Articles of the Anglican Communion and in order to graduate, a student needed to assent to these.

Chapter Three of *Loss and Gain* reflects on this idea of "too viewy" and it is Newman's fictional opportunity to consider the perils of any complex, minute examination of motives, of private judgments and multiple views. When a person penetrates a world like politics or religion, or the multiple world of motivations and intentions in consciousness for the first time, "all that they find there meets their mind's eye as a landscape addresses itself for the first time to a person who has just gained his bodily sight...there is no perspective (*Loss,* 15)." Connections and relationships between names, persons and events are not made. There is no sense of history; the present stands as "round and full, like the moon" and passes before the person like the wind, nothing makes an impression, nothing penetrates, no name, event or person takes on any significance. There is no consistency to arguments; they are indirect, random and change from day to day; they diverge and converge; nothing comes to a point. There is no center in which the mind can sit and on which private judgement can rest and decisions proceed.

Reding reasons that it could appear that these people are "unfettered, moderate, dispassionate, that they observe the mean, that they are not "party men;" when in fact they are the most helpless of slaves; for our own strength in this world is to be subjects of reason and our liberty to be captives of truth (*Loss*, 16)."

And Newman captures this state in this interior monologue (*Loss*, 203) where Charles admits that he wants to be settled in some church, whether English or Roman, but he is so confused at this time that he doesn't even know what Christianity is. "All the paper arguments in the world are not equal to giving one a view in a moment (*Loss*, 203)." Coming to have a point of view, a perspective, a conviction about something, which may be synecdochically significant for the person's life or may just be another metaphoric self asserting itself at a particular time, is a metonymic process that is separate from but conjoined with intellectual conclusions made from premises in syllogisms. Charles can't *will* to believe in a moment nor can he "achieve" belief by logical argument.

In paper arguments, the "words signify the argument on the paper," they stand for "things" rather than represent his feelings, intentions and the convictions of his heart. In the *Apologia* Newman says that he "had a great dislike of paper logic....pass a number of years, and I find myself in a new place; how? the whole man moves; paper logic is but the record of it (*Apologia*, 136)." He concludes in the monologue that he must allow the intellectual-emotional inquiry into his motivations and intentions, goals and ideals, to proceed freely at its own pace. Paper arguments have their own metonymic glue which may only be a part of the explanation of an action.

The character "Freeborn" in *Loss and Gain* says to Charles:

> 'First, it is evident that it is not mere belief in facts, in the being of a God, or in the historical event that Christ has come and gone. Nor is it the submission of the reason to mysteries; nor, again, is it that sort of trust which is required for exercising the gift of miracles. Nor is it the knowledge and acceptance of the contents of the Bible. I say, it is not knowledge, it is not the assent of the intellect, it is not historical faith, it is not dead faith: true justifying faith is none of these---it is seated in the heart and affections' (101).

Both Charles and Newman, like Eliot's Becket, are torn with the fear that they may be "doing the right [exterior] thing for the wrong [interior] reason." A "lust for salvation that is ultimately egoistic" may inspire their conversions. The characters in *Loss and Gain* want to know "what Charles' means" as do the persons in Newman's life want to know what he means and intends. What are their views and why do they hold them? Are they trying to win salvation and justify themselves before God? Are they trying to make a good impression on earth and get a better job? Or are their words and actions motivated by heartfelt convictions and affections that are in effect inexpressible? Newman was trying to do what Derrida argues is well nigh impossible: to get to the core, the center and construct it. Newman's confessional defense more realistically set the various metaphoric perspectives in a comparative-contrastive gestalt where he is always aware that there is one metonym (possibly a synecdoche, depending upon its significance to the whole) piece missing yet at the same time, he is quite conscious that he is doing the right synecdochic thing in relation to his life and religious convictions.

Conclusion

In this final chapter on Cardinal Newman, I have attempted to show how his autobiographical writings contain various narrative units and voices that synecdochically unify and balance themselves as in an autobiography, metaphorically compare and contrast as in a memoir, and metonymically reveal, explain and defend as in a confession or apology.

The documents construct an autobiographical portrait of a man who saw himself as one who could achieve some degree of certitude with regard to his faith and his conversion by means of an intellectual analysis of probabilities and possibilities. He was always the student and scholar *par excellence* and this is his predominant, synecdochic image of himself. At the same time, another voice in the documents confesses to the impossibility of metonymically constructing such a consistent, certain portrait because he also recognizes the obvious inconsistencies and gaps about his conversion. His inexplicable recognition of his need for a private judgement and a private place in his own heart (*cor ad cor loquitur*) is the metonymic image that is confessional, apologetic. But he does proceed to defend his right to remember, categorize, and evaluate the metaphoric variety of personal motivations, intentions and voices in his life according to his own private judgement and the right to act on that judgement. He remembers the details of various crises and attempts to compare and contrast them as perspectives among perspectives, varieties of voices and events.

Near the end of his life, Newman returned to the time and place, where the religious road diverged in the woods and he chose Roman Catholicism over Anglicanism in the 1830's. He returned to the time when he wrote the fictional account of such a choice in *Loss and Gain* in 1848. He also returned to the time when he was called to defend his conversion in the *Apologia* in 1860 and he finally returned to it when he wrote some documents for his biographer in the 1870's. Each time he returned to these points of decision where the two roads converged or diverged in the wood and he realized, like Wordsworth or DeQuincey, that the one he chose made all the difference. In each return, he comes to a nexus, a deeper sense of himself, so he is able to expose the various levels of inconsistency and conflict inherent in the conversion and asserts his right to determine his own motivations and intentions, to choose which way he wants to go based upon his right to judge and decide privately about certain things.

> I took the one less traveled by,
> And that has made all the difference.[14]

Notes

1. Robert Frost, "The Road Not Taken," *The Norton Anthology of American Literature*, Volume II, edited by Ronald Gottesman, Laurence Holland, David Kalstone, Francis Murphy, Hershel Parker, and William Pritchard (New York: W.W. Norton and Company, 1979), 1117.

2. John Henry Newman, *John Henry Newman Autobiographical Writings*, edited by Henry Tristram (New York: Sheed and Ward, 1956), 49. All further references will be to this edition.

3. John Henry Newman, *Loss and Gain: The Story of a Convert*, edited by Alan G. Hill (Oxford University Press, 1986), 2. All further references will be to this edition.

4. John Henry Newman, "*Apologia Pro Vita Sua*, edited by David DeLaura (New York: W.W. Norton and Company, 1968), 29. All further references will be to this edition.

5. Harry Epstein, "The Relevance of Newman's Apologia to its Modern Reader," (*Southern Humanities Review*, 10), 208, 212.

6. "The Basic Texts of the Newman-Kingsley Controversy" in *Apologia Pro Vita Sua*, edited by David DeLaura, (New York: W.W. Norton and Company, 1968), 297.

7. Charles Kingsley, "What, Then, Does Dr. Newman Mean?" in *Apologia Pro Vita Sua*, edited by David DeLaura (New York: W.W. Norton and Company, 1968), 310.

8. T.S. Eliot, *Murder in the Cathedral*, (New York: Harcourt, Brace and Company, 1935), 44.

9. *The New Jerusalem Bible* (New York: Doubleday and Company, 1985), Matthew 21:31 on p. 1644.

10. Jan B. Gordon, "Wilde and Newman: The Confessional Mode," (*Renascence* 22), 185.

11 Sydney Mendel, "Metaphor and Rhetoric in Newman's *Apologia*," (*Essays in Criticism*, 23), 369.

12 John Henry Newman, "Note C: On Wisdom and Innocence," in *Apologia Pro Vita Sua*, edited by David DeLaura (New York: W.W. Norton and Company, 1968), 233 ff.

13 John Henry Newman, "Wisdom and Innocence," in *Victorian Literature: Prose*, edited by G.B. Tennyson and Donald J. Gray (New York: Macmillan Publishing Company, Inc., 1976), 280 ff.

14 Frost, 1118.

Conclusion

A Philosophy of Autobiographical Writing: A Metaphysics of Presence

Individuals render themselves, their consciousness and personality, present in a special, unique way in autobiographical writing. In this conclusion, I would like to frame a "metaphysics of presence"[1] using the writings of Jacques Derrida and Edmund Husserl as my points of departure and in so doing develop a systematic philosophy that constitutes autobiographical writing.

Edmund Husserl's construction of the phenomenological bracket is one system which can constitute autobiographical writing. Narratives and narrative voices are systematic constructs of authors. Jacques Derrida's deconstruction of phenomenological brackets and written narratives is another system.

I would like to use Samuel Beckett's *Malone Dies* and *Endgame* as my illustrations of Derrida's deconstructionism although my earlier considerations of Tristram Shandy and Hermione Gart also apply. James Boswell's dual narration of his first meeting with Samuel Johnson are examples of phenomenological brackets or constructs.

"Consciousness offers itself to thought as self-presence, says Derrida, "the self perceives itself as present to itself through thought and consciousness."[2] Jane Tompkins puts Derrida's same sentiment in other words: "I think "consciousness" by thinking that I am in some way present to my "self":"[3] Derrida's metaphysics of presence is a "self-proximity that gives privileged position to the absolute now, the life in the present, the living present...."[4] The very essence of presence <u>is</u> presence....A principle of identity is the founding principle for a philosophy of science or a metaphysics of presence which is a presence of consciousness, a "Being as *presence*,"[5] embodied by the words used in an autobiographical document.

Samuel Beckett's Malone or Hamm are in just such positions of presence. Malone is portrayed on his death bed and he is attempting to recapitulate his life by re-telling it in stories and Hamm is merely sitting on the stage, unable to move, telling his story. They are each present to their lives but their lives are a series of disorganized, incoherent, deconstructed stories. Their lives are not neat packages of constructed narratives representing a meaningful life.

As Gayatri Spivak says in her introduction to her translation of *Of Grammatology*: "Derrida's trace is the mark of the absence of a presence, an always already absent present,..."[6] She writes in her introduction that his is an "ethics of presence, an ethic of nostalgia for origins,...a science of presence."[7] And Derrida himself says in *Of Grammatology*: "I have identified logocentrism and the metaphysics of presence as the exigent, powerful, systematic and irrepressible desire for such a signified."[8] Questions of origins, he says, carry with them a "metaphysics of presence." Malone and Hamm are made present in the autobiographical documents, *Malone Dies* and *Endgame* but not like Boswell is made present in *The London Journal* or the *Life of Johnson*.

In order to establish this metaphysics of presence which constitutes autobiographical writing, I will define the key terms that Derrida uses to support the system: the always already absence and presence of a force at a center; the construction and deconstruction dilemma; the free interplay of traces and differences; and the natural attitude versus the Husserlean natural standpoint and illustrate these in *Malone Dies*.

Derrida's "natural attitude"[9] is that which respects the deconstructive-constructive freeplay of the different traces in consciousness which constructs and deconstructs of necessity and will involve a violence, a destruction of the natural attitude of respect, done to the force and center of that consciousness when consciousness attempts to construct an autobiographical narrative of its traces and differences. For Derrida, as each narrative of a life story is constructed, rendered present to consciousness, it signifies the absence of some other part of the life story.

"Natural writing [in keeping with the natural attitude] is that which is in communion with the unity of breath and voice; the pneumatological and the grammatological."[10] The science of language and the metaphysics of presence that Derrida is talking about must recover the *natural*---that is, the simple and original---

> ...*natural* bond of sense to the sense and it is this that passes from sense to sound: "the natural bond," Saussure says, "the only true bond, the bond of sound (p.46 [p. 25]. The natural bond of the signified [concept or sense] to the phonic signifier would condition the natural relationship subordinating writing [visible image] to speech.[11]

The situation that Beckett sets up in *Malone Dies* is that in which Malone, similar to the man in Beckett's *Company*, is aware that he is dying and wants to tell his life story. But before he begins to narrate his life story, Malone says that he needs to recapitulate his "present state"[12] at which point he admits that he does not remember how he got to his present state. He says that there is a major "hiatus (5)" in his recollection process and there are no "discernible traces (5)" to put it back together again. This is a Derridean "natural attitude" or perspective. Like the characters in Godot, Malone attempts to remember "the last thing I remember (5)" but to no avail. He describes himself as quite "neutral and inert...not worked into a state...natural at last...drawing no conclusions, neither hot nor cold (1)." He would like to "take everything in in a single [Husserlean] glance," but instead he must "look long and fixedly and give things time to travel the long road that lies between me and them (64)," which is the Derridean natural attitude.

Inscribing the life story on paper in narrative is an example of what Derrida calls a violent "rupture" of these "natural attachments."[13] Lawrence Watson says that "the individual returns to the phenomenon itself, the particular life experience, as a phenomenological object of consciousness...where the individual reflects on the experience...and transforms what was originally the *natural attitude* into the *phenomenological attitude*."[14] An autobiographer's "natural attitude" of respect for the sequence of events in the life story is an attitude which plays with the various traces left in memory about the particular experience from the past. The violence occurs when an autobiographer forces the construction of a system, a narrative, to represent the essence of the particular experience or even the life itself. The autobiographer writes a narrative of the experience and in so doing renders the life, the consciousness of the experience narrated, present at the same time that the narrative renders absent other traces of the experience not included in the construct. Derrida's natural attitude is discarded when the autobiographer assumes what Watson calls the Husserlean "phenomenological attitude" or "natural standpoint" and sets out to write an autobiographical narrative of a particular experience.

A first act of violence in *Malone Dies* is his remembrance of a "mood (6)" which gradually brings him back to his young days "in fits and starts (6)." Malone is very aware that these "fits and starts" are violent as he attempts to tell stories about his parents and childhood and as he tells the stories, he admits that "this is awful (14);" the storytelling is a way to relieve what he calls "the tedium (9)," that is itself tedious. He is doing a violence to himself and his natural attitude in this attempt to construct stories about himself and his life. As he tells the stories, he realizes ever so sharply and realistically, violently, that there is "nothing to signify (12)." He emerges from his reveries "tired and pale (16)." He feels that instead of constructing himself and his life, he is losing it "by a thousand ways (17)."

> A thousand little things to report, very strange, in view of my situation, if I interpret them correctly. But my notes have a curious tendency, as I realize at last, to annihilate all they purport to record (88).

The violence is in the synecdochic, idealizing self-invention itself, not so much in the metaphoric, metonymic remembering and re-telling. The construction of a self in a story is a violent act, fraught with "stinging air, inaccessible boon, rapture into vertigo, the letting go, the fall, the gulf, the relapse into darkness, the nothingness...to another self (18-19)."

Any deconstructive freeplay of traces and differences at the center ceases when the narrative is constructed. Just as the person is made present in the representation of consciousness in the narrative so some of the person is absent from the construct and the autobiographer must return to the natural attitude of respectful, deconstructive freeplay when a new part of the self is discovered in reading or hearing the self's own attitude.

The natural attitude or point of view is that which respects the ongoing process, the movement of becoming, until which time the autobiographical consciousness feels the need to bracket or construct a system or story about some experience. For Derrida, unlike Husserl, this constructing is a violent process of "dismantling and dispossession" or "dissimulation or oppression of the other by the same."[15] Being dissimulates itself in its occurrence and originally does "this first violence" to itself in order that it might state itself and appear real; in order to be a "first epiphany of Being."[16] The autobiographical piece of writing "is the dissimulation of the natural, primary, immediate presence of sense to the soul within the logos."[17]

Derrida elaborates the key notion of "trace" in his article on "Freud and the Scene of Writing" where he indicates that he got the idea of "trace" from Freud's writings, and most especially Freud's idea of the Mystic Writing Pad.[18]

> The trace is not only the disappearance of origin---within the discourse that we sustain and according to the path that we follow it means that the origin did not even disappear, that it was never constituted except reciprocally by a non-origin, the trace, which thus becomes the origin of the origin.[19]

> There is an illumination, a flash of light which inundates us. This flash, however, is not at all lasting, it is already hidden at the very moment it represents itself to the mind. Yet it leaves traces (*vestigia*) or impressions (*impressiones*) in our memories which constitute a kind of prelinguistic and purely mental writing.[20]

The following from *Malone Dies*, I think, illustrates the concept of "trace:"

> I shall tear a page out of my exercise-book and reproduce upon it, from memory, what follows, and show it to him to-morrow, or to-day, or some other day, if he ever comes back. 1. Who are you? 2. What do you do, for a living? 3. Are you looking for something in particular? 4. Why are you so cross? 5. Have I offended you? 6. Do you know anything about me? 7. It was wrong of you to strike me. 8. Give me my stick. 9. Are you your own employer? 10. If not who sends you? 11. Put back my things where you found them. 12. Why has my soup been stopped? 13. For what reason are my pots no longer untied? 14. Do you think I shall last much longer? 15. May I ask you a favor? 16. Your conditions are mine. 17. Why brown boots and whence the mud? 18. You couldn't by chance let me have the butt of a pencil? 19. Number your answers. 20. Don't go, I haven't finished. Will one page suffice? There cannot be many left. I might as well ask for a rubber while I'm about it. 21. Could you lend me an India rubber (102)?

According to Derrida, Freud discusses the mind or the psyche in terms of the three levels of conscious perceptions, unconscious recordings and preconscious, pre-verbal sensations. Freud's mystic writing pad is his metaphor for describing how perceptions are imprinted on the mind. "The alterity of the unconscious makes us concerned not with horizons of modified---past or future---presents) but with a "past" that has never been present,..."[21] (because it has been inscribed in the unconscious, subconscious or preconscious realms).

The cover sheet of the writing pad records the initial perceptions and intuitions on consciousness at the time that the experience is occurring but then some of these perceptions and intuitions are imprinted permanently on the wax slab (unconscious/preconscious) underneath the cover sheet. When the perceptions are recorded and the cover sheet is lifted, they are erased and the cover sheet is a *tabula rasa* again, ready to receive new perceptions and intuitions from new experiences. But the wax slab underneath, the metaphor for the unconscious and preconscious, has retained some of these writings as traces which intersect and overlap as they accumulate.

The "palimpsest" of the Middle Ages is an earlier version of this same thing. Writing surfaces were scraped or washed and used again but the traces still remained and modern chemical methods make it possible to recover some of these texts.[22] Thomas DeQuincey uses the palimpsest image, like Freud's mystic writing pad, as a metaphor of the mind which is an interlace of intersections, much like a road map.

> What else than a natural and mighty palimpsest is the human brain?...Everlasting layers of ideas, images, feelings, have fallen upon your brain as softly as light. Each succession has seemed to bury all them before. And yet, in reality, not one has been extinguished...Yes, reader, countless are the mysterious handwritings of greed and joy which have inscribed themselves successively upon the palimpsest of your brain;...They are not dead but sleeping.[23]

Derrida considers these "traces" recorded on the palimpsest, the mystic writing pad of the mind, and calls them the "grammes"[24] that appear as writing on a piece of paper in an autobiographical narrative. He talks about the traces in consciousness as these grammes on the piece of paper as "breaches" or paths, which break through upon each other and conduct to other traces. Meaning is created by "enregistering" it to an "engraving, a groove, a relief, to a surface whose essential characteristic is the infinitely transmissible."[25]

> Freud forges the hypothesis of "contact-barriers" and "breaching" (*Bahnung*, lit. pathbreaking) of the breaking open of a path (*Bahn*)...Breaching, the tracing of a trail opens up a conducting path...breaching without difference, resistance, is insufficient for memory.[26]

This "breaking a path against resistance, rupture and irruption becoming a route, is a violent inscription of a form."[27] Derrida compares this breaking a path, breaching, to the furrow that a ploughman makes in a field which opens the land for cultivation and fertilization just as the furrow made by the writer are the lines written on the pages of paper, opening the mind to cultivation and fertilization of thought.[28]

As Malone progresses with his four stories, these become traces of who he is. He asserts that "before he is done, he shall find the traces of who he was (52)" and he will do this by recollecting this "inventory (4)," as he calls it, on himself which are the traces that he can leave behind when he dies. He will "state the facts, without trying to understand, to the end (77)."

Autobiographers write their narratives, which narratives are themselves "traces," or "grammes." The trace intersections in the palimpsest of the mind and memory which appear as the grammes (the words, clauses, sentences, phrases, narratives, the autobiographical documents themselves) on the written page are ways of separating and breaking apart the trace experiences in consciousness. This setting apart and arranging and constructing into autobiographical narratives on written pages is a violent process that forces the self into a narrative mold which does not really represent it. What is not respected and is forced into the mold is the force at the center which is never reached but always approximated. The effort to get to this force and center and separate it from the "always already"[29] consciousness is a violent act. The paths resist and counter each other; one ruptures the other. The paths, the traces, the inscriptions, the grammes on the page are ruptures on the text of the mind as they are on the paper. One narrative opposes, complements or reveals another. Malone feels that he "became very old before he found himself there (8)." The "dinning together of the noises into one continuous buzzing sound frustrates him (31-32)" because he can no longer discern traces and differences. He can no longer decompose, deconstruct or construct. He is in that "always already," metaphysical present that I am saying is the basis for autobiographical documents.

This inaccessible force at the center, an unreachable origin, is never present for Derrida except in the interplay of these differences among traces in the conscious, subconscious, preconscious, unconscious mind. The trace is the "simulacrum"[30] of a something dislocated from itself, displaced, "under erasure;"[31] it is and it is not. As Gayatri Spivak says:

> "The sign must be studied "under erasure" always already inhabited by the trace of another sign which never appears as such."[32]

Conclusion 227

The narrative units in an autobiographical document are traces which synecdochically juxtapose with each other and metonymically differentiate and re-connect with each other or metaphorically replace one another as representative of the person.

The autobiographical document and its narrative units themselves are rupturous, violent events for the autobiographer; some moreso than others. An autobiographical document or a narrative unit in a document is a violent act because it attempts to give voice to an "untouchable, untranslatable, absolute nonpresence,"[33] the ferment and internal dialogue and discernment, between conscious, unconsciousness, preconscious traces and attempts to express them in writing and in so expressing them, destroys them, makes them completely other and absent.

> ...irreducibility of intentional incompleteness, and therefore alterity; and by showing that since consciousness is irreducible, it can never possibly, by its own essence, become self-conscious,...[34]

In "Genesis and Structure," Derrida makes the point that the structure, the text, is motivated by this dynamic activity or movement, of discourse, of the being at its center, the source, the force but this dynamic activity stops, the process of becoming stops, when it is forced into an Husserlean bracket or box, into a "state" of being, an object, that is not becoming; the autobiographical writer is still moving and growing and the autobiographical document becomes something quite alien to the autobiographer because it represents someone whom the autobiographer is not any more. The naming in the document represents the chain or "system of roots"[35] of differences linked into a narrative and in all the diversity of the interlink and network, the thing, the autobiographer, is never the same. "Linguistic identity does not reside in substance; it resides in relationality...Identity...is a function of positioning within a system."[36]

Malone, Beckett's own fictional creation, himself speaks of this unreachable center as an "accumulation of darkness which thickens, bursts and drowns everything (13)." The force at the center continually eludes Malone. The stories do not adequately represent him; in fact, they distort him. His intention is to "enounce clearly, without additions or omissions, all that this interminable prelude has brought me...treasures derived from the same source...the forms, the stories, are many in which the unchanging seeks relief from its formlessness (21)." He says that the words and images "run right through his head, pursuing, flying, clashing, merging endlessly (22)." He wants to make this last effort to understand "the night, storm and sorrow, the catalepsies of the soul (23)" but he says it all goes "clean out of his head (51)" as soon as it comes in. He has one "little private idea" after another. "Perhaps they are all the same," he says, these private "ideas are so alike, when you get to know them (52)....All these parts are intimately and even indissolubly bound up together (66)," and to separate them is a kind of violence. He "supposes that the wisest thing, now is to live it over again, meditate upon it and be edified (82)." Writers often speak about their fictional characters as persons, individuals in their own rights, who actually dictate to the author how they want their story written.

The rupturous event, the violent act, for autobiographers like Malone or Hamm, is the attempt to inscribe and structure the indeterminate center of the self, to separate the self from the system of relations. The metaphoric, infinite substitutions (stories that are alike or similar) which never signify the force at the center (the essence, the movement) are violent actions which attempt to totalize by adding up a bunch of seminal traces, Hamm's "millet grains,"[37] or Malone's "lentils (39)" (narrative units, autobiographical stories) and naming them.

The unconscious and preconscious compilation of traces, like the conscious ones from which the autobiographical narrative is written, are also a network of weaves of their own meanings and forces which affect the way that the conscious mind of the autobiographer brackets those weaves and traces into narrative. The articulation, the vocalization of these traces by means of the words of the narrative is essentially the idea behind my assertion here that autobiographical writing embodies a metaphysics of presence and consciousness. Derrida admits that the interlace and weave of traces and differences in unconscious, preconscious and conscious mind in an "always already" present, "energetic" act of becoming is essentially inaccessible and irreducible.

> Rousseau...articulates the chain of significations...on the classical metaphysics of the entity as *energy*, encompassing the relationships between being and time in terms of the now as being in action (*energeia*):[38]

> "*Energeia* of speech (a word's capacity to make the image of the thing present to the mind),..."[39] through the "eternal return" and the re-writing, re-editing, re-vocalizing, new traces and differences are discovered, always "supplementing and compensating for what is lacking in the previous articulation" in an attempt to bracket the "plenitude,"[40] the fullness, the essence of a particular experience or person when in fact there will always be some trace that is absent.

> ...this sequence of supplements...is an infinite chain, ineluctably multiplying the supplementary mediations that produce the sense of the very thing they defer: the mirage of the thing itself, of immediate presence, of imaginary perception.[41]

This "movement of supplementary representation approaches the origin as it distances itself from it."[42] As Hamm recapitulates his life in *Endgame*, he wants to be "put right in the center (27);" he wants to get to the beginning, the origin, but comes to realize that "the end is in the beginning (69)" as he tells the story of his childhood relationship with his father which has radically affected his life, his perspective, and has determined how he has proceeded to his "end."

Derrida's roundtable discussion in *The Ear of the Other* of Nietzsche's problem of the "eternal return"[43] accents this idea that on "the basis of this unfolding of the same as *differance*, we see announced in the sameness the *differance* and repetition in the eternal return."[44] But, "rather than a repetition of the same, the return must be selective within a differential relation of forces."[45]

Derrida uses the Tower of Babel example from the bible to illustrate this untranslatable confusion.[46] God interrupts and deconstructs the tower and in so doing he insists that people not impose a single meaning or structure but that they must submit to an untranslatable plurality. All they must do is keep trying to translate meaning and experience the differences. Attempts at translation in order to establish links, a network of traces. The ears, eyes and voices of the others within the self and outside see, hear and speak the multiplicity and difference in the selves. Beckett's Malone echoes Derrida:

> ...to put the index on the subject and the little finger on the verb, in the way his teacher had shown him [Husserlean bracket] and sorry he would make no meaning of the babel raging in his head, the doubts, desires, imaginings and dreads (16).

Malone says that he "tells himself so many things" and then wonders, with Vladimir in *Godot*, "where the truth is in all this babble (62)?" The self is always seeking the "asemic" kernel "beneath the shell of the text,"[47] the core, the center which eludes absolute, untouchable non-presence. "The totality of hereditary characteristics are enveloped in the germ."[48] If such a center can be touched, the person feels that he or she will experience wholeness and integration. Derrida quotes Jean Pepin who said that "hermeneutics is not so much a return to an uncovering by way of exegesis, the kernel or hidden meaning within the shell of the text, but an act of extroversion, a natural vocalization of that kernel."[49] When the autobiographer engages in this freeplay, there is the truth that this center probably won't be touched but the autobiographer also risks facing the void there, the absence of the parts that have died or never existed where they should have existed, e.g., feelings and attitudes that most people have, others may have missed. The autobiographer may attempt to fill the void or represent what is perceived as the center, the core, the kernel in various narrative units but will discover that the narrative not only does not capture what is trying to be represented but what is represented is a mere tangential trace on the circumference of the center. He eternally returns looking for that synecdochic narrative that will establish a differential of forces from which something new can be drawn, which may be the center. The radical alterity, the always present void within, surrounded by multiplicity, is of great concern to autobiographers like Hamm or Malone because it suggests that there are parts of the self in the unconscious, subconscious and preconscious mind which will always be radically other and there are parts of the unconscious, subconscious, preconscious and conscious mind which are identifiably blank. The autobiographer realizes that there were events in childhood which have been traced in the unconscious or subconscious to which the autobiographer feels that he was not really present or involved because his conscious mind had not yet developed.

Derrida makes the point in *The Ear of the Other* that when a person confronts various kinds of voids within, when the person meets a radical emptiness or nothingness inside, the natural desire is of course to fill it with something, someone, to create a presence. Malone realizes that he is proceeding towards his death, his final, eternal "absence" so he wants to leave "something," someone, behind to fill the space, the absence, after he leaves. The end of *Malone Dies* suggests most explicitly the autobiographical metaphysics of presence that I have been attempting to articulate in this conclusion. Throughout the document, Malone has been telling various stream of consciousness stories, one story leading to another. The document suggests a freeplay of different traces and memories from which Malone constructs his various narratives. His natural attitude is that he will tell these stories as he proceeds to his death but the realization of his death and subsequent absence gives an urgency to his story-telling and thus a "violent" desire to get at the source, his center, of who he really is. He never does get there and the end of the document suggests that the freeplay is still going on. He said earlier in the document that he would tell these stories and fill his time until the end, unless the storytelling activity continues this way after he dies as well, which the ending of both this book and Sartre's *No Exit* suggest, i.e. that there is no ending, just a "getting on with it." Hamm wonders if he is getting on; if something is happening; if he is making meaning; if he himself is meaningful. And throughout the texts of *No Exit* and *Endgame* the getting on is being done, the meaning is being made, and the suggestion is that it continues after the text (and by extension, after the life) has ended.

> Gurgles of outflow.
> ...The night is strewn with absurd
>   absurd lights, the stars, the beacons, the buoys, the lights of earth and in the hills the faint fires of the blazing gorse. Macmann, my last, my possessions, I remember, he is there too, perhaps he sleeps. Lemuel
>   Lemuel is in charge,...he will not touch anyone anymore, either with it or with it or with it or with or
>   or with it or with his hammer or with his stick or with his fist or in thought in dream I mean never will he never
>   or with his pencil or with his stick or
>   or light light I mean
>   never there he will never
>   never anything
>   there
>   anymore (119-120)

This passage actually portrays what Derrida calls traces and differences, pieces and fragments which go to make up a narrative and this narrative breaks down into incoherent pieces on its way to another kind of organization not represented. Ostensibly, it fades into silence and then picks up again on a later page.

The construction of an autobiographical document is an expansive, creative, active freeplay of traces, a metaphysics of presence. The autobiographical document, as a repository of truths and definitive statements, will always break down and give way to a new logic, a new synthesis, an interpretation and vision, thus multiple autobiographies and multiple metaphoric narratives. This freeplay becomes work for Derrida when it is forced into a particular structure. The person discourses with the multiple selves around the indeterminate center affirming that center by recognition of its continued absence.

Malone says "strictly speaking, it is impossible for me to know, from one moment to the next, what is mine and what is not, according to my definition (79)." His definition, constructions of himself, continually deconstruct and change. He "wonders why he should go on drawing up the inventory corresponding only faintly to the facts, and if he should not rather cut it short and devote himself to some other form of distraction (79)," some other construction, which would be of "less consequence (79)." Or should he "simply wait," doing nothing, or "counting perhaps." As he arrives at definitions of who and what he is, he deconstructs them as he wonders if they are really his or if the definition itself is at fault (80).

In "La Parole Soufflee," Derrida's words suggest to me that autobiographers "vainly seek a place that is always missing."[50] If the presence articulated in the autobiographical narrative implies an absence, then a process of deconstructing the presence in the narrative needs to be undertaken in order to perceive the absent parts. The traces present reveal the traces and connections hidden. If traces and differences can freely dialogue with each other and construct a text, they can also dialogue with each other and deconstruct that text. The constructive act is as violent a rupture as is the deconstructive one. The autobiographical document as a construction asks to be deconstructed to the extent that it fails to capture some other trace, some other presence, some other consciousness, some other voice. Once the person or situation is captured as an entity, a product, a passive, static, stagnant noun, then the reality of a living being, an active verb, is lost. Malone realizes that if he "ever stops talking it will be because there is nothing more to be said, even though all has not been said, even though nothing has been said (63)....For my stories are all in vain, deep down I never doubted, even the days abounding in proof to the contrary,...(60)...And perhaps there is none, no morrow any more, for one who has waited so long for it in vain. And perhaps he has come to the state of his instant when to live is to wander the last of the living in the depths of an instant without bounds...(59)," a frustratingly unreachable center. Malone knows that essentially he is waiting to die and it is "vain" to suspect that he is telling these stories or constructing a self for any other reason than to fill up the time while he waits (68).

Hamm captures the same sentiments in *Endgame*. He does construct some Husserlean narratives, however incoherent, but most of his time is spent either lamenting that he can't get up or wondering when "this farce will end (14, 23, 32, 45)" or feeling that "something [he] is taking its course (13, 32, 42)," a key sentiment in the play.

He feels like a "speck in the void;" surrounded by "infinite emptiness (36)" in which he occasionally "has an idea (46-47)" like Gogo and Didi "have a conversation or a fight." These ideas occasionally emerge as narratives in his attempt to "put things in order....create a little order (57)," a construct. His desire to create a little order through storytelling is like Vladimir's attempt to re-tell the events of the day and both experience this activity as a "prolonged creative effort (61)" while others may hear it as the "chronicle you've been telling yourself all your days (58)."

Hamm then feels "absent, always. It all happened without me. I don't know what's happened (74)" and Clov asks him if it really matters anyway (75). There is "nothing to say" except "a few words to ponder in the heart (79)" which might elicit some "compassion (76)" from the hearer where the "heart is in the head (18)" of both narrator and hearer.

With Pozzo, Hamm realizes that "we breathe, we change! We lose our ears, our teeth! Our Bloom! Our ideals! (11) ...One day, suddenly, it ends, it changes, I don't understand, it dies, or it's me (81)" and where is all the truth, the meaning, in all the babble and change except perhaps in this heartfelt compassion elicited.

Endgame, like *Godot*, *No Exit* and *Malone* ends as if it is beginning. In *Godot* and *No Exit*, they continue to get on with it. Malone's voice gradually fades as if the volume is being turned down and Hamm says "since that's the way we're playing...let's play it that way...(84)."

In what I believe to be prototypical, autobiographical documents, like Beckett's works or Sterne's *Shandy* or Doolittle's *Hermione*, the self is a person comprised of multiple others in conversation, each listening to the others; the person tells the life story to the other selves who listen and take their turns telling their version. These "ears of the others"[51] within seem to divide irreducibly, Zeno-like, such that each of them is not only radically other but "irreducibly secondary."[52] I believe that Boswell's narration of his first meeting with Johnson or Malone's or Hamm's narratives of their parents are paradigmatically Husserlean constructs while their commentaries on their own narrative constructs as they tell them are instruments through which they make themselves present.

The key ideas that makeup this metaphysics of presence in relation to autobiographical writing are that the *natural attitude* of the autobiographical writer is one which constructs the self (fictional or not) in narratives and then deconstructs the self made *present* in the narratives and in so doing draws attention to various *absences* in the *freeplay* of *traces* and *differences* represented in the multiple narratives and narrative voices and perspectives. The process of writing these autobiographical narratives is a *rupturous, violent* one because it attacks the ongoing process of movement, dialogue, growth and becoming being voiced at the *center* at the same time that the document and its narrative units find their source and origin in this *force* at the unreachable center.

Each of the autobiographies and narratives that I have used throughout this book exemplify elements of both a Derridean deconstructive or Husserlean phenomenological stance. There is always something missing, not quite clear, another point of view, another voice, that can be taken, embellished and heard. Some of the person is rendered present but rarely, if ever, the whole, the center. The phenomenological object that is rendered present in a good autobiographical narrative is the dialogue of voices and perspectives which are forces within the individual and are a small part of what constitute the person's unreachable center. Besides illustrating the philosophical tenets of an autobiographical metaphysics of presence, the narratives that I have selected illustrate the importance of the mimetic and diegetic voices of the writers in the texts.

Notes

1 Jacques Derrida, *Of Grammatology*, (Baltimore: The Johns Hopkins University Press, 1974), 74.

2 Jacques Derrida, *Margins of Philosophy*, (The University of Chicago Press, 1972), 16.

3 Jane Tompkins, "A Short Course in Post-Structuralism," (*College English*, 50, 7, November, 1988), 746.

4 Derrida, *Of Grammatology*, 309, 311.

5 Jacques Derrida, *Writing and Difference*, (The University of Chicago Press, 1978), 207, 213, 279.

6 Gayatri Spivak, "Translator's Introduction" to *Of Grammatology*, (Baltimore: The Johns Hopkins University Press, 1974), xvii.

7 Spivak, xix, xxi.

8 Derrida, *Of Grammatology*, 49.

9 Derrida, *Writing and Difference*, 144.

10 Derrida, *Of Grammatology*, 17.

11 Derrida, *Of Grammatology*, 35.

12 Samuel Beckett, *Malone Dies*, (New York: Grove Press, 1956), 12. All references will be to this edition.

13 Derrida, *Of Grammatology*, 46.

14 Lawrence C. Watson, "Understanding a Life History as a Subjective Document: Hermeneutical and Phenomenological Perspectives," (*Ethos*, 4, 1976), 99.

15 Derrida, *Writing and Difference*, 82, 129.

16 Derrida, *Writing and Difference*, 147, 149.

17 Derrida, *Of Grammatology*, 37.

18 Derrida, *Writing and Difference*, 223.

19 Derrida, *Of Grammatology*, 61.

20 Jacques Derrida, *The Ear of the Other: Otobiography, Transference, Translation*, translated by Peggy Kamuf, edited by Christie MacDonald, (New York: Schocken Books, 1985), 80-81.

21 Derrida, *Margins of Philosophy*, 21.

22 William Flint Thrall, Addison Hibbard and C. Hugh Holman, *A Handbook to Literature*, (New York: The Odyssey Press, 1936), 336-337.

23 Thomas DeQuincey, *Tales and Prose Phantasies*, Volume XIII, *The Collected Writings of Thomas DeQuincey*, edited by David Masson, (Edinburgh: Adam and Charles Black, 1890), 510.

24 Derrida, *Writing and Difference*, 205.

25 Derrida, *Writing and Difference*, 12.

26 Derrida, *Writing and Difference*, 200-201.

27 Derrida, *Writing and Difference*, 214.

28 Derrida, *Of Grammatology*, 287.

29 Derrida, *Writing and Difference*, 74, 165, 178, 211, 213, 219, 226. *Of Grammatology*, 7, 9, 47, 66, 73, 84, 106, 112, 280, 289-290, 304.

30 Derrida, *Margins of Philosophy*, 24.

31 Derrida, *Of Grammatology*, 60.

32 Spivak, xxxix.

33 Derrida, *The Ear of the Other*, 114-115.

34 Derrida, *Writing and Difference*, 120.

35 Derrida, *Of Grammatology*, 102.

36 Tompkins, 737.

37 Samuel Beckett, *Endgame: A Play in One Act followed by Act Without Words: A Mime for one Player*, (New York: Grove Press, 1958), 70. All references will be to this edition.

38 Derrida, *Of Grammatology*, 311.

39 Derrida, *The Ear of the Other*, 137.

40 Derrida, *Writing and Difference*, 212.

41 Derrida, *Of Grammatology*, 157.

42 Derrida, *Of Grammatology*, 295.

43 Friedrich Wilhelm Nietzsche, *Ecce Homo* and *The Birth of a Tragedy*, (New York: The Modern Library, 1927), 69, 95, 107.

44 Derrida, *Margins of Philosophy*, 17.

45 Derrida, *The Ear of the Other*, 45.

46 Derrida, *The Ear of the Other*, 98.

47 Derrida, *The Ear of the Other*, 80, 113.

48 Derrida, *Writing and Difference*, 23.

49 Derrida, *The Ear of the Other*, 136.

50 Derrida, *Writing and Difference*, 178.

51 Derrida, *The Ear of the Other*, 35, 49-51.

52 Derrida, *Writing and Difference*, 178.

Bibliography

Adams, Henry. *The Education of Henry Adams: An Autobiography.* Boston: Houghton Mifflin Company, 1961.

Albee, Edward. *Who's Afraid of Virginia Woolf?* New York: Atheneum Press, 1975.

Angelou, Maya. *I Know Why The Caged Bird Sings.* New York: Bantam Books, 1970.

"The Basic Texts of the Newman-Kingsley Controversy." in *Apologia Pro Vita Sua.* Edited by David DeLaura. New York: W.W. Norton and Company, 1968.

Bates, E. Stuart. *Inside Out: An Introduction to Autobiography.* New York: Sheridan House, 1937.

Beckett, Samuel. *Endgame: A Play in One Act followed by Act Without Words: A Mime for One Player.* New York: Grove Press, Inc., 1958.

---. *Malone Dies.* New York: Grove Press, Inc., 1956.

---. *Company.* London: Jack Calder, 1980.

---. *Waiting for Godot.* New York: Grove Press, Inc., 1954.

Blasing, Monica. *The Art of Life: Studies in American Autobiographical Literature.* Austin: The University of Texas Press, 1977.

Boswell, James. *London Journal: 1762-1763*. New York: McGraw-Hill Book Company, Inc., 1950.

---. *Life of Johnson*. Oxford University Press, 1980.

Bree, Germaine "Autogynography," *Southern Review*, Volume 22, #2, April, 1986.

Bruss, Elizabeth. *Autobiographical Acts: The Changing Situation of a Literary Genre*. Baltimore: The Johns Hopkins University Press, 1976.

Burke, Kenneth. "The Four Master Tropes." *A Grammar of Motives*. Los Angeles: The University of California Press, 1969.

---. *A Rhetoric of Motives*. Los Angeles: University of California Press, 1969.

Capote, Truman. *In Cold Blood: A True Account of a Multiple Murder and Its Consequences*. A Signet Book: New American Library, 1965.

Chatman, Seymour. "The Structure of Narrative Transmission," in *Style and Structure in Literature*, ed. Roger Fowler, Cornell University Press, 1978.

Cooke, Michael G. "'Do You Remember Laura?' or, The Limits of Autobiography." *Iowa Review*, ii, 1978.

Cox, James M. "Autobiography and America." *Virginia Quarterly Review*, 47, #2, 1971.

DeQuincey, Thomas. *Tales and Prose Phantasies*. Volume XIII of *The Collected Works of Thomas DeQuincey*, ed. David Masson. Edinburgh: Adam and Charles Black, 1890.

---. *Confessions of an English Opium Eater. Volume I of The Works of Thomas DeQuincey.* London: The New Universal Library: George Routledge and Sons Limited.

Derrida, Jacques. *Of Grammatology*, trans. Gyatri Chakravorty Spivak. Baltimore: The Johns Hopkins University Press, 1974.

---. *The Ear of the Other: Otobiography, Transference, Translation.* Trans. Peggy Kamuf, ed. Christie McDonald. New York: Schocken Books, 1985.

---. *Margins of Philosophy.* The University of Chicago Press, 1972.

---. *Writing and Difference.* The University of Chicago Press, 1978.

Donohue, Denis. *Ferocious Alphabets.* Boston: Little, Brown and Company, 1981.

Doolittle, Hilda. *Hermione.* New York: New Directions, 1927.

Eakin, Paul John. *Fictions in Autobiography: Studies in the Art of Self-Invention.* Princeton University Press, 1985.

Eliot, T.S. *Murder in the Cathedral.* New York: Harcourt, Brace and Company, 1935.

Epstein, Harry. "The Relevance of Newman's *Apologia* to its Modern Reader." *Southern Humanities Review*, 10.

Finney, Brian. *The Inner I: British Literary Autobiography in the Twentieth Century.* Oxford University Press, 1985.

Fischer, David. "The Braided Narrative: Substance and Form in Social History." *The Literature of Fact: Selected Essays from the English Institute.* Edited by Angus Fletcher. New York: Columbia University Press, 1976.

Foster, Dennis. *Complicity in Confessional Narratives*. Cambridge University Press, 1987.

Frost, Robert. "The Road Not Taken." *The Norton Anthology of American Literature*. Volume II, edited by Ronald Gottesman, Laurence Holland, David Kalstone, Francis Murphy, Hershel Parker, and William Pritchard. New York: W.W. Norton and Company, 1979.

Frye, Northrup. *Anatomy of Criticism: Four Essays*. Princeton University Press, 1957.

Garrett, George. "Crime and Punishment in Kansas: Truman Capote's *In Cold Blood*." in *Truman Capote's In Cold Blood: A Critical Handbook*. Edited by Irving Malin. Belmont, California: Wadsworth Publishing Company, Inc., 1968. Reprinted from *Esquire*, LXV, June, 1966.

Genette, Gerard. "Boundaries of Narrative," *New Literary History* 8 (1) Autumn ,1976.

Gordon, Jan B. "Wilde and Newman: The Confessional Mode." *Renascence* 22.

Gosse, Edmund. *Father and Son: A Study of Two Temperaments*. Edited by Peter Abbs. New York: Penguin Books, 1983.

Goodwin, James. "Narcissus and Autobiography." *Genre*, Volume 12, Spring, 1979.

Greeley, Andrew. *Confessions of a Parish Priest: An Autobiography*. New York: Simon and Shuster, 1986.

Gross, John. A Review of Christopher Nolan's Autobiography *Under the Eye of the Clock* in *The New York Times*, February 26, 1988, Section C.

Hampl, Patricia. "Defying the Yapping Establishment." *The New York Times Book Review*, March 13, 1988.

Hemeren, Goran. "Intention and Interpretation in Literary Criticism." *New Literary History* 7, 1, 1975.

Howard, Jane. "Horror Spawns a Masterpiece." *Life* 60, January 7, 1966.

Husserl, Edmund. *Ideas: General Introduction to Pure Phenomenology*. London: Collier MacMillan Publishers, 1962.

Ionesco, Eugene. *Four Plays: The Bald Soprano, The Lesson, Jack, or The Submission, The Chairs*. Trans. Donald M. Allen. New York: Grove Press, Inc., 1958.

Joffee, Linda. "A Voice from a Mute World Sings." *The Christian Science Monitor*, January 27, 1988.

Kahler, Erich. *The Inward Turn of Narrative*, trans. Richard and Clara Winston. Princeton University Press, 1973.

Keller, Helen. *The Story of My Life*. New York: Doubleday and Company, Inc., 1954.

Kellogg, Robert and Robert Scholes, *The Nature of Narrative*. London: Oxford University Press, 1966.

Kermode, Frank. *The Sense of Ending: Studies in the Theory of Fiction*. Oxford University Press, 1966.

Kingsley, Charles. "What, The, Does Dr. Newman Mean?" in *Apologia Pro Vita Sua*. Edited by David DeLaura. New York: W.W. Norton and Company, 1968.

Kingston, Maxine Hong. "Shaman." *The Woman Warrior: Memoirs of a Girlhood Among Ghosts.* New York: Vintage Books, A Division of Random House, 1977.

Labov, William, Paul Cohen, Clarence Robins and John Lewis. *A Study of Non-Standard English of Negro and Puerto Rican Speakers in New York City*; Co-operative Research Project No. 3288. Volume II: *The Use of Language in the Speech Community.* Printed and distributed by the U.S. Regional Survey, 204 N. 35th Street, Philadelphia, Pennsylvania, 19104, 1968.

Langbaum, Robert. *The Mysteries of Identity: A Theme in Modern Literature.* New York: Oxford University Press, 1977.

Lanser, Susan Snaider. *The Narrative Act: Point of View in Prose Fiction.* Princeton University Press, 1981.

Lejeune, Philippe. "The Autobiographical Contract." in *French Literary Theory Today: A Reader.* ed. Tzvetan Todorov, trans. R. Carter. Cambridge University Press, 1982.

Loesberg, Jonathan. *Fictions of Consciousness: Mill, Newman and the Reading of Victorian Prose.* Rutgers University Press, 1986.

Mansell, Daryl. "Unsettling the Colonel's Hash "Fact" in Autobiography." *Modern Language Quarterly*, xxxvii, 1976.

Marcus, Steven. "The Psychoanalytic Self." *Southern Review*, Volume 22, #2, April, 1986.

Martin, Jay. *Who Am I This Time: Uncovering the Fictive Personality.* New York: W.W. Norton and Company, 1988.

Martin, Wallace. *Recent Theories of Narrative.* Cornell University Press, 1985.

Mailer, Norman. *The Armies of the Night*. A Signet Book from New American Library, 1968.

Mayoux, Jean-Jacques. "Variations on the Time-Sense in *Tristram Shandy*," in Laurence Sterne *Tristram Shandy: An Authoritative Text, The Author of the Novel, Criticism*. edited by Howard Anderson. New York: W.W. Norton and Company, 1980.

McCarthy, Mary. "A Tin Butterfly." *Memories of a Catholic Girlhood*. New York: Harcourt, Brace Jovanovich Publishers, 1957.

Mellard, James M., *Doing Tropology: Analysis of Narrative Discourse*. Chicago: University of Illinois Press, 1987.

Mendel, Sydney. "Metaphor and Rhetoric in Newman's *Apologia*," *Essays in Criticism* 23.

Mill, John Stuart. *Autobiography of John Stuart Mill*. New York: Columbia University Press, 1924.

Miller, Arthur. *Timebends: A Life*. New York: Grove Press, 1987.

Nabokov, Vladimir. *Speak, Memory: An Autobiography Revisited*. New York: G.P. Putnam's Sons, 1947, 1948, 1949, 1950, 1960, 1966.

Neuman, Shirley. *Gertrude Stein: Autobiography and the Problem of Narration*. The University of Victoria Press, 1979.

The New Jerusalem Bible. New York: Doubleday and Company, 1985.

Newman, John Henry. *Apologia Pro Vita Sua*. Edited by David DeLaura. New York: W. W. Norton and Company, 1968.

---. *John Henry Newman Autobiographical Writings*. Edited by Henry Tristram. New York: Sheed and Ward, 1956.

---. *Loss and Gain: The Story of a Convert*. Edited with an introduction by Alan G. Hill. Oxford University Press, 1986.

---. "Wisdom and Innocence. *Victorian Literature: Prose*. Edited by G.B. Tennyson and Donald Gray. New York: MacMillan Publishing Company, Inc., 1976.

Nietzsche, Friedrich Wilhelm. *Ecce Homo and The Birth of a Nation*. New York: The Modern Library, Inc., 1927.

Nolan, Christopher. *Under the Eye of the Clock: The Life Story of Christopher Nolan*. New York: St. Martin's Press, 1987.

Norton, Anne. "Writing, Violence and Revolution in Memory." The 1987-88 William Andrews Clark Lecture Series: Violence and Order, Revolution and Constitution: Bicentennial Reflections," Los Angeles, May 27, 1988.

Olney, James. "A Theory of Autobiography." *Metaphors of the Self: The Meaning of Autobiography*. Princeton University Press, 1972, 3-50.

Pascal, Roy. *Design and Truth in Autobiography*. Harvard University Press, 1960.

Pike, Burton. "Time in Autobiography." *Comparative Literature* 28, 1976.

Pison, Thomas. "Wordsworth's Autobiography: The Metonymy of the Self." *Bucknell Review*, 23.ii,1977.

Pizer, Donald. "Documentary Narratives as Art: William Manchester and Truman Capote." *Journal of Modern Literature* 2.

Renza, Louis. "The Veto of the Imagination: A Theory of Autobiography." *New Literary History*, 9.1, Autumn, 1977.

Said, Edward. "On Repetition." *The Literature of Fact: Selected Essays from the English Institute*. Edited by Angus Fletcher. New York: Columbia University Press, 1976.

Searle, John. *Speech Acts: An Essay in the Philosophy of Language*. Cambridge: Cambridge University Press, 1969.

Searle, John R. and Daniel Vanderveken. *The Foundations of Illocutionary Logic*. Cambridge University Press, 1985.

Spacks, Patricia Meyer. *Imagining a Self: Autobiography and Novel in Eighteenth Century England*. Harvard University Press, 1976.

Spengemann, William C. *The Forms of Autobiography: Episodes in the History of a Literary Genre*. Yale University Press, 1980.

Spivak, Gayatri. "Translator's Introduction" to *Of Grammatology*. Baltimore: The Johns Hopkins University Press, 1974.

Stanton, Domna. "Autogynography: Is the Subject Different?" in *The Female Autograph*. V. 12-13 of the *New York Literary Forum*.

Sterne, Laurence. *Tristram Shandy: An Authoritative Text, The Author of the Novel, Criticism*. edited by Howard Anderson. New York: W.W. Norton and Company, 1980.

Sturrock, John. "The New Model Autobiographer." *New LIterary History*, 9, 1, 1977.

Tanner, Tony. "Death in Kansas." *Truman Capote's In Cold Blood: A Critical Handbook*. Edited by Irving Malin, Belmont,

California: Wadsworth Publishing Company, Inc., 1968. (Reprinted from *The Spectator*, CCVIII, March 18, 1966.

Thrall, William Flint, Addison Hibbard and C. Hugh Holman, *A Handbook to Literature*. New York: The Odyssey Press, 1936.

Tompkins, Jane. "A Short Course in Post-Structuralism," *College English*, 50, 7, November, 1988.

Trilling, Diana. "Capote's Crime and Punishment." in *Truman Capote's In Cold Blood: A Critical Handbook*. Belmont, California: Wadsworth Publishing Company, Inc., 1968. Reprinted from *Partisan Review*, XXXIII, Spring, 1966.

Watson, Lawrence. "Understanding a Life history as a Subjective Document: Hermeneutical and Phenomenological Perspectives." *Ethos*, 1976, Volume 4.

White, Hayden. "The Value of Narrativity in the Representation of Reality." *Critical Inquiry*, 7, 1980.

Williams, Tennessee. *The Glass Menagerie*. New York: A Signet Book of the New American Library, 1945.

Winterowd, W. Ross. *The Rhetoric of the Other Literature.* forthcoming University of Southern Illinois Press, 1990.

Wordsworth, William. *The Fourteen Book Prelude*. Edited W.J.B. Owen. Cornell University Press, 1985.

---. *The Prelude: 1799, 1805, 1850*. A Norton Critical Edition of Authoritative Texts and Contexts and Reception and Recent Critical Essays, edited by Jonathan Wordsworth, M.H. Abrams, and Stephen Gill. New York: W.W. Norton and Company, 1979.

---. "Ode" Intimations of Immortality from Recollections of Early Childhood," in *The Norton Anthology of English Literature*, Volume Two, fourth edition by M.H. Abrams, E. Talbot Donaldson, Hallett Smith, Robert M. Adams, Samuel Holt Monk, Lawrence Lipking, George H. Ford, David Daiches. New York: W. W. Norton and Company, 1962, 1968, 1974, 1978.

Index

absence 33, 55, 80, 84, 100, 156, 220, 221, 230-233
accidental murder 137
Adams, Henry 5
After the Fall 114
Albee, Edward 139, 141, 151, 183
Alkon, Paul xi
Allport, Gordon 138
"always already" 226, 228
Ambrose 201
Angelou, Maya 18, 20, 71, 109
Anglican 195, 197, 205, 207, 209, 211-213
Anselm 201
Antioch 201
antiquity 197, 198, 201
Apologia Pro Vita Sua 136, 189, 194, 195, 197, 207, 210
Arabian knight 102
Aristotle 7
Armies of the Night 139, 163 ff.
associationism 25
associative 10
Athanasius 201
Augustine 164, 201
autobiographer(s) 5, 8, 10-12, 14, 18-20, 52, 57, 69, 71, 72, 75, 85, 109, 117, 122, 131, 139, 159, 164, 189, 198, 202, 206, 222, 223, 227, 228, 230, 231
autobiographical account 81
   act 18, 21, 26, 28
   assumption 22
   attempt 14
   consciousness 227
   document 13, 22, 24, 32, 50, 51, 57, 58, 71, 75, 76, 82, 93, 102, 112, 117, 170, 182, 189, 220, 226, 227, 232, 233
   documents 52, 58, 139, 181, 190, 220, 226, 234
   enterprise 24
   ideal self 192
   literature ix, viii
   memorabilia 182
   metaphysics of presence 231, 235
   order 206
   piece of writing 1, 173, 183, 223
   pieces 176
   poem 99
   portrait 215
   preface xi, vii ff.
   statement viii, 139, 140, 179
   statements 180
   stories 228
   testimonies 178
   theory 13, 103
   writing viii-xi, 1 ff., 4, 10, 13, 21, 79, 130, 135, 182, 189, 206, 208, 219 ff., 220, 228, 235
   writings x, 184, 189-191, 208, 215
autobiographies, fictional 21 ff., 50, 57
   non-fictional, 50 ff.
autobiography viii-x, 2 ff., 4, 11, 51, 54, 56, 61, 72, 79, 81, 117, 164, 173, 174, 194, 196, 215
"autobiography proper" 1, 14, 17, 21, 159, 190
autobiography *simplex* and *duplex* 5
autobiography, defined, 13
   ontological, 10

Autobiography (Mill's) 20, 61, 69, 70

Barton, Ralph 54, 57
Baltimore 52
baptism 22, 82, 121, 123-125
Basilian Fathers, xi
Bastille 68
Batts, Mr., 203
Becket-complex (Eliot) 205, 214
Becket, Samuel xi, 2, 10, 11, 19, 33, 35-37 ff., 41, 49, 50, 52, 76, 80, 86 ff., 87, 92, 139, 219-221, 227, 230
Bertrand, Virginia, xi
bible 73, 207, 209, 214, 229
Bierman, Karen, xi
biographer 109
biographical 108
biography ix, 81, 191, 192
blindness 92
Bonaventure 201
Boston 52
Boswell, James ix, xi, 2-13, 219, 220, 234
bracket 11, 18, 25, 28, 29, 33, 42, 53, 54, 56, 68, 71, 87, 92, 158, 197, 219, 223, 227, 229
Braille 51
breaches 225
Bruss, Elizabeth 156
Burke, Kenneth 137-138, 149, 155, 157, 169, 170, 177

Cambridge 101
Camus, Albert 119
cancer 82, 121-123
Capote, Truman 139, 140, 176-178, 180-183
Carey, John 57
casuistry 137
Celestius 202
certainty 47, 58, 196, 212
certitude 184, 194-197, 199, 201, 211, 215
Chairs, The 19, 41 ff., 57, 71

chaos 20, 21, 29, 30, 52, 70, 104, 111, 112
Chatman, Seymour 8
Chicago Sun-Times 174
childhood 71, 79-81, 83, 84, 99, 100, 105, 112, 123, 130, 145, 177, 182, 222, 229, 231
Christianity 67, 168, 169, 171, 198, 203, 213
chronological 87, 139
chronology 2, 6, 7, 108, 195
Church fathers 198, 201
Cieslinksi, John xi
Clarke, Michael Murray and Susan xi
Clov 234
Clutter family 140, 177, 180
Cody, Cardinal 171, 173-176
Coffin trick 96
Company 33, 37 ff., 41, 89, 221
Comte, August 67, 68
confess to 183, 184
confesses 141, 164, 174, 204, 215
confessing 190, 207
confession 17, 18, 21, 79, 85, 135 ff., 145, 154, 161, 164, 166, 173, 174, 199, 209
  "proper" 2, 190
  fictional 141 ff.
  defined, 13, 139, 182-183, 206, 215
confessional attempt 14
  consciousness 183
  defense 170, 192, 194, 196, 214
  event 158
  explanation 160
  insight 158
  mode 182
  revelation 170
confessions 14, 156, 183, 184
  fictional 141 ff.
  non-fictional 156 ff.
Confessions of a Parish Priest 139, 170 ff., 173
Confessions of an English Opium-Eater 139, 156 ff., 161, 163

Index 253

confessor 8, 14, 131, 189, 198, 206
Connecticut 114, 121
connective 4, 6
connector x, 207
consciousness 6, 10-12, 17, 21, 23,
    24, 25, 26, 28, 34, 35, 37-43, 46,
    50, 56, 58, 60, 61, 67-76, 81, 90,
    95, 99, 100, 102, 106-108, 111,
    115, 120, 122-125, 162, 171-172,
    180, 181, 191, 195, 202, 207,
    213, 219, 220, 221-228, 233
    act of consciousness 8, 21, 24,
        31, 32, 42, 44, 49, 53, 54, 55,
        56, 65, 68, 70, 73, 79, 80, 88,
        101, 113, 161, 169, 173,
        183
    autobiographical 18, 198, 223
    criminal 177, 182
    intentional-motivational 165
    narrating 18, 22
    other 233
    personal 201
    phenomenal 64
    self-consciousness 10, 27, 32, 36,
        52, 58, 63, 83, 103, 105, 190,
        194
    state of consciousness 20, 21, 29,
        30, 42, 44, 49, 57, 59, 62, 64,
        65, 79, 80, 93, 112, 156-157,
        164, 169, 176, 177, 183
    unified 190, 192, 199, 206
constitutional 156
constitutive 137, 209, 210
continuous presence 10, 11
Cooke, Michael 18, 20, 67, 68
cor ad cor loquitur 215
"crisis in my mental history" 61
criterial list 65
Cullen, Dr. 193
Curran, Charles 202

daimon 4-5
Darwin, Charles 4, 5
Davies 2, 3, 5, 7, 9, 12
Debating society 65
Declaration of Independence 69

deconstruction 219, 220
DeQuincey, Thomas 85, 119, 139,
    140, 156 ff., 162-164, 183, 216,
    225
Derrida, Jacques 1, 2, 26, 68, 79-81,
    84-87, 111, 211, 214, 219-235
desire, Boswell 5
    centrality of 152
    college 193
    death of 73
    for child 144, 154
    gestalt of 151
    heroic 143
    interior 125, 150
    loss of 61, 62, 155
    natural 85, 103
    order 234
    original 115
    publicity 164
    real 155
    say the right thing 167
    scale of 154
    signification 220
    synecdochic 156
    to learn
    truth 203
    unity 201
    violent 231
    written 81
Destito, Connie xi
dialogue 6, 32, 33, 40, 41, 83, 84, 91,
    98, 102, 104, 165, 166, 167, 197,
    202, 227, 233-235
Didi (Vladimir) 85, 86, 234
diegesis 6, 7
diegetic act 80
    additions 13, 59, 142
    aspect 108
    assertion 19, 194
    behavior 147
    bracketing 28, 92
    commentaries 80, 183
    commentary 9, 20, 47, 48, 82, 98,
        108, 145, 150, 154, 162, 164,
        167
    commentator 8

comments 25, 49, 59, 71, 93, 99, 109, 169, 183, 200
confession 147
connection 107
construct 25
convictions 140
creating 45
creations 28
creativity 113
device 99
elements 95
evaluation 48
evaluator 86
explanation 136, 140
examination 80
exposition 46
fact 53
focus 122, 131
gestalt 3
information 55-6
insight 96
interpretation 99
language 58
narrator 58
one 9, 53, 61
point(s) 22, 26-28, 56, 70, 75, 81, 96, 98
postscripts 82, 129
purely 9
realization 20
remembering 90
representation 200
retrospect 43
selection 27
sense 44
sequence 2, 98
series 65
stance 95
statement(s) 49, 116, 182
study 65
summations 192
diegetically analyzed 80, 157
   attempt 170
   brackets 61, 42, 113
   changed 110
   combined 107

comments 8, 20-22, 37, 81, 90, 140, 176, 183
compares 112
connects 177
considers 203
divides 19
edited 19
evaluates 94
explaining 140, 170
expanded 142
explore 170
expose 177
expresses 191
imagines 48, 181
justify 183
named 19
needs 45
organize 76
perceives 30
pick 52
reflects 96
remember 146
represented 7, 82
say 49
seen 193
select(s)(ing) 20, 59, 61
separate 76
tells 155
unites 53, 76
justify 183
"Directing the Intention" 137
discourse x, 10, 24, 58-60, 75, 223, 227
divisibility 36
dogma 125, 171, 198, 202
Doolittle, Hilda (H.D.) 19, 30
drama (play, stage) 1, 86, 92, 95, 139, 141, 165, 183
dream 53, 87, 92, 157, 232
Dunn, James 171
duration 25
dynamo 5

Ear of the Other, The 84, 229-231
"ears of the others" 234
Earle, William 18, 20, 23, 58, 75

Index

Ecce Homo 81, 102
Egan, Susanna 21
Eliade, Mircea 172, 173
Eliot, T. S. 205, 214
Endgame 35, 219, 220, 228, 229, 231, 233, 234
equivocate 136
"Essay on Government" 66, 67
"Essay on Some Unsettled Questions of Political Economy" 70
Estragon (Gogo) 86-92, 130
eternal(ly) return(ing) 81, 83, 84, 86, 92, 102-104, 113, 117, 143, 229

Fall, The 119, 120
fancifulness 28
Father and Son: The Clash of Two Temperaments 121
Federal Grand Jury 174
feudal 67
fictional account 215
    adventures 97
    alter ego 102
    behaviors 156
    boy 143
    characters ix, 2, 114, 119, 228
    Charles 191, 196, 212
    children 154
    colonel 45
    creation 1, 92, 178, 227
    device 72
    dinner 181
    documents 75
    group 181
    hero 195
    idea 197
    intentions 152
    myth 112
    opportunity 112
    people 97
    piece 19, 183
    portrait 114, 189
    protagonist 20
    re-creation 45 (a fiction in a non-fiction)

representation(s) 113, 114, 189, 190, 194
set 152, 156
son 142, 144
story 119, 151
subject 142
surety 196
technique 72
words 156
writings xi
Zarathustra 103
fictionalize(d) 46, 47, 110, 205, 208
fictionalizing 93, 116, 208
fictionalization 57
fictionally give 203
    portray 52
    re-arranged 113, 151
film 114, 116-118
Fischer, David 105, 138, 139
Fleischmann, Avrom 21
"Four Major Tropes" 138
Franciscan spirituality 5
"Freeborn" 214
"Freud and the Scene of Writing" 223
free clauses 2
freeplay 220, 223, 230-232, 235
French Revolution 68
Freud 79, 83, 223-225
Frost, Robert 189, 216
Frye, Northrup 18, 21

Gala, Ed xi
Garrick 2, 9, 13
Gart, Hermione 18, 19, 30 ff., 39, 41, 49, 50, 57, 69, 76, 92, 219, 234
"Genesis and Structure" 227
Genette, Gerard 6
genre x, 1, 13
gestalt 145, 155, 163, 169, 170, 183, 201
    comparative-contrast 214
    diegetic 3
    intentional 140, 142, 152-3
    internal 137-138, 151, 156

metonymic 161
ghost(s) 109-112

Glass Menagerie, The 80, 93 ff., 98
God 32, 47, 48, 101, 120, 123, 125, 145, 171, 172, 209, 211, 212, 214, 229
Gogo (Estragon) 85, 86, 234
Goodwin, James 79, 82, 83, 85, 86
Gosse, Edmund 82, 109, 121 ff., 130
Grammar of Assent 196
A Grammar of Motives 136-138
grammes 225, 226
grandfather 120, 121, 128
Grasmere 99, 107
Greeley, Andrew 139, 140, 170 ff., 183
Gregory 202
gross anatomy of motives 138
Gusdorf, Georges 19, 20, 68, 75

Hamm 220, 228-231, 233, 234
handicap 51, 52, 60, 72, 75, 76
Heidt, Ruthanne xi
Hermeren, Goram 138
hermeneutics 230
Hermione 92 ff.
hero 61, 110, 124, 148, 175 (tragic), 195 (fictional)
heroine 32, 52, 108, 109, 111
heroism 56, 63, 112
hierarchy 67, 138, 160, 162, 163, 168, 170, 171, 177
Hilary 201
Hill, Alan 195
historical development 68, 197, 198
  inevitability 148, 150, 153
  interpretation 197
  overview 202
  past 11
  proof 89
  record 85
  summary 200
history ix, 6, 19, 20, 61, 67, 104, 142, 150, 166, 167, 171, 191, 194, 198-204, 206, 213

humor 28, 203
Husserl, Edmund 1, 2, 12, 31, 43, 70, 219 ff.
hysterical pregnancy 150, 151, 154

I Know Why The Caged Bird Sings 20
Ilative sense 196
illocutionary-locutionary 6, 8, 11, 138, 156
illusion, of certainty 196
  as created 96
  as fiction 97, 154, 155, 180, 183, 189, 190
  magician 95
  as mimesis 95, 97
  movies 97
  of Roslyn 116
  as (coffin) trick 96, 144
imitation 6, 7, 46, 89
In Cold Blood 139, 140, 176 ff., 178, 183
incandescence 34, 36
Indian 178
Industrialism 5
infallibility 119, 200, 202
integrity 197, 205
intention 54, 65, 136-138, 140, 142, 144, 145, 149, 150, 154, 156, 157, 161, 163, 164, 169, 198, 227
intention, directing the 137, 174
intention, formal-material 136-137, 149-150, 157, 169, 209-210
Ionesco, Eugene xi, 19, 41, 52, 76, 139
Ireland 190, 193, 206
irony 42, 152
Irvingites 202, 203

Jerome 201
jesuitical 204
Joachism 68
John Paul II 202
Johnson, Samuel ix, xi, 2-5, 7, 9-13, 219, 220, 234

Index

journey(s) 26, 29, 34, 51, 52, 65, 72, 76, 83, 142, 208
Joyce, James 58, 60
Judaism 203
Julian 203

Kaata, Ragnhild 54
Kansas 177, 178
Keller, Helen 18, 20, 50 ff., 56, 61, 71, 75, 76, 157
Kermode, Frank 68, 70, 204
kinesis 5
Kingsley, Charles 197, 204, 205
Kingston, Maxine Hong 81, 82, 86, 108 ff., 112, 113, 130
Kitchen, Dr. 203
Kohut, Heinz 79-80, 83, 84 (kohutian 92)
Kung, Hans 202

Labov, William 2, 42
Lake District 99-103, 105, 109
Langbaum, Robert 83, 85
Lanser, Susan Snaider 8
"La Parole Soufflee" 233
Lazar, Moshe xi
Life of Johnson ix, 3, 7, 220
linear progression 11, 138-9
logocentrism 220
London Journal ix, 3, 7, 220
Lord Eglinton 3
Lord Nelson 159, 162
Loss and Gain: The Story of a Convert 189-191, 194-201, 203, 205, 207, 212-214, 216
Lucky 86-92
"Lying and Equivocation" 136, 208
Lynd family, the xi
Lyrical Ballads 100

Macaulay, Thomas 66
Macbeth 36
magician 95-98
Mailer, Norman 139, 140, 163 ff., 182, 183, 205

Malone 92, 219-222, 224-228, 230-234
Malone Dies 39, 49, 219-222, 224, 231
Malvolio 95-98
Manchester 119, 140, 157-159, 162, 163
Mansell, Darryl 11
Marceau, William xi
Marcus, Steven 79, 83, 85, 86
marginal(ized) 172, 173, 175
Marguerite 75
Marmontel 62-65
Martin, Jay xi, 120
Mayoux, Jean-Jacques 18, 20, 25, 75
McCarthy, Art xi
McCarthy, Kevin 129
McCarthy, Mary 82, 95, 126 ff., 176
McCarthy, Preston 129
McCarthy, Sheridan 126, 127
medieval virgin 5
Meehan, Joseph 20, 57-59
Mellard, James 5
memoir(s) 14, 79 ff., (81, 82, 85, 86, 92, 98, 103, 108, 117, 119, 120, 130), 139, 173, 183, 184, 189, 190, 192, 194, 196, 215
 "proper" 1, 21, 190
 defined 13, 17, 76, 85, 135
 fictional 86 ff.,
 non-fictional 99 ff.,
Memoires (Marmontel) 62
memoirist 8, 14, 79 ff., 81, 83-85, 103, 115, 123, 131, 179, 189, 198, 206
 metaphoric 76, 98
memories 12, 29, 33, 45, 50, 54, 80-82, 86, 95, 100, 101, 105, 108, 112, 113, 118, 121, 129, 130, 157, 171, 182, 206, 223, 231
Memories of a Catholic Girlhood 82
memory, abyss 93, 117
 activity in 23-26, 94, 172
 failed, destroyed 46, 83, 196
 fixed 50, 85, 90, 91, 99, 109, 205
 mimetic 96

narrator's 130
nook 108
of a day or time 53, 68, 69, 113, 160, 191
overlap 86, 99, 107, 225
palimpsest 116
power 171, 195
re-created 59, 112, 162, 206, 224
reduces 81, 87
re-turn 102-103
unreality
traces 25, 43, 222, 226
Mendel, Sydney 209
metaphor(s) ix, x, 2, 4-6, 10, 91, 101, 104-106, 112, 121, 130, 131, 135, 180, 183, 195, 212
  boxing 143
  boots, bone, kick 89
  death 39
  doctrinal conflict 200
  loss 106
  memory 93
  narrative as 184
  overlap 86
  palimpsest 17, 185, 225
  period in history 5, 67
  sequence 87
  writing pad 224
metaphoric account 81
  action 106
  branches 198
  contrast 119, 190
  diversity 199, 202
  divisions 198
  experiences viii, 81
  explanation 106
  forms 98
  image 98-99
  non-fictions 121
  parts 83
  perspectives 200, 214
  points 202
  pole 4
  remembering 222
  replacement(s) 1, 6, 17, 82, 103, 107, 117, 120, 130, 170, 172, 183
  representation(s) 103, 104
  re-telling 222
  scenes 80
  sea 31
  self 84, 195 ff., 213
  stories 81
  substitutions 228
  sub-sects 199
  variables 11
  variety 215
  versions 80, 98, 144
  vocations 170
  voices 170
metaphorically compare 7, 215
  re-creating 11
  replace viii, ix, 4, 68, 117, 227
  represent 106-7
  similar 102
metaphors 4, 5, 67, 86, 87, 89, 93, 101, 120, 129, 131, 135, 180, 183, 184, 195, 200, 212
metaphysics 10
metaphysics of presence 219-221, 228, 231, 232, 235
metonym 13, 112 (significant part), 121 (of self), 141 (puzzle), 199 (missing piece), 208, 212 and 215 (as synecdoche)
  bits 120
  clarity 161
metonymic coherence 161
  confession 158
  connection 17, 87, 156, 159
  connector x, 207
  development 5
  elements 162
  events 6
  experience x
  explainer 207
  similarity 2
  facts 154

fictions 121
force 197, 211
fragments 180
gestalt 161
glue 163, 180, 198, 199, 202, 214
image 215
incidents 2
link 2, 170
meaning 89
moment 206
parts 24
pieces 120
period 68
perspective 206
point 208
pole 4
process 213
remembering 222
revelation 155, 168
self 206 ff.
sequence 86-88, 107
statement viii
unity 206
vigor 140
voices 170, 206
metonymical relationships 4
metonymically capture 87
    connect 7, 135, 136, 140, 170, 201
    constructing 215
    differentiate 227
    explain 170
    linked 85, 170
    read 11, 107
    re-discovering 11
    reveal 215
metonymies 5
metonyms 67, 104, 135, 136, 141, 183, 208
metonymy 2, 4, 5, 104
Mill, J. S. 61 ff., 71
Miller, Arthur 82, 113 ff., 120, 131
millet grains 35-37, 92, 228
mimesis 6, 7, 28, 95

mimetic accuracy 109
    act 20
    activities 20, 80
    alliance 183
    associations 19
    chaos 75, 130
    chronology 2, 6
    circumstances 98, 181
    clarity 113
    comments 22
    consciousness 31, 56
    detail(s) 28, 42, 45, 95, 110, 113, 141, 154
    device 167
    elements 159
    embracing 90
    events 45, 82
    evidence 45
    experiences 19, 25, 59, 70, 81, 99, 104, 109, 113
    fictions 98
    illusion 97
    interaction 80, 183
    memory 96
    one 8, 9, 162
    re-enactments 194
    re-telling 3, 155
    reality 49, 130
    replication 70
    reporting 44
    represent(ation) 22, 73
    sequence(ing) 2, 7, 22, 43, 44, 48, 49, 61, 71, 73, 82, 88, 89, 98, 108, 113, 141, 162, 197
    series 19, 20, 98
    state 157
    statement 182
    storytelling 90
    tracing 28
    triviality 28
    words 140
mimetic/diegetic sequence 2
    discourse 75
mimetically act 140
    connect 20

communicate 48
describes 112
doing 22
exemplifies 28
experienced 20
explore 170
narrate 71, 122
portrays 20, 139
read 3
re-constructs 53
re-experienced 99
recalls 19
remember 81
reports 8
represent(s)(ed) 7, 21, 27, 37, 48, 74, 107
reveals 170, 183
sees 95
shows 75
speaking 93, 140
Misfits, The 82, 113-117, 119, 120
Monroe, Marilyn 82, 114 ff., 116, 120, 121
monologue, interior 158, 162, 207, 213, 214
motivation, constitutive 210, 161, 135, 148, 157, 160-161
  compulsive 180
  distorted 62, 96, 138, 155-56, 163, 169, 177
  explained 14, 139, 166-7, 183, 216
  formation of, examination of 69, 153, 161-2, 180, 214
  gestalt, hierarchy 6, 138, 142, 154, 163, 168, 209, 213, 215
  initial 51
  interior 24, 42, 62, 136, 137, 141, 145-6, 149, 158, 196, 210
  non-fictional 151
  strength of 50, 54, 56, 161, 163
  synecdochic 161
  unrecognized 126, 135, 142, 144, 150, 152, 153
  for writing 85, 147, 198
motive 130, 140, 153, 163, 166, 176

apparent 140, 176
clarifying 139, 151, 164, 170, 213
distorted 163, 177, 205
first, important 153
gestalt 163, 183
honorable 166
other 142, 150, 167
real, non-fictional 144, 204
Mount Temple Comprehensive School 58
movies 97
"My Illness in Sicily" 193
Myers, Uncle 126 ff., 176
mystery 121, 122, 212
Mystic Writing Pad 223-225
myth 79, 112, 173-176
mythic 44
mythical 115, 121
mythological 108, 110
mythologize(ing) 108

Nabokov, Vladimir 80, 93-95, 102, 113
namelessness 19-20
naming 19-20, 31, 39, 56, 61, 68-69, 76, 227, 228
narcissistic 83
narcissistic self-objectification 83
Narcissus 79
narrates 94, 164
narrate(s) (to narrate) ix, x, 2, 7, 10, 23, 24, 90, 94, 95, 97, 104, 122
(mimetically) 130, 141, 177, 221
autobiographer narrates 71, 164
consciousness narrates 49
DeQuincey narrates 158
George narrates 147
Gosse narrates 121
Helen narrates 51
it narrates 4
Mailer narrates 140
Martha narrates diegetically 141
Mill narrates 61, 70
Miller narrates 120
McCarthy narrates 82
mother narrates 111

Tom narrates 95, 97, 98
Tristram narrates 24
Nabokov narrates 95
Newman narrates 190
narrated 19 (mimetically), 104
  (series), 121
  event being narrated 1, 6, 8, 11,
    23-24, 139
  experience is narrated 12, 222
  Hermione narrated 32
  history to be narrated 191
  incidents narrated 13
  period narrated 67
  roles narrated 121
  scene narrated 3
narrating 2, 68, 102
  act of narrating (Wordsworth) 8,
    21
  consciousness 17, 18-22
  moment 11
  present 23
  protagonist 135
  the narrating 69
  Tom is narrating 98, 140
  Tristram is narrating 22
  voice(s) 1, 10, 20, 52, 61, 80, 85,
    93, 135, 162, 170, 176, 183
narration, the 1, 6-8, 18, 20, 29, 51,
  104, 111, 117, 41, 142, 159, 181
narration, dual 2, 219
narrative(s) viii-x, 3, 11, 31, 38, 53,
  64, 76, 82, 85, 87, 89, 92, 96,
  101, 109, 116, 120, 121, 122,
  144, 151, 159, 160, 178, 208,
  223, 226, 228
  autobiographical 6, 13, 138, 140,
    162, 221, 222, 225, 226, 228,
    233, 235
  Boswell 10, 12
  braided 105
  childhood 107
  confessional 136, 137, 139, 154,
    158, 162, 164, 167, 169, 170,
    180, 183, 184
  diegetic 71
  fictional 139, 144, 156, 205

historical 205
Husserlean 233
intercalated 23
longer viii
metaphoric 5, 78, 82, 86, 99,
  105, 115, 190, 232
metonymic 4, 86, 115, 135, 164,
  170, 176, 184, 189, 190
mimetic 69, 71, 142, 154, 167,
  177
multiple 235
non-fictional 72, 140, 143
particular x
synecdochic 4, 17, 41, 42, 52, 71,
  75, 86, 105, 119, 125, 189,
  230
verbal 19
voice(s) diegetic, mimetic 1
written 219
narrative act 8, 106
  bits 22
  elaboration 12
  explanation 107
  fictions 190
  memories 108
  method 25
  mimetic sequence 3
  mold 226
  point 20, 21
  present 10
  progression 1
  re-creations 107
  re-telling 18, 144
  remembrance 108, 115
  representations 117
  sequence 3, 43
  simple 6, 191
  subverts 22
  unit(s) 2-3, 13, 21, 26, 42, 61, 71,
    72, 111, 112, 117, 130, 163,
    184, 190, 215, 227, 230, 235
  unites 18
  versions 190
  voice(s) 1, 23, 61, 79, 99, 102,
    113, 135-6, 157, 169, 181,
    219, 235

narrator 6-8, 10, 17, 20-22, 52, 57-59, 69, 72, 75, 76, 87, 95, 113, 130 (consciousness), 140, 146, 148, 158, 234
narrator, diegetic 2, 72
natural attitude 220-223, 231, 235
natural standpoint 12, 30, 31, 101, 162, 220, 222
Necessity 28, 69, 70, 2220
neurochemistry 35
Newman, John Henry Cardinal 4, 14, 62, 136, 137, 149, 155, 157, 169, 170, 184, 189, 190-215
Nicea 201
Nicene Creed 201
Nietzsche 79, 81, 84, 102-104, 229
No Exit 88, 231, 234
Nolan, Christopher 18, 20, 56 ff., 61, 71, 75, 76
non-fictions, metaphoric 121
non-fictional autobiographies 50 ff., 57
    confessions 156 ff.
    desire 144, 151
    documents 75
    events 151
    eye 116
    memoirs 99 ff.
    motives 144, 151
    narration 1, 72, 140, 142
    novel 140
    piece 76
    representation 113
    speech 181
    story 152
    writer 1, 2, 8, 13
Norton, Anne 68-69
Norway 54
Notre Dame 174, 175

O'Connor, Paul xi
octopus 30, 31, 34, 35
Of Grammatology 220
Olney, James 4, 5
opium 163
orator 42, 45, 48, 57, 165

organic 31 (sense of self), 67-68 (history), 71 (whole)
organically 199
Oriel 191, 193
other, the: another act 64-65
    character/person 58, 59
    speech 48
    system 219
    bump into each other 26
    break through each other 225
    care for each other 90
    complement the other 81
    counter each other 226
    each other, one after another, 145
    each other's strangeness 179
    "ear of the other" 229, 231
    heroic 164
    juxtapose and reconnect each other 226
    love self as other 79
    multiple other acts 79
    not himself but another 46
    one in the other 46
    "the other" 102, 112, 137, 199-200
other aspects 55
    buried voices 53, 183, 184, 202
    churches 199
    desires 144
    documents 177
    facts 87
    half 33
    literature 164
    memories 121
    mimetic interactions 183
    mothers 112
    motivations 126, 142, 152, 167
    narrative units 190
    narrators 148
    parts 221
    perspectives 205
    points of view 148
    reasons 233

Index

self 84
states 63, 158
stories 97
times 70, 114, 130
traces 222
voices (buried) 53, 183, 184, 202
words 136
others in *Company* 38
paired with each other 169
precede and follow others 67
radically other selves 83
replace the others 76, 82, 99, 107-8, 115-6, 117, 130, 172, 193, 204, 226
separating 30
substitute for each other 98, 101, 105
tamper with 36
"that cantankerous other" 37
"to another of that other or of him. Or of another still. To another of that other or of him of another still" 38
variety of others within 104
wax and wane with each other 40
Oxford 57, 195, 212
Oxford Movement 207

palimpsest 17, 18, 23, 25, 27, 56, 76, 85, 116, 135, 183, 224, 225, 226
Paris 43
Pearson's theory of kinesis 5
pentad 138
Pepin, Jean 230
Perloff, Marjorie xi
"perspective among perspectives" 138, 177
Petrarch 201
Pharisee 207, 209, 210
phenomenological attitude 222
bracket 219
data 43, 48
investigation 65
object 221, 235
residuum 43

stance 235
truth 12
Pison, Thomas 4
Plato 6, 7, 68
possibility 91, 94, 153, 161, 166, 209
postscripts 82, 95, 129
Pozzo 86 ff., 130, 234
preconscious 23, 224, 226-228, 230
Preface, Autobiographical vii ff.
Prelude, The 4, 80, 99, 107
priest 139, 140, 170-173, 183, 202
Princeton University 68
Pringle 3
privacy 126, 166, 199, 208, 209
probability(ies) 194, 195, 197, 199, 201, 202, 207, 215
psychoanalysis 83
"Psychoanalytic Self, The" 83
Pygmalion 34

quadriplegia 20, 56
quadriplegic 20, 56-58, 60, 76
Quixote, Don 102

Radcliffe College 54, 55, 57
rape 71-73, 108
"ray(s) of light" 62 ff., 67, 68, 70
reality 6, 7, 17, 31, 34, 36, 49, 57, 68, 69, 94, 96-99, 116, 120, 122, 130, 131, 151, 155, 180, 183, 189, 190, 212, 225, 233
Reding, Charles 189, 191, 194-200, 202-207, 212, 213-4
Reformation 67-68
Reno 116
Republic, The 6
restricted clauses 2
retrogressive 23, 103
Reynolds, Charles xi
Reynolds, Joshua 12, 13
rhetoric xi, 148
Rhetoric of Motives 137
Rhetoric of the Other Literature, The 164
rhetoric of religion 169
rhetorical flourish 28

rhetorically 140, 184
right to private judgement 206 ff.
Ritter, Thelma 116
Roman Catholic 197, 202, 203, 209, 211, 212
Rosary College 175
Roslyn 114-116, 118
Rousseau, Jean-Jacques 164, 228

Said, Edward 104
Saint Paul's Cathedral 159, 160, 162
Saint-Simonian school 67-68
Santayana, George 177
Sartre 88, 231
Scotland 3-5, 7-8
Schultheis, Kathy xi
selbstbessinung 41
Shafer, Ingrid 171
Shakespeare 36, 95-98
shaman 81 ("Shaman") 110-112
Shandy, Tristram 10, 11, 18, 19, 21 ff., 41, 49, 57, 59, 69, 76, 88, 219, 234
simultaneity 23
Sliwa, Olga Kravechenko xi
Smith, Perry Edward 139, 140, 176 ff., 181-183
Speak, Memory 80, 93
speech(es) 39, 42-48 (orator in *The Chairs*), 51 (Keller), 65 (Mill), 138 (figures of), 164-168 (Mailer), 180-181
speak(s)(ing) 6, 7, 20, 29, 37-39, 42, 50, 51, 53, 54, 56, 71, 74, 75, 80, 93, 94, 154, 161, 165, 180, 181, 221, 228, 229, 232
Spiritual Elixir 203
Spivak, Gyatri 220, 226
stance 8, 24, 69, 95 (diegetic), 198, 205, 206, 235
status 8, 32 (heroic), 143, 172
Stein, Gertrude 10, 11
Sterne, Laurence 19, 52, 234
Story of My Life, The 19, 50
Strasberg, Lee and Paula 114, 119
Sturrock, John 85

subconscious memories 50
  truth 144
  realm 224
  mind 79, 226, 230, 231
Sullivan, Annie 53
synecdoche(s) 2, 4, 5, 52, 59, 65, 86, 87, 91, 93, 101, 104, 112, 121, 136, 163, 170, 183, 193
significant synecdoches 183
synecdochic account 81
  additions 52
  attitude 23, 161
  autobiography 158
  awareness 130
  chapter 65
  commentary 52
  contribution x
  core 71
  crisis 65
  deletion 52
  desire 156
  document 184
  event 17, 19, 50, 59, 131, 158, 200
  examples 52
  experience x, 20, 50, 62, 81, 99
  fact 5, 86-7
  fatality 44, 160
  form 85
  generalizations 11
  goals 49
  history 19
  idealizations ix
  image 4, 19, 31, 99, 164, 193, 215
  impact 197
  incidents 2
  insight 119, 160, 180
  intentions 161
  meaning 89
  metonym 212
  moment 75, 204
  motivations 161
  narrative 41, 52, 71-2, 75, 86, 105, 115, 119, 125, 184, 189-90, 230

Index

narrative unit 3
nature 102
need 211
one vii, 184
oneness 198
part 4
perception 180
period 67-8, 206
piece 4, 92
point 28
portrait x, 61, 131
preference 170
reality 120
realization 158
representation 107, 180
resonances 112
roles 121
self (selves) 191 ff., 195, 204, 206
self-invention 222
sequence 107
significance 23, 27, 161, 183
stages 67
statement 42
story 5, 81
subject 51
surety 195
thing 215
thread viii, 72
title 53
turn 194
unfolding 6
 unification 124, 170, 190
unity 4, 56, 76, 196-8, 202, 203
voice 170, 172
synecdochically hang 88
   joined 23
   juxtapose 227
   remember 146
   renewing 11
   represent x, 87
   selected 5
   significant 213
   unify 117, 215
   unite 7
synecdochist 123
synecdochize 205

tabula rasa 43, 224
taxonomy 138
Tertullian 201
Thirty-Nine Articles 212
"thick present" 19-21, 24, 25, 30, 75-76
time, about this time 119
   all the time 127, 148
   around the time 94
   as a time of 193
   at one time 203, 207
   at the time 53, 74, 93, 98, 117, 144, 183-4, 191
   at the time of writing 52, 119, 122, 123, 169, 224
   at the present time 33, 36, 96, 117, 119, 172, 174, 177-182, 197, 211, 215
   back and forth in 10
   each time 81, 216
   of the time 212
   fill his time 231, 233
   first time 101, 213
   flow of events in time 25, 114
   for that time 211
   from the time 191, 199
   give time 221
   at certain times 70
   co-exist in 11
   in time 68, 104, 166
   lifetime 45
   many times 43
   (an)other times x, 32, 106
   at no time 38, 55
   a particular time 23, 130, 200, 213
   remember the time 105, 158
   separate time periods 43
   up to this time 59
   this time 89-90, 120
   "timebends" 113 ff., 120
   Time magazine 163-4, 167
   time of death 48
   time to die 49
   time checks us 29
   time has left marks 46

time-sense 18
  to the time 215-16
  at which time 39
  until which time 63, 154, 223
  very long time 43
Timebends 113-115, 120, 121
Tompkins, Jane 219, 227
Tower of Babel 229
trace(s) 3, 11, 22, 25, 26, 29, 39, 43, 45, 86, 92, 183, 220-230, 231, 232, 233, 235
Tractarian Movement 191-193, 204, 212
transition(al) viii, 30, 57, 61, 67-70
transitional 68, 70, 198, 204
Tristram 18, 19, 21-30, 41, 49, 57, 59, 69, 76
Tristram, Henry 189-193, 206
Tuscon 172
Twelfth Night 95, 98

unconscious 23, 79, 83, 84, 144, 147, 150, 211, 224, 226, 228, 230, 231
Under the Eye of the Clock 20, 57 ff.
"Unmaking of a Cardinal, The" 173, 175

Vatican I 201
Vatican II 176, 202
violence 68, 71, 76, 126, 220, 222, 223, 228
violent 26, 74, 75, 177, 180, 221-223, 225-228, 231, 233, 235
Virginia Woolf 10, 139, 141, 142
Vladimir (Didi) 36, 86-92, 130, 230, 234
voice, the 36-41
  adult 71
  another x, 215, 235
  apologetic 208
  confessional 207, 212
  diegetic 2, 8-9, 19, 30, 31, 41, 45, 46, 53, 61, 62, 75, 76, 82, 87, 89, 100, 113, 119, 128, 135, 139, 158, 162, 167, 184
  each 203
  first 8
  inner 52
  mimetic 6, 8-9, 17, 20, 30, 45, 50, 53, 59, 71, 80, 82, 87, 93, 94, 113, 135, 139, 140, 158, 162, 164, 176, 177, 183, 198
  mimetic/diegetic 2, 6, 7, 17-18, 50, 75, 76
  see "narrative"
  one 4
  own 165
  past 206
  particular x, 184
  poetic 81
  predominant 61, 183
  present narrating 183
  present 19, 23, 85
  second 8
  some 183
  see "synecdochic" 14, 170, 172
  third 9
  tone of 55
  unified 23, 194
  unique 1
  unrecognized 1
  "voice above the voice" 9
given voice 21, 75, 140, 177, 227
voices(ed)(as verb) 6, 19, 22, 29 (re-voiced), 72, 108, 126, 129, 235
voiced, mimetically 19
  perspective 129
voices, buried 184
  comparative-contrastive 194
  different 170, 190
  diegetic 1, 7, 12, 13, 16, 62, 78, 86, 98, 134, 167, 190, 235
  interactive 103
  marginal 172
  metonymic 11, 14, 194, 207
  Mill's 72
  mimetic/diegetic 1, 7, 12, 13, 16, 59, 75, 78, 86, 98, 134, 141, 167, 190, 235
  mimetic 6, 9, 13, 17, 59, 80, 82, 100, 119, 131, 140, 141, 184, 200

multiple 21, 23
other 85, 202, 233, 229
re-created 104
remembered 85
replacement 103
separate 19, 37
three 53, 76, 99, 140, 170, 173, 224
varieties 130
various 208
void 33, 38, 40, 80, 81, 84, 85, 87, 100, 103, 111, 112, 234

Waiting for Godot 80, 86 ff.
Waletsky, Joshua 2, 42
warrior 81
"What Exactly Does Dr. Newman Mean?" 204
Whispering Gallery 119, 159, 161, 162
White, Andrea, xi

Who's Afraid of Virginia Woolf? 139, 141
Who Am I This Time? 120
wholeness 35, 36, 104, 184, 230
Widow Wadman 29
Wilde, Oscar 173
William Andrews Clark library 68
Williams, Tennessee 80, 93
Wingfield, Tom 80, 93 ff., 113, 130
Winterowd, Ross xi, 164
"Wisdom and Innocence" 210
Woman Warrior, The 81
Wordsworth 4, 64, 66, 80, 81, 99 ff. 113, 130, 138, 157, 215

Yeats, W. B. 60

Zarathustra 102-103
Zeno 35, 234
Zosimus 202